Asian Diasporas

T0351491

Hong Kong University Press thanks Xu Bing for writing the Press's name in his Square Word Calligraphy for the covers of its books. For further information, see p. iv.

Asian Diasporas

Cultures, Identities, Representations

Edited by

Robbie B. H. Goh and Shawn Wong

香港大學出版社

HONG KONG UNIVERSITY PRESS

Hong Kong University Press
14/F Hing Wai Centre
7 Tin Wan Praya Road
Aberdeen
Hong Kong

ISBN 962 209 672 7 (Hardback)
ISBN 962 209 673 5 (Paperback)

Secure On-line Ordering
http://www.hkupress.org

British Library Cataloguing-in-Publication Data
A catalogue record for this book is available
from the British Library.

Printed and bound by Condor Production Co. Ltd., in Hong Kong, China

Hong Kong University Press is honoured that Xu Bing, whose art
explores the complex themes of language across cultures, has written
the Press's name in his Square Word Calligraphy. This signals our
commitment to cross-cultural thinking and the distinctive nature of
our English-language books published in China.

"At first glance, Square Word Calligraphy appears to be nothing more
unusual than Chinese characters, but in fact it is a new way of rendering
English words in the format of a square so they resemble Chinese
characters. Chinese viewers expect to be able to read Square Word
Calligraphy but cannot. Western viewers, however are surprised to
find they can read it. Delight erupts when meaning is unexpectedly
revealed."

— Britta Erickson, *The Art of Xu Bing*

Contents

Acknowledgements

This collection of essays arose out of a conference on "Asian Diasporas and Cultures" held at the National University of Singapore from 5 to 7 September 2001. The conference would not have been possible without the funding and administrative support of the Department of English Language and Literature and the Centre for Advanced Studies of the National University of Singapore.

A research grant from the Faculty of Arts and Social Sciences supported the conference as well as the work that went into this volume.

Thanks are also due to the colleagues who helped organize the conference and supported it in various ways, the graduate student helpers, and all the participants whose intellectual input has helped shape the present volume.

Introduction

The Culture of Asian Diasporas: Integrating/Interrogating (Im)migration, Habitus, Textuality

Robbie B. H. Goh

The claim that Asian diasporas are cultural phenomena would in all likelihood meet little or no objection — except, of course, for the problem of what precisely is meant by "culture"? In what ways can an understanding of cultural influences, transformations, and representations affect the study of those major transnational human movements that are the foci of diaspora studies? What kinds of relationships can be posited between the "hard" data of migration statistics and histories, housing and employment analyses of migrant workers, and the like, on the one hand; and the "soft" data of literature written by diasporic writers, representations of race in the context of immigration, the psychology or mentality of diasporas, and related material, on the other hand?

The present volume attempts to argue for the importance of a wider range of cultural documents — "high" literary texts, popular writings and public discourses, film and media texts, architecture and spatial design, the various cultural elements that shape identity politics and consciousnesses — in the analysis of diasporic movements. As Chuh and Shimakawa (2001: 5) observe, "In order to understand the phenomenon of globalization, it is necessary to 'globalize' academic practices by thinking across disciplinary and areal boundaries." Such cultural documents play a crucial role in acknowledging the complexity of diasporic identities, particularly in the present age of "global citizens" who face, and represent, a multiplicity of competing allegiances, claims, rights, and duties (Holston and Appadurai 1999; Sassen 1999). Until very recently, diaspora studies arguably did not pay sufficient attention to issues of global claims and rights, in part because these are often regarded as the privileged domain and condition of the "corporate and media elites" of global capitalism (Sassen 1999: 100). In turn, in the popular conception, immigration is regarded as the influx of lowly qualified members of a workforce who, it is commonly assumed, will take on low-paying jobs (if they are at all successful in gaining employment), live in abject conditions, and contribute to urban problems like crime and the creation of ghettoes. Thus a recent article on "Who Gains from Immigration?" in *The Economist*, which considers the impact of immigration on Britain's economy: while acknowledging that immigrants to Britain are "both more and less skilled," the article in the main pursues the argument that immigrants "are generally prepared to work at lower wages" (*Economist* 2002: 56). Consequently, immigration adds supply pressures in those less desirable occupations for which immigrants compete and lowers those wages; the net result is that "immigration makes business and most people a bit better off, and some of the poor poorer" (*Economist* 2002: 56).

While this argument is hardly surprising in an article concerned with the economic results of immigration, it is representative of a type of discourse and consciousness which reifies transnational human movement in terms of labor and wages; social effects, where they are considered at all, usually focus on ills such as the loss of "public safety" and "cultural identity," an increase in crimes, and an overburdening of welfare systems and provisions in the receiving nations (Sung 2001: 11). This reifying tendency is not merely a discourse of the popular press and media, nor is it merely a result of immigration-centered analyses and accounts. As Van Hear (1998: 5, 13–6) observes, scholarly accounts of "diaspora" tend to cluster around notions of "forced dispersions," memories of the homeland and a desire to return there, socioeconomic "disparities between places of origin and destination," laws and policies that prohibit or permit migration/immigration, "macropolitical economy," and the like. Despite the differences between these accounts, and their usefulness for scholarly analysis, they nevertheless tend to regard diasporas as mechanistic, static, and divisive. The emphasis on migratory flows and their various parameters narrows the notion of "diaspora" to a set of systemic causes not unlike the machinery of a global "invisible hand" (admittedly a complex one, incorporating interventions by various agencies and authorities) moving counters from a "push" area to a "pull" one. It is in turn tempting to see such migratory flows as divisive bipolarities set up between the original and host countries, played out in various oppositional terms such as "home" and "alien place," "self" and "other," "crisis spot" and "asylum," "poor" and "rich," and so on. Studies and anthologies such as *Ideas of Home* (Kain 1997) and *Narrating Nationalisms* (Ling 1998) are thus perhaps unfortunately titled, since they seem to hypostasize notions of a "homeland" or a discrete "national boundary" — notions which come under the most pressure in contemporary transnational conditions.

Van Hear's review of the scholarship is part of his argument for a more inclusive understanding of "New Diasporas," one which accepts more complexly fluid, multiple, and recurrent movements, which result in "transnational communities" rather than in relatively static displacements of laborers and asylum seekers (Van Hear 1998: 1, 6). To this necessary call for a more fluid notion of diasporic movements may be added a call for more fully textured studies of diasporic lives and lived experiences. As Yeoh and Huang (1998: 584) observe, scholarship on "Third World female migrants" has tended to view these individuals "first and foremost as *workers*," to the neglect of issues pertaining to their "lives beyond their work." This equation of female migrant workers with labor tends to skew research in the direction of "macroperspective" topics such as the role of remittances as "measures to overcome deficits in [national] balance of payments," the "structural causes" of growth in the supply of such workers, the "productive relations" and "work conditions" within which they work, and so on (Yeoh and Huang 1998: 584). Yet these conditions of labor and employment are also affected by, and affect, not only the workers' engagements with and movements in public space, but employers' attitudes to their domestic servants, the public image and representations of the latter, spaces and praxes, dialectical negotiations of freedom and power between employer and servant, cultures of consumption formed by these migrant workers (Yeoh and Huang 1998), and other related factors pertaining to the social identities, movements, and discourses by and of such groups.

Nor can diasporic "lived experience" simply be equated with housing and the related politics of space – with the main tropes that often emerge in studies of "race and ethnicity in the city." Pinderhughes's (1997: 76) survey of recent scholarship notes that the pressure on American cities of "immigrants in larger numbers and from all corners of the globe" has resulted in a focus on the "complex and ... conflictual" nature of "urban politics" among increasingly "bifurcated and differentiated" racial groups. Pinderhughes's indication of future research directions moves away from the "limitations of the socioeconomic status model" toward an increased awareness of the complex developing "institutions" and "experiences" among the different racial and ethnic groups, and of the asymmetrical experiences that often arise within a single group as well (1997: 85, 86). A different analysis of the existing scholarship, by Ratcliffe (1997), notes the "inability of the literature" to convincingly theorize race and housing in urban Britain, particularly in light of the often imprecise racial and ethnic terms employed in census-based analyses, and the tendency to focus on relatively simple data categories such as housing tenure, dwelling type, location, number of occupants, and household income. While there may be "little disagreement about the *existence* of major inequalities in the housing market" (Ratcliffe 1997: 87) and the racialized bases for such inequalities, there is certainly a need to add substantially to the fronts on which research on race and urbanism is conducted.

Racial segregation, either in housing or in more generalized spatial politics and policies, continues to be a dominant area of research. Thus, for example, Goldsmith (2000: 49) sees a pattern of the segregation in European cities of "dangerous classes" of "darker skinned" immigrants either in "city centers" of "on the outskirts" — a pattern which reproduces the racial segregations of American cities. Other studies do not only indicate existing spatial and power patterns, but also contest the rigidities of racial segregation by importing notions of changing social identities, representations, and praxes in the lives of minority groups and their interactions with the white majority. Starting with spatial tropes such as the "Chinese takeaway" small business (Parker 2000), the "Asian gang" zone of violence (Alexander 2000), or Miami as a city characterized by "Cuban immigration" (Croucher 1997), these studies are not content with reconstructing patterns of racial segregation and confinement, but typically invoke a wide range of cultural documents — media and public discourses, popular music, architecture and spatial symbolisms, food culture, and others — to argue for the "constructed" and "negotiated" nature of ethnic social identities and spatial interventions.

The key theoretical strand contributed by many of these newer studies of diasporic and ethnic identities thus seems to be the dynamic acts of cultural construction involved in social processes, and consequently the necessarily fluid, multiple, and often overdetermined nature of diasporic conditions. The replacement of divisive and static notions of diasporas with an acknowledgment of the recurring movements, conflictual desires, and mixed and multiple loyalties and affiliations that actually characterize such human transnational processes, is an important step in this new theoretical orientation. So too is the gradual balancing out of the predominant emphases on migration-as-labor, and housing and spatial segregations and exclusionary "power geometries" (Parker 2000: 75). Yet the movement toward a theory of dynamic diasporic cultures and social identities still requires the crucial input of theories of textual, discursive, and symbolic negotiation and contestation. Much of this theoretical ground is inextricably bound to the critical theory of poststructuralist and postmodernist culture and society — to the awareness of the constitutive role of multiple and complex narratives in contemporary social identities and positions (Lyotard 1992: 149).

A number of major strands in this textual and theoretical ground become vital to diasporic studies: firstly, the "dialogical" nature of social identities, as reflected in textual forms and structures (Bakhtin 1981: 3–13); this not only allows for an understanding of the ways in which political and social identities are contested via narrative forms, but also confers a terminology and theoretical framework for plural social identities coexisting and interacting with each other. Contemporary diasporic conditions are indeed akin to a "polyglossia" (Bakhtin 1981: 12) in which there are undoubtedly dominant majority voices, but ones that do not silence or invalidate a multiplicity of more marginal positions whose narratives constitute a challenge to the dominant. The polyglossia is not merely an allegory of ethnicity in the global city, but an actual model of diasporic relations; developments in communications technology, such as e-mail, webpage services, desktop publishing, digital filming, inexpensive and accessible long-distance telephoning and mobile phone networks, constitute new media narratives through which a multitude of new social identities and positions may be voiced. These proliferating voices constitute a more pragmatic challenge to social dominants than the more overt avenues of policy, political power, and economic control.

Secondly, postcolonial literary and cultural studies add a particular set of nuances to the understanding of diasporic conditions by their insistence on the necessarily mixed and "hybrid" nature of newly independent nations in the new world order, as well as by their theorizing of the diachronic dimension of cultural influence. Bhabha's (1994: 2) well-known formulation of the "location of culture" as an "interstitial" space, where "the intersubjective and collective experiences of nationness, community interest, or cultural value are negotiated," is fundamentally dialogical in that it blurs the hard and fast distinction between dominant and marginal cultures, colonizing and colonized positions. This condition is not only true of the formerly colonized nation, but also of migrants, immigrant societies, and global diasporic contexts, as Bhabha himself observes (1994: 139). Hybridity thus becomes a "metaphor" not merely for the modern nation, but for a complex "form of living" which is constituted by "social and textual affiliation[s]" (Bhabha 1994: 140) — a form which can be found beyond the nation, among the ethnically diverse, transnationally oriented citizens of contemporary global zones. From this perspective, formerly colonized nations are critically hybrid due to the diachronic development of their "institutions at the core of culture": their architectural and spatial forms, their social and political institutions, their terms and phrases, above all their consciousness and modes of thought which are infused with the language structures of the former colonial masters (King 1976: 41–66).

Space and time thus intersect in multiple and complex ways in the logic of postcolonial cultures, making it unremunerative to identify definitive moments of social influence and transformation. The production of a specific spatial trope — the church, the public square or garden, the town hall, the ghetto, the red-light district — is not confined to the period of actual physical construction, but incorporates the entire span of cultural influence and cultural production. This once again has a bearing on the question of diasporas: historical transnational movements, and indeed historical cultural influences of a broad variety, play their part in more recent diasporas and the construction of social identities. Diasporic space and time cannot be regarded as isolated phenomena (the marginalized ethnoscape, the crisis moment of mass emigration, and the like), but must be seen as an interactive "critical space" (Virilio 1998: 58, 59) in which the speed, volume, diachronicity, and diversity of multiple subjective transactions and interventions (in travel, communications, media and commodity consumptions, and other acts) constantly recreate and renegotiate the social sphere and its significance.

In many ways this dynamic and fluid notion of diasporic culture is exemplified by contemporary Singapore: the former British colony, which gained independence in 1965, has a fundamentally diasporic population and society, with the majority of its inhabitants descended from Chinese, Indian, and other immigrants who came to work in the late nineteenth century and thereafter. While modernization and nationhood have resulted in many signal successes, a number of recent factors and developments contribute to create conditions of multiple "pulls" and allegiances: firstly, Singapore's policy of emphatic "multiculturalism" paradoxically stresses racial and linguistic differences among its citizens (Chua 1998: 190), thus in some ways recalling the different migrant origins of different groups of citizens. This is exacerbated by cultural mechanisms which divide along the different vernacular lines: religions and rituals like Islam, Hinduism, Buddhism, ancestor worship/veneration; media texts like Bollywood films or Hong Kong television and film; and the language, literature, and popular writing of "mother" countries like India and China. Secondly, legacies of British colonial rule — the use of English as the language of education and government, a heavily exposed English literary tradition, media influences, elements of British education (such as the dominant influence, until very recently, of the Cambridge G.C.E. 'O' and 'A' Level examinations), colonial architecture, and so on — engage dialectically with vernacular social identities, exerting a diachronic influence from a different cultural source. These conditions are of course heightened by Singapore's present push toward "world city formation," and its economic and cultural engagements with global cities, markets, and centers (Perry, Kong, and Yeoh 1997: 18). The result is not only a fundamentally and inextricably hybrid culture and society, but also in some ways an "unsettled" nation whose population is constantly reminded of migrant pasts and present transnational possibilities and affiliations.

Singapore thus exemplifies similar forms of "unsettled settlements" in Asia, Africa, and the Pacific — in the former colonies (or otherwise subjects of colonial interventions) whose historical mandate of imperial trade and commodity production resulted in significant diasporic movements and racial-cultural hybridity, and whose brief histories as independent nations have been marked in many ways by a perpetuation of significant past influences and the uncertainties of global competition. Certainly the diasporic particulars (the periods of mass diasporic movements, origins and destinations, languages and cultures involved, media influences, and so on) pertaining to Kuala Lumpur, Lagos, Manila, Hong Kong, Johannesburg, Mumbai, Sydney, Jakarta, and other such cities differ from those of Singapore and from each other. Yet they share a particular historical affectedness — a characteristic marking by external political and economic forces, and by fundamental cultural influences — that makes them markedly conscious of and subject to transnational movements and patterns. Where the consciousness of a discrete national identity, a heritage of the past, a sense of "rootedness" and "home" are often missing or problematized, as they are in many of these places, then an essentially diasporic culture prevails, whether manifesting itself in actual large-scale migrations and immigrations, or else in national or group imaginings of some other home, or in other dislocating phenomena.

It is thus not untimely for the appearance of a volume such as the present one, which seeks not only to interrogate some of the *idées fixes* which often dominate diaspora studies, but in the process also to turn the focus away from immigration and ethnicity problems in North American and European locations toward an examination of the endemic and persistent diasporic cultures of Asia-Pacific zones. By the same token, it is not inappropriate that the genesis of this volume lies in an international conference on "Asian Diasporas and Cultures" held at the National University of Singapore in September 2001. It was perhaps the conference's sense of place — the history, institutions, spatial logic, languages, and cultures of Singapore — that contributed something to the fundamentally dynamic and multidisciplinary sense of "diasporic culture" that these select papers attempt to analyze. Most, if not all, of the contributors have lived and worked in the unsettled and hybrid places that are the logical subjects for studies that rely on newer definitions of diasporas and transnational communities. Diasporas are by nature wideranging and far-flung subjects of study, and no one volume can lay claim to being an exhaustive study. Yet the range of papers in this volume is itself part of an attempt to redefine diasporas, moving away from static locales (hypostasized "homes" and "away places"), and toward intermediary cultural mechanisms, social networks, and "third spaces" that characterize many contemporary transnational structures.

The main emphases are on the diasporic cultures associated with India and China — arguably two of the most far-reaching and numerically significant transnational networks of the long modern era (of European colonialism, industrialization, and world trade). Certainly there are other diasporic phenomena with equivalent claims for scholarly attention, including those of the Jewish and Latino peoples. Yet once again a certain correcting of balance is necessary: while Jewish and Latino (among other) diasporic movements and networks are entirely significant in and relevant to Europe and North America, they are less significant in the Asia-Pacific region (which has come in for less scholarly attention) than the Indian and Chinese ones. A study of Asian diasporic cultures cannot entirely ignore America, of course, but the condition of Asian communities in the U.S. will then form only one part of a global diasporic picture, rather than the exclusive or main focus that it constitutes in many of the studies of "Asian-American cultures."

In an enquiry of this nature, "location" becomes highly problematic, the site of contested identities and acts of power, imaginary recreations, and fluidly "interactive" (in Virilio's sense) subjectivities. Robbie Goh's essay on "Diaspora and Violence" in this volume points to the interpenetration of cultural representations of ethnicity and the spatial logic of multiracial hot spots such as the Chinatown areas of Birmingham and Vancouver. Film, literature, popular culture images such as advertising, and spatial symbolisms and the everyday experiences of space collectively cause violent disjunctions that rupture the apparent seamlessness of the landscape. Diasporic texts thus work across the fixities of location (nation, city, "home" and "away") to articulate the tensions inherent in these multiple affiliations and contested relations. In a similar way, Ann Brooks's essay foregrounds and juxtaposes Chinese diasporic communities in the very different locations of Singapore, Britain, and Australia, to show how a "flexible citizenship" (Ong 1999) is created out of the differentiated pulls of local politics, nationalism, and global socioeconomic networks. What results is a set of "complex subjectivities" nominally grouped around a particular ethnic transnational network, but in reality divided along lines of gender, socioeconomic privileges and powers, class identities, and other such particularities. Regina Lee's account of three kinds of diasporic "psychological states, or forms of consciousness" is both an attempt at a taxonomy of theoretical approaches, and a recognition of the multiple strategies and means involved in the production of diasporic identities. Once again, the problematic discourses and projects of "the nation" are compromised by these diasporic strategies, but so too are the static and exclusionary categories ("self" and "other," "the past," "presence," "interior" and "exterior") that are the products of nationalisms.

The dislocation of national boundaries in the name of racially inflected social identities is in turn related to the production of "cultural citizenship," as opposed to a more tightly defined citizenship constituted by sociopolitical rights and privileges. Wenche Ommundsen's study of the Chinese community in Australia notes the duality of cultural citizenship: on the one hand, it is a flexible notion which facilitates the study of "culturally complex and inclusive communities," and may pave the way for a recognition of new kinds of citizen rights and responsibilities. On the other hand, however, it also constitutes yet another friction point in multicultural societies like that of Australia (and for that matter in many other nations), as a prescription for multicultural inclusivity that may provoke conservative reactions. At stake in this clash of different kinds of citizenship is the role of cultural parameters associated with diasporas — ethnicity, cultural difference, plural social identities and affiliations — within the existing tolerances even of modern immigrant nations like Australia.

In the light of questions thus raised, "hybridity" in diasporic conditions becomes problematized, not necessarily for reasons of irrelevance, but because it implies a more positive and constructive social condition than may be warranted in many locales. Rebecca Sultana's reading of Bharati Mukherjee's "attempt to become an American writer" goes against the laudatory grain of critics who see her as speaking for cosmopolitan writers, and as offering a positive image of the immigrant both in her personal life and in her dramatically hybrid, transnational fictional characters. Sultana's reading of Mukherjee is thus a paradigm for reading the absences and silences in celebratory transnational discourses; these must be informed by a critical reinsertion of the "conflicting locations of 'home,'" the real dualities of identity and culture, the problematic particularities of transnational dislocation. The cautionary note sounded by this reading of Mukherjee is salient in a wider context: literature may play a vital role in diasporic culture, but not necessarily in rationalized and constructive ways; the critical project of reading ideologically motivated gaps and silences in such literatures may be as important, if not more so, than authorial intentions.

The return of the exile, the diasporic writer's confrontation with what is left behind, is precisely the topic of Carol Leon's essay on Michael Ondaatje. Ondaatje's return to his homeland after an absence of twenty-five years — a return recorded in his *Running in the Family* — offers a postmodern critique of settled migrant identities and positions. This postmodern narrative thus offers a form for inserting several of the key disjunctions characteristic of diasporic movements: the split between biographical and symbolic fathers and sons, the conflict of memories and desires and of history and subjective reconstructions, the "binary between self and other." In contrast and yet also in complement to Sultana's treatment of Mukherjee, Leon's reading of Ondaatje's postmodern autobiography-travelogue suggests how the complex tensions of diasporic identities can be articulated, if only in suitably open and multivalenced narrative forms.

"Distance" is obviously a crucial concept in the phenomenon of diasporas, and yet also one that is difficult to theorize. Relative notions of distance are involved in complex imaginings of "home" and "away," "community" and "isolation," "self" and "other." Diasporic movements emphasize distance (in going away from the "homeland") but paradoxically also reiterate closeness and return (in reconstructions of and desires for the home, and in networking mechanisms to approximate the homeland community). Monti and Mittapalli consider the question of diasporic distance from an intertextual perspective, analyzing figures of the migrant, exile, Hindu religion, notions of caste, and other tropes in the works of transnational Indian writers like Rao, Mistry, Seth, Ghosh, and others. While nostalgic reconstructions of the homeland are often read into the works of émigré writers, it is also the writers' sense of distance from India that permits their textual critiques of the "strictures and the forbidding regulations ... that continue to harness the lives of Hindus." Monti and Mittapalli, like Sultana and Leon, are wary of the tendency to see "hybridization" as a comfortably affirming condition. Their reading of diasporic Indian writing shows how the writers' experience of distance, and their fictional accounts of this experience, constitute an act of power that enables the creation of a "postcolonial hegemony" and a corresponding "ethical other."

Another notion of diasporic distance emerges in Jeffrey Partridge's essay, which reads Shirley Lim's *Joss & Gold* against the grain of the "claiming America" strand of Asian-American writing. Distance is crucial to Lim's project, both in her own placement (as an ethnic Chinese who grew up in Southeast Asia and who now lives and works as an academic in the U.S.), as well as in the "tripart setting of the novel" (Malaysia, New York, Singapore). In significant part because of its translocational tropes and agenda, *Joss & Gold* thus represents Asian-American literature's "heteroglossic phase," in opposition to the older model of "ethnic nationalism" (Li 1998: 191, 196). Walter Lim's reading of Russell Leong has similarities to Partridge's paper, in positioning Leong against a larger strand of Asian-American writing and experience concerned with "generational travail" (Amy Tan and Maxine Hong Kingston are perhaps the best known representatives of this strand). Like Shirley Lim, Leong is as much interested in Southeast Asia as he is in America as a site of immigration and cultural transformation. Another distancing device is Leong's use of "deviance" — sexual deviance from social norms (of heterosexuality, monogamy, and so on), as well as the Asian immigrant's deviation from traditional cultural practices and attitudes. Such distancing tropes are part of Leong's concern, not with the more static notions of location and identity often produced in diasporic conditions, but with the fluid and often unsettling conditions of transnational identities in a global context.

The duality of diasporas — simultaneously an estranging distancing, as well as a perpetuated connectivity — is the subject of Bishop's and Phillips's essay on the military "insignia" that are borne by all diasporic movements. This essay in some ways links with Goh's article, in seeing symbolic violence as the underlying condition of transnational and transcultural relationships. For Bishop and Phillips, the "insignia of the military" are a way of conceptualizing the complex technologies and mechanisms (such as electronic financing and markets, digital and telecommunications, state sovereignties) that simultaneously sponsor and give birth to diasporic dispersals, and yet also connect and transform diasporic communities into new orders, allegiances, and identities.

Diasporic cultures are the reality of the global order and its technologies and institutions. Scholarship has the burden of attempting to document, theorize, and analyze the often rapid and intertwined social developments associated with transnational movements and communities. While no volume can claim to be an exhaustive study of such fluid and rapidly developing phenomena, there should nevertheless be an attempt to reflect and engage with the pace of diasporic developments through a theoretically informed, critically flexible, and multidisciplinary approach. It is hoped that the present volume will contribute to contemporary diasporic studies in precisely that spirit.

1

The Uncertain Configurations of a Politics of Location: The Intersection of Postcolonial, Feminist, and Nationalist Discourses in Understanding Chinese Diasporic Communities

Ann Brooks

Global shifts in the movement of peoples have led to the destruction of old nations and the formation of new ones. It is maintained in this chapter that emerging diasporic movements and communities have the potential for "surfacing" a range of new cultural and ethnic identities. It is further maintained that such new identities carry new conceptions of subjectivity and political subjecthood and require a rethinking of traditional analytical frameworks. Diasporic movements and their theorization can be seen to advance debates in this area. Within this chapter Chinese diasporic communities in Singapore, Australia, and Britain provide a focus for analysis and a backdrop to a reassessment of frameworks of analysis. This chapter examines the intersection of postcolonial, nationalist, and feminist discourses in providing a framework for understanding the complexity of Chinese diasporic movements in contemporary Singapore, set against a backdrop of political and cultural change in Southeast Asia. The theorization of diaspora advances the relationship between postcolonial theory and contemporary capitalism and provides a clearer understanding of the relationship between diaspora, nation, and postcolonial perspectives.

The chapter aims to achieve three things: firstly, it provides a theoretical critique of the limitations of traditional binary frameworks encapsulated in postcolonial and nationalist discourses; secondly, it provides a brief empirical study of the Chinese diaspora in Singapore and considers issues around the creation of new cultural identities; thirdly, the chapter also considers issues of hybridity and identity for Chinese diasporic communities in Australia and Britain and shows how the intersection of postcolonialism and feminism combined with a theorization of diaspora has opened up possibilities for a new conceptualisation and analysis of diasporic spaces.

The first part of the chapter examines some of the debates emerging around postcolonial, diasporic, and feminist discourses and shows how these frameworks can act in a mutually corrective way.

POSTCOLONIALISM: A CONTESTED DISCOURSE

Debates around what is understood by postcolonialism have shown the concept to be a highly contested one in theoretical terms. The emphasis for writers such as Said (1993) and Spoonley (1995) of postcolonialism is its rejection of colonialism and its accentuation of the process of decolonization. Said understands the process to be far more than a reaction to imperialism, and to provide "an alternative way of conceiving human history" (Said 1993: 260). Said is seeking to restore a notion of community and identity, "not confined to the orthodoxies of ethnic particularism" (Spoonley 1995: 49) but one which offers a reconceptualization of society as liberating.

Hall (1996) agrees that the "post-colonial" refers to a general process of decolonization, and he acknowledges the "universalizing" aspects of the concept, in terms of its high degree of abstraction. In this, Hall recognizes the postcolonial signals an interrogation if not subverting of the colonizer/colonized binary. However, Hall goes on to show that the "postcolonial" highlights a shift in the representation of such relations. As Hall states, "in terms of any absolute return to a pure set of uncontaminated origins, the long-term historical and cultural effects of 'transculturation' which characterized the colonizing experience proved, in my view, to be irreversible" (Hall 1996: 246). Suleri agrees, maintaining that the "entire post-colonial project usually posits precisely the impossibility of that identity ever being 'uncontaminated'" (Suleri 1995: 135). However, Hall urges caution around the assumptions that can be drawn from a critique of essentialism, noting, "it is too tempting to fall into the trap of assuming that because essentialism has been deconstructed *theoretically* therefore it has been displaced *politically*" (Hall 1996: 249).

Hall raises the question of whether the "postcolonial" has been confusingly universalized. Writers like Sara Suleri (1995) clearly think that it has. She comments, "where the term once referred exclusively to the discursive practices produced by the historical fact of prior colonization in certain geographically specific segments of the world, it is now more of an abstraction available for figurative deployment in any strategic definition of marginality" (Suleri 1995: 274). Hall acknowledges that there has been some "careless homogenizing" around the postcolonial going on, and the phrase has been applied widely and sometimes inappropriately. However, as Hall comments, "are we not all in different ways, and through different conceptual spaces (of which the post-colonial is definitively one) desperately trying to understand what making an ethical political choice and taking a political position in a necessarily open and contingent political field is like, what sort of 'politics it adds up to'?" (Hall 1996: 244).

POSTCOLONIALISM AND THE CURRENT CRISIS OF CONCEPTUALIZATION

The "postcolonial" and the various intellectual and cultural positions associated with it have provided a valuable terrain to test out some critical premises within the contemporary transformations in global relationships. As Dirlik (1997: 502) notes, we are dealing with a new world situation created by the transformations of global capitalism which has "disorganized" earlier conceptualizations of global relations, "especially the relations comprehended earlier by such binarisms as colonizer/colonized, First/Third Worlds, or the 'West and the rest.'" As Dirlik notes, unlike other 'posts,' postcolonialism claims this as its special provenance:

> to achieve an authentic globalization of cultural discourses: by the extension globally of the intellectual concerns and orientations originating at the central sites of Euro-American cultural criticism; and by the introduction into the latter of voices and subjectivities from the margins of earlier political and/or ideological colonialism. ... The goal, indeed, is no less than, the abolition of all distinctions between center and periphery,

and all other "binarisms" that are allegedly a legacy of colonialist ways
of thinking, and to reveal societies globally in their complex heterogeneity
and contingency. (Dirlik 1997: 501)

Understanding the critical premises of postcolonialism has been
valuable in understanding the uncertainty created by the reconfiguration
of the politics of location generated by the transformations of global
relationships. An example of this is the appeal of postcolonial thinking
to intellectuals from "settler societies." As Dirlik notes: "A changing
global situation in recent years has transformed earlier identifications
with Euro-America in these societies to new kinds of regional affinities
— most clearly in the case of Australia, which seeks to remake itself as
an 'Asian' society" (Dirlik 1997: 511). New Zealand has followed a very
similar pattern in defining itself in postcolonial terms and allies itself
with the South Pacific cluster of nations as opposed to Asia or Europe.
Australian postcolonial theorists Ashcroft, Griffiths, and Tiffin (1989) —
enthusiastic proponents of the postcolonial idea, particularly in literature
— understand all countries affected by the imperial process from the
moment of colonization to the present day as postcolonial, including
African countries, Australia, Bangladesh, Canada, Caribbean countries,
India, Malaysia, Malta, New Zealand, Pakistan, Singapore, South Pacific
Island countries, and Sri Lanka.

Another group, identified by Dirlik, whose intellectualism, while
different from postcolonial intellectuals, also signifies a shift in
conceptualizations in current intellectual/cultural positions, are Chinese
intellectuals. The latter, whose position is encapsulated in the so-called
Confucian revival of recent years, as Dirlik (1997: 511) notes, obviously
do not describe themselves as postcolonial, as their point of departure is
the "newfound power of Chinese societies within global capitalism,
which, if anything, shows in their efforts to suppress memories of an
earlier day when China, too, suffered from Euro-American hegemony."
I argue later in the paper that a theorization of diaspora and an
understanding of diasporic movements advances the relationship
between postcolonialism and the current transformations in global
relations, and in particular clarifies issues around complex subjectivities
for Chinese diasporic communities. This is an important development
because, as Dirlik comments, "since postcolonial criticism has focused
on the postcolonial subject to the exclusion of an account of the world

outside of the subject, the global condition implied by postcoloniality appears at best as a projection onto the world of postcolonial subjectivity and epistemology." Despite these limitations,

> "post colonialism" is expressive of a current crisis in the conceptualization of the world — not just a crisis in the ideology of linear progress but a crisis in the modes of comprehending the world associated with such concepts as ... the "nation-state".... Crossing national, cultural, class, gender and ethnic boundaries, moreover, with its promise of a genuine cosmopolitanism, is appealing in its own right. (Dirlik 1997: 516)

Issues of nationhood, gender, ethnicity, and class have all been issues that have not only preoccupied postcolonial thinking, they have also been central in understanding feminist thinking as it has engaged with a range of intellectual and epistemological discourses in its understanding of transformations in global relations.

CONVERGENCE AND DIVERGENCE IN THE INTERSECTION OF POSTCOLONIAL AND FEMINIST DISCOURSES

The last decade has produced an interesting debate on the significance of the postcolonial for feminist analysis and vice versa. There are a number of points of convergence and divergence in the intersection of feminist and postcolonial discourses. Feminism and postcolonialism share a number of similarities and objectives, which can act as mutually corrective strategies. There are also parallels in the history and political concerns of feminist and postcolonial discourses. Both feminist and postcolonial discourses advance philosophical positions which "seek to reinstate the marginalized in the face of the dominant" (Ashcroft ed. 1995: 249). Feminist and postcolonial theory also have a history of theorizing which addresses sets of binary relationships. "Early feminist theory, like early nationalist post-colonial criticism, was concerned with inverting the structures of domination, substituting, for instance, a female tradition or traditions for a male-dominated canon" (Ashcroft ed. 1995: 249). However, feminist theory, like postcolonial criticism, has moved on from "such simple inversions in favour of a more general questioning of forms and modes, and the unmasking of a spuriously author/itative on which such canonical constructions are founded" (Ashcroft ed. 1995:

249). Regardless of parallels in the historical emergence of contemporary feminism and postcolonial theory and despite having "theoretical trajectories demonstrating striking similarities" as well as having "followed a path of convergent evolution," there was little significant interest in the mutual interaction of these two discourses until recently. However, over the last ten years there has been "increasing interest not just in their parallel concerns but in the nature of their actual and potential intersections" (Ashcroft ed. 1995: 249). This aspect of feminist and postcolonial theory has only been adequately theorized relatively recently and I have written about this more fully elsewhere (Brooks 1997).

NATIONALIST AND FEMINIST DISCOURSES

The recent "dialogue" between postcolonial and feminist discourses needs to be set in the context of the more extensive relations between nationalist and feminist discourses and movements. The relationship between nationalist and feminist discourses is a complex one, and historically, in the Third World, feminist and nationalist movements have emerged in tandem, as Heng (1997) observes, either as anticolonial or anti-imperialist struggles or as part of reform movements or religious-nationalist/cultural-nationalist revivalist movements. Heng notes that the failure to articulate the relationship as one of contestation as well as cooperation has resulted in a widely held view of a "triumphant nationalism that makes its gains and wins its accomplishments at the expense of a subordinated feminism" (Heng 1997: 31). There is little doubt that despite a lack of historical documentation of the intersection of nationalism and feminism, women have provided a mechanism for embedding a concept of collective mobilization within a framework of community groups and have contributed to anchoring "the national(ist) imaginary." Heng comments that "given feminism's uneasy status in the Third World, its problematic relations with nationalism, and (like nationalism) its relatively brief genealogy, Third World feminism has been especially liable to manipulation by nationalists for its symbolizing potential, and as a capsule instance of the encroachment of modernity and/or Westernization" (Heng 1997: 133).

The parallel development of nationalist and women's movements in the form of anticolonial independence movements in countries such as China, Indonesia, Malaysia, and Singapore frequently produced a number of women nationalist political leaders in the forefront of anti-imperialist struggles. Heng notes that "feminism in Singapore and Malaysia arose as a subset of nationalist politics, so that the hierarchical relationship of feminism to nationalism ... was plainly visible at the outset" (Heng 1997: 35). The contradictory position of Singapore in relation to its colonial past and contemporary postcolonial politics combined to create a deeply ambivalent position for women in relation to the Singaporean state, where women are frequently seen as central in ideological reproduction, at the same time as being exploited in the framing of the relationship between nationalism and sexuality.

This contradictory attitude was apparent in the emergence of the first postcolonial government in Singapore led by the People's Action Party (PAP).[1] As Heng notes, "significantly, the theme of female emancipation enabled the essentially reform-minded PAP, whose leadership was dominated by English-educated elites, to present itself in powerfully revolutionary terms, the ideological resonance of which echoed and approximated the revolutionary discourse of their competitors, the Chinese-educated and China-backed Communists" (Heng 1997: 35). However, once in power the attitude of the PAP toward women and women's issues has been contradictory, with women caught in the maelstrom of ideological, economic, and political tensions characterizing Singapore's position in the region. In this context it is important to understand the contradictory location of Singapore in its framing of an "imagined national identity."

A NATIONAL IMAGINED COMMUNITY

The history of Singapore as a thoroughly "settled" multiracial society by definition provided a deeply entrenched sense of insecurity in terms of satisfying a need for a strong postcolonial national identity. Ang and Stratton (1995: 182) show how Singapore's lack of claim to "indigenous authenticity" reinforced its sense of isolation in terms of its participation within "an imagined Asia" and in particular in relation to "Malaysia and Indonesia, who defined *their* postcolonial national identities precisely on the basis of discursive claims to indigenous territorial belonging." Singapore, thus, in its own terms and those of its neighbors, "suffers from an originary identity deficit." As Ang and Stratton show, "it cannot lay claim to a myth of indigenous origin (which is the case for Malaysia), nor to a history of heroic struggle for independence against colonial oppression (as is the case with Indonesia), which in these two, and in other contexts, have provided the basis for a transcendental legitimation of the postcolonial nation state" (1995: 184).

As a result, Singapore is characterized by a complex racial and cultural hybridity, framed by a Western legacy, expressed in its dominant language, bureaucratic structures, and multiracial population consisting of Chinese, Malay, Indian, and Other. While it can be argued that this hybrid character has given Singapore a significant economic strength in the region, it has, for the Singaporean government, been a paradoxical strength. "It is precisely this reality of hybridity, with its related dynamics of cultural impurity, mixture and fusion, which presents a problem in the dominant global cultural order, where historically nation-states have been supposed to have pure and unified, if not homogenous national cultures, a national culture created through the intervention of an authentic Asianness" (Ang and Stratton 1995: 183). This has resulted in the Singapore government becoming one of the most significant proponents of what Ang and Stratton define as "a new *self-Orientalization*" or what Heng and Devan define as an "'internalized orientalism' of state narratives ... whereby a timeless Confucian paternal essence is defined as embodying the nation" (Heng and Devan 1995: 195).

"ORIENTALISM" AND "AMBIVALENCE" IN CONTEMPORARY SINGAPORE

The legacy of "Orientalism" in the context of contemporary Singapore has a particular inflection which reflects its contradictory postcolonial identity as "both non-Western and always–already Westernised, neither truly Western nor authentically 'Asian'" (Ang and Stratton 1995: 180). As Ang and Stratton note, "the ambivalent positioning of Singapore exemplifies the exclusionary effects of the binary logic of Orientalist discourse" (1995: 180). The East/West binary established by this discourse is problematized by the "politics of location" characterized by the uncertain configuration of contemporary Singapore. As Ang and Stratton observe, the discursive construction of "Singapore" both unsettles the narrative legacy of Orientalism which underpins this renewed ideological investment in the binary oppositioning of "East" and "West." We want to suggest that the discourse of the East/West divide is essential for an understanding of Singapore, not only because it lies at the historical origin of Singapore as a colonial construct, but also because ... it is structurally constitutive of Singapore as a modern, national cultural entity. (1995: 179)

Central in this thinking around *"self*-Orientalization" is the Singaporean government's conceptualization of Singapore within an "imagined Asia" and in particular the ways in which Singapore has positioned itself within debates around "Asian values" and the construction of a "national imagined community."

"INTERNALIZED ORIENTALISM": CONFUCIAN VALUES AND NATIONAL IDENTITY

In order to create a Singaporean national identity the government has attempted to create an "authentic" Chineseness which is highlighted in the emphasis of all Chinese learning to speak their officially defined mother tongue, Mandarin. Heng and Devan (1995: 203) define "the retrieval of a superior, 'core' Chinese culture in the name of a fantasmatic 'Confucianism'" through the promotion of Mandarin, "the preferred dialect of the ruling class of imperial China, as the master language of Chineseness" as an aspect of offsetting the potential danger of contamination by the West.

The particular concerns held by the Singaporean government to maintain an "authentic" Chinese culture through aspects of Confucianism, as revealed in the emphasis on Mandarin, is related to English being the language of instruction. This, argue Heng and Devan, makes Singapore more vulnerable to Western influence, unlike Japan, Taiwan, and Korea. As Heng and Devan note, "the dominance of English was institutionalized after decolonization by Lee's [Kuan Yew] own government which established it as the preferred language of education and business, and as the *de facto* language of government: a privileged medium of access to Western science and technology which augmented the nation's attractions to multinational capital" (1995: 204).

This has proved to be an enormously successful strategy, providing the kind of reassurance for global capitalist investment that other regional centres like Hong Kong have not been able to provide since "handover" to China in 1997. As Heng and Devan note, "the paradigms of economic and corporate management and their protocols of rationality serve at once as the model and chief beneficiary of the state's pastoral power submitting citizens to a structure of values which best subtends, with minimal fuss and resistance, the efficient working of state corporatism and multinational capital" (1995: 207). The combination of what I have called a *post(modern)* Confucianist ethos with the demands of the "new economy" have produced what they call an "internalized Orientalism" which they maintain "allows the definition of an idealized Chineseness fully consonant with the requirements of a modern market economy" (Heng and Devan 1995: 207).

GLOBAL CAPITALISM, "FLEXIBLE CITIZENSHIP," AND THE CHINESE DIASPORA

The relationship between global capitalism and Chinese diasporic movements has been explored recently in the work of Aihwa Ong (1999). I have already shown that theorizing diaspora advances the relationship between postcolonialism and global capitalism by reinserting a complex subjectivity around Chinese diasporic communities. Ong develops just this paradigm by focusing on the concept of "flexible citizenship." In her study of the "flexible citizenship" of Chinese global capitalists, Ong (1999: 3) suggests that we consider the "transnational practices and imaginings of the nomadic subject and the social conditions that allow his flexibility." As Ong states, the Chinese global capitalists she describes are not simply "adroitly navigating the disjunctures between political landscapes and the shifting opportunities of global trade." Rather, their "very flexibility in geographical and social positioning is itself an effect of novel articulations between regimes of the family, the state and capital" (Ong 1999: 3). Ong is concerned with "human agency and its production and negotiations of cultural meanings within the normative milieus of late capitalism" (1999: 3). By "flexible citizenship" Ong is referring to the "cultural logics of capitalist accumulation, travel and displacement that induce subjects to respond fluidly and opportunistically to changing political-economic conditions"; in other words, Ong is interested in the way in which Chinese subjects are regulated by a range of practices "favoring flexibility, mobility and repositioning in relation to markets, governments and cultural regimes" (1999: 3). There are implications here for the relationship between Chinese diasporic communities and nationhood as well as subjectivity. As Ong notes: "if ... we pay attention ... to the *transnational practices and imaginings* of the nomadic subject and the social conditions that enable his flexibility, we obtain a different picture of how nation-states articulate with capitalism in late modernity" (1999: 3).

The relationship between transnationality, global capital, and the feminization of labor is a particularly interesting one in the context of Southeast Asia. As Ong notes, "in Asia, transnational flows and networks have been the key dynamics in shaping cultural practices, the formation of identity, and shifts in state strategies" (1999: 17). Transnationalism takes on a particular inflection in the context in the so-called Asian tiger economies, given the history of diasporan trading groups such as the ethnic Chinese, who play a major role in relation to transnational Asian capitalism. As Ong states:

> Global capitalism in Asia is linked to new cultural representations of "Chineseness" ... in relation to transnational Asian capitalism. ... The changing status of diasporan Chinese is historically intertwined with the operations and globalizations of capital. ... " (1999: 7)

These aspects of transnationalism have clear implications for the economies of Chinese diasporic communities in Singapore and Hong Kong.

Diasporic Chinese within the region have played and are playing a key role in the emergence of a "new flexible" capitalism in the region. In addition, as Ong argues:

> Many formerly colonized countries in Southeast Asia are themselves emergent capitalist powerhouses that are "colonizing" territories and peoples in their backyard or further afield: Indonesia has invaded and colonized East Timor, while Malaysian, Singaporean, and Hong Kong entrepreneurs are factory managers in China, timber barons in New Guinea and Guyana, and hotel operators in England and the United States. These strategies of economic colonization by countries formerly colonized by the West represent new forms of engaging dissent at home and capital abroad. (Ong 1999: 35)

Ong goes on to note that her interest in the study of Chinese subjects is also concerned with how global capitalism in Asia is linked to new cultural representations of "Chineseness" in relation to transnational Asian capitalism. As she observes, "the changing status of diasporan Chinese is historically intertwined with the operations and globalizations of capital and their cultural experiences" (Ong 1999: 7). However, it is important to acknowledge, as Ong (1999: 13) notes, "academic interest in how diasporas shape racialized, gendered, sexualized and oppositional subjectivities is often tied to scholars' attempts to shape their own cosmopolitan, intellectual commitment." Regardless of this, the combined emphasis of theorizations around both the postcolonial and diasporic subject have resulted in a position where, as Dirlik (1997: 506) notes, "attention needs to be shifted from national origin to subject-position; hence a 'politics of location' takes precedence over politics informed by fixed categories" such as the nation. The theoretical framing of debates around diasporic Chinese communities and subjectivities has been significantly advanced by the intersection of feminist diasporic perspectives with the postcolonial. The theoretical implications of such analysis are explored in the final section of this chapter.

OPENING UP SPACES FOR POSTCOLONIAL FEMINISTS

Much of the work which has been drawn on in this chapter and elsewhere from postcolonial feminist perspectives tends to operate within a fairly conventional feminist model drawing on the Western "grand narrative tradition" within feminism of relying on categories such as race (Heng and Devan 1995), nationality/nationhood (Ang and Stratton 1995), or patriarchy (Stivens 1998) as the basis of analysis. This tends to formulate fairly rigid patterns of analysis which fail to identify spaces where alternative perspectives can be articulated. Such analyses are as a result overly deterministic in their outcomes. I would advocate a more fully "postcolonial feminist" perspective where the intersection of postcolonial conceptualizations with feminism provides opportunities for the opening up of spaces within which alternative models can be developed. The intersection of postcolonialism and feminism framed within and contextualized by an understanding of the theorization of diaspora produces some interesting possibilities for an analysis of the Chinese diaspora in countries such as Australia and Britain. As Ong (1999: 15) notes, "in a sense, the diasporan subject is now vested with the agency formerly sought in the working class and more recently in the subaltern subject."

POSTCOLONIAL FEMINIST SPACES AND THE CHINESE DIASPORA

The concept of "postcolonial" space(s) and the opportunities it opens up for the development of new subject positions and new places from which to speak has been particularly valuable for a number of feminist theorists writing and working from diasporic experiences. Magdalene Ang-Lygate (1997) considers the significance of the "postcolonial" for "charting the spaces of (un)location," that is, for developing a feminist theorizing of diaspora. Ang-Lygate, by birth a Malaysian Chinese, describes herself as an "immigrant Chinese woman in postcolonial British society" (Ang-Lygate 1997: 169). She recognizes that Eurocentric feminist discourse was silent about transnational diasporic experiences, such as her own, and lacked both a knowledge and understanding of such experiences.

Ang-Lygate understands the framing of identity as complex, and she resists systems that perpetuate uniformity and "monovocality" and that fail to acknowledge "the hybrid influences of culture, politics, history and language that stem from post-colonial traditions" (1997: 170). She distinguishes between spaces of (un)location which she defines as "uncharted territories where the shifting and contextual meaning of diaspora reside — caught somewhere between, and inclusive of, the more familiar experiences of (re)location and (dis)location" (Ang-Lygate 1997: 170). She defines (re)location as concerned with the processes of emigration and (dis)location to represent the realities and experiences of immigrants.

She draws attention to the difficulties of using a language that, while available in the literature, does not explain the location from which she is writing. As she notes, "I have had to use permutations ... words such as 'black,' ... diasporic, immigrant, visible minority, ethnic, non-white, women of colour, 'Third World' women, ... native (female) Other — all of which are individually wanting and inaccurate" (Ang-Lygate 1997: 170). Having acknowledged the inappropriateness of much of the language available, she warns feminist scholars against a neglect of "unproblematized and unlocated struggle" (Ang-Lygate 1997: 170). She notes that "given the legacy of white supremacy and a pathological denial of difference, it is all the more vital that the complex realities of (un)location are not silenced through a lack of suitable vocabulary" (1997: 170).

She highlights the problematic around the conceptualization of "Asian." The term "Asian" also has very different meanings in different contexts. In Britain, it refers to "peoples who originate from the Indian subcontinent," whereas in the United States, while it applies to this group, it also applies to peoples from "Southeast and Pacific Asian countries such as Japan, Korea and the Philippines" (Ang-Lygate 1997: 172–3).

The lack of an appropriate language to frame identity forces diasporic groups to adopt identities which deny the complexities of everyday experiences and realities of diasporic communities and movements. In addition, as Ang-Lygate (1997: 173) points out, "the privileging of 'race' or descent over and above other social categories and the adoption of a 'black' identity may discourage such groups of women from a recognition of multiple identities and subjectivities." For example, the experience of racialization is different for "black" women and "black" men.

One of the reasons why there has been a failure in the development of an appropriate language and conceptual repertoire to explain diasporic identities and experiences is a failure at the level of theory. "For example, when Edward Said (1978) claimed that 'black' peoples are orientalized and demonized as 'heathens,' 'pagans,' 'uncivilized,' 'barbaric' and so on, in eurocentric narratives of anthropology, religion and colonialism, his ... argument failed to include a gendered analysis" (Ang-Lygate 1997: 173). Building on Said's model, Ang-Lygate shows how drawing on a conception of "multiple identities allows a more constructive argument that 'black' women are not only racialized but also sexualized, exoticized and eroticized — all at the same time" (Ang-Lygate 1997: 173).

A further dimension which complicates identity for Chinese women is the issue of authenticity. The term "Chinese" is itself problematic as it imposes "a unilateral homogeneity on Chinese peoples and fosters the myth of 'authentic ethnicity'" (Ang-Lygate 1997: 178). In other words, these concepts carry "racialized stereotypes" and support an essentialist notion of identity that ignores historical and geographical diversity. The relationship between "authenticity" and "Otherness" is an important one. Ang-Lygate shows how conceptions of "Otherness" are unproblematic when "'authenticity' is demarcated and controlled by a dominant western discourse." However, Otherness is seen as subversive when it moves outside "dominant defined identity enclosures" (Ang-Lygate 1997: 180). Trinh T. Minh-ha (1991: 74) discusses the concept of "inappropriate Others" to refer to those who resist definitions of Otherness and whose understanding of difference draws on their own perspective rather than as defined by dominant discourses. A recent novel by the writer/novelist Hsu-Ming Teo, *Love and Vertigo* (2000), explores the diasporic experience for the Singaporean Chinese family, and women in particular, in the Australian context. This novel highlights the complexities of a gendered analysis in the fragmentation of identity within the framework of the Chinese diasporic family.

HYBRIDITY AND CHINESE IDENTITY

The issue of authenticity and Chineseness is taken up by Ien Ang (1992, 1993, 1996) who has explored the relationship between identity and Chineseness particularly in the context of the Chinese diaspora and its positioning in the multicultural context of Australia. At a political level Ang sets out to "deconstruct the essential Chinese subject to carve out a space for overseas Chinese people in which they can claim their own hybrid sense of identity *as* Chinese without having to apologise that they are not pure and authentic" (Ang 1993: 19). In theorizing a conception of Chineseness, Ang maintains that such categories should not be seen as fixed but "as an open and indeterminate signifier whose meanings are constantly renegotiated and rearticulated in different sections of the Chinese diaspora" (Ang 1993: 19). As Ang indicates, what it means to be Chinese varies from place to place and by patterns of settlement; there are, in other words, many different Chinese identities.

The conception of the pure and essential Chinese subject, "the absolute norm for authentic Chineseness" that overseas Chinese people are confronted with, is one that owes much to China's recent history. The creation of a unified and holistic Chinese culture emanated from the defeat of Chiang Kai-Shek's Nationalist army in mainland China in 1949 and the subsequent installation of the Nationalist government in Taiwan. As Ang notes, the emergence of "the discourse of Chineseness" in the context of the Taiwanese nation-state is "thoroughly ideological." She argues that "one of the political effects of this official intervention of 'traditional Chinese culture' in post-war Taiwan is a 'reanchoring [of the] indigenous Taiwanese population to the mythic origins of Chinese civilisation'" (Ang 1993: 22).

The concept of Chineseness in Taiwan "has been constructed as the hegemonic, universal identity imposed on everyone, leaving no space for difference and diversity, for the assertion of non-Chinese identities" (Ang 1993: 24). Ang maintains that states such as Australia that vigorously promulgate multiculturalism create "the space for the representation of a cultural diversity which is not publicly available in nation-states which define themselves in terms of a single and homogeneous national identity" (Ang 1993: 24).

In a further development of the relationship between multiculturalism and the framing of Asian identity in the context of Australia, Ang (1996) considers the issue of "ambivalence" in relation to multiculturalism. In the Australian context, the narrative of multiculturalism is a "narrative of progressive transformation" in which the nation is seen to be moving from "a racist exclusionary past to a multicultural inclusionary present" (Stratton and Ang 1994: 132). Ang points out that underlying the narrative of multiculturalism in Australia is a subtext which has as its emphasis "integration with Asia." As Ang points out, "this does not mean that people of diverse 'Asian' origins living in Australia are no longer constructed as other to the Australian self but ... that the *status* of the otherness has changed" (Ang 1996: 37).

In the context of multicultural Australia, Ang maintains that being Asian means occupying a position some way between inclusion and exclusion, in the ambivalent space of what Bhabha describes as "almost the same [as us] but not quite" (Bhabha 1994: 86). As Ang observes, "if the ambivalence of multicultural discourse creates a space, itself replete with ambivalence, in between sameness and otherness, then it is a space in which minority subjects are both discursively confined and symbolically embraced" (Ang 1996: 46).

CONCLUSION

This chapter has examined the intersection of postcolonial, diasporic, and feminist discourses for an analysis of new conceptualizations of diasporic spaces. The Chinese diasporic community has been examined within the context of contemporary Singapore and the limitations of traditional binary frameworks have been highlighted. The relationship between the Chinese diaspora and issues of national identity in Singapore have also been explored. Conceptualizations of "hybridity," "authenticity," and "ambivalence" as aspects of a postcolonial feminist theorizing of diaspora have provided a framework for analysis of Chinese diasporic communities in Britain and Australia. It is maintained in this paper that the theorization of diaspora advances debates around postcolonialism and feminism and opens up possibilities for an understanding of complex subjectivities for Chinese diasporic communities.

2

Diaspora and Violence: Cultural/Spatial Production, Abjection, and Exchange

Robbie B. H. Goh

"I can see you don't understand Americans, Pooley — or blacks for that matter. Those Yardies in Brixton shoot you as soon as look at you. I know about them." (Ruth Dudley Edwards, *Matricide at St. Martha's*)

"Forget it, Jake — It's Chinatown." (Roman Polanski, *Chinatown*)

Episode 1: On 5 August 2001 in Glasgow, 22-year-old Firsat Yildiz, a Turkish Kurd asylum seeker, was stabbed to death by attackers who (according to a companion of the victim) "hurled racist insults ... in Scottish accents" (Lee 2001b: 15). The incident took place in the Sighthill housing estate, where the government had housed 3,500 asylum seekers in ten run-down high-rise blocks, and which had become a target of the resentment of the neighboring Scottish communities.

Episode 2: On 23 June 2001, in Burnley, Lancashire, the attack on a Pakistani taxi driver by a group of white youths armed with hammers led to a riot in which 100 Asian youths went on a rampage, destroying shops and public property. About 8 percent of Burnley's population is Asian. The ultra-right-wing British National Party (BNP), which was involved in this and other racial clashes, garnered 11 percent of the vote in the most recent general election. During the riot, Muslim youths torched a shop selling pornographic material and alternative lifestyle clothing (Lee 2001a: 9).

Episode 3: In Sydney, a series of gang rapes on Caucasian girls by teenagers from the city's Lebanese community provoked retaliatory threats against Muslim women and abusive behavior toward Muslims. The Imam of a mosque in the city was quoted as saying that the Muslim community would "strike back at attacks on its women" (*Straits Times*, 27 August 2001: 11).

Such accounts of violent episodes involving immigrant communities in recent years can be multiplied manifold, and added to the toll of violence whose more spectacular and memorable incidents include the attacks on shopkeepers of Korean descent in Los Angeles during the Rodney King riots in 1992, repeated attacks on immigrants of Turkish and African descent by skinheads in Germany, and attacks on the property and persons of the ethnic Chinese (regardless of whether they were "totok" or "peranakan," recent immigrants or acculturalized longstanding citizens) in Indonesia during the May 1998 riots.

As spectacular and newsworthy as such episodes may be, violence as a fundamental aspect of immigrant and transnational movements does not fully register within much of diaspora studies, with the exception of the crisis in the homeland which is the original cause for the "collective forced dispersion" of the diasporic group (Chaliand and Rageau 1995: xiv). Yet this recognition of the sociopolitical disruption that often spurs diasporic movement is then elided within the schema of transnational communities and networks, where the emphasis instead is often on continuity and consolidation: the maintenance of a "strong sense of identity" over space and time that is tantamount to a "global tribalism," or the "economic synergy" of "diaspora capitalists" (Kotkin 1993: 6; Lever-Tracy, Ip, and Tracy 1996: 8). Considered as a phenomenon of urban sociology and spatial analysis, the violent disruption of diasporic links often fails to emerge within the discussion of "global cities" and their creation of a corresponding "global citizenship" that is in many ways at odds with "nations as the important space of citizenship" (Holston and Appadurai 1999: 3). Where factors of ethnicity and power are acknowledged within the abstracting terms of "global citizenship" and "cosmopolitanism," they tend to be manifested in terms that still imply the subject's continuity and functionality within the global economic enterprise: thus Sassen (1996: 192) speaks of multiple ethnic identities in global cities like New York, Paris, and London as "the amalgamated 'other'" within a "dominant economic narrative." Goldsmith's (2000: 41, 45) useful analysis of the political and spatial manifestations of racism in American cities focuses on the relegation of black Americans to "segregated" and "marginal" roles, from which they are viewed at a "safe distance" by whites; it is not until the very end of his article that he touches briefly on the issue of violence, and even then does not link the disjunctive force of such violence to the racial logic of the city itself.

In media and cultural studies, where race and ethnic identities are central themes, there is generally a greater recognition of injustice in representations, but less analysis of the role of violence in ethnic representations or of its function within a cultural logic of diasporic cultural negotiation and exchange. Earlier scholarship in this area tended to focus on racial stereotyping and the propagation of images of inferiority attached to ethnic groups. Hartmann and Husband (1974: 36, 44) see in British media of the 1960s and 1970s the perpetuation of a quasi-scientific and "Victorian" perspective of the black man as biologically or culturally inferior, which thus also serves as a justification for white dominance or control. Both Solomos (1989) and Saggar (1992) observe the history of violent race riots in Britain, but tend to see these as consequences or justifications of the racist immigration policy in Britain — as "examples [used in the media] of the dangers of unrestricted immigration" (Solomos 1989: 60) — rather than as integral parts of an immigrant experience and process. More recent media studies have tended to focus on issues of empowerment and growth: thus, on the one hand, the rising prominence of ethnic producers of media texts, for example black directors in Hollywood (Wilson and Gutierrez 1995: 89); and on the other hand, the growing communications networks among groups such as the diasporic Chinese, which promise to create a "global" audience and "common cultural region" (Cunningham and Sinclair 2001: 35).

While it seems certain that recent developments in transnational networks transform older forms of racism as they also challenge older forms of nationality and citizenship, and at least in this respect potentially empower ethnic minorities, it is less certain that such networks foster continuous cultures and inclusive spaces under the aegis of the "cosmopolitan" citizen and the "global city." Celebratory accounts of seamless diasporic networks, the economic successes of certain migrant groups, their integration into the "multicultural" fabric of their host nation, are discourses which, while they feed into the ideology of global capitalism and its notions of borderless and inclusive profits, are in some danger of slanting the diasporic experience. As Hall (2000: 210–1) points out, the ideology of "multiculturalism" associated with "liberal-constitutional, 'modern,' western nation-states" is motivated (among other things) to "assimilate," "manage," and "integrate" ethnic and cultural difference into the sociopolitical mainstream. At the level of representational discourses, then, such a multiculturalism produces signs of inclusivity that, while not denying the differences of race and ethnicity, attempt to fit these into functional roles within the machinery of global capitalism. As Deleuze and Guattari (1984: 185) argue, an "alliance is representation itself," a recoding of difference into the abstract logic of social and economic exchange and serviceability. The discourse of global diasporic networks incurs a representational cost; it works to cover its own processes of recodification, and thus entails a certain false consciousness, part of which is expressed as "myths" of diasporic entrepreneurship, of immigrant business successes, and of multicultural assimilation.[1]

The discourse of seamless networking fails, among other things, to account for the phenomenon of violence that constantly recurs in connection with diasporas. Nor is this discourse salvaged by the implication that violence is incidental and isolated, attached to crisis moments such as civil disorder in the homeland ("exile") and immigration disorders ("criminal activity," "welfare abuses," "race riots"). Such a fragmentary view thwarts the understanding of diasporas as "processes" (Sassen 1999: 111), replacing this with a sanitized conception of idealized cosmopolitan citizens removed from actual contexts of transnational movements and the problems thereof. Such denials — the work of "repression" caused by the "State desire" for seamlessness (Deleuze and Guattari 1984: 221) — constantly run up against the articulations of diasporic violence in the spatial logic of cities, in the symbolic logic of various cultural texts that refer to transnational human processes, and of course in the endemic physical violence that occurs in various stages of the diasporic process.

THE BUSINESS OF PLEASURE: DESIRE, ETHNICITY, CITYSCAPES

One of the dominant scenes in the narrative of immigrant success is the ethnic business area — the Chinatowns in many anglophone nations being prime examples — which in many ways is held up as the model of seamless ethnic integration into the white host culture. Once again the "myth" of Chinese entrepreneurship is significant here, feeding into a broader perception of Asian immigrants as hardworking and contributing to the prosperity of their adopted country, and fostering a strategy of assimilation into the mainstream business life of the city.[2] One token of this preferential assimilation in many global cities is the close proximity of Chinatowns and their business establishments to the busy city nexus: thus London's Soho, Birmingham's Hurst Street, Vancouver's Chinatown just outside of the Gastown tourist/shopping belt, Chicago's Chinatown south of downtown, Melbourne's Chinatown close to the central shopping area, and so on.

This desire for Chinese goods and businesses relies, among other things, on the creation of the ethnic business district as a safe, family-oriented, and fun place. There is thus in one form of discursive production a conspicuous erasure of all traces of violence, indeed of much of the problematics and potential confrontations caused by ethnic difference. This is evident not only in the kind of tourist material represented by the "FindFamilyFun" webpage, which depicts Vancouver's Chinatown largely as a family "adventure" whose main attractions are shopping and eating ("FindFamilyFun" 2001); it is also part of the spatial organization and presentation of the Chinatown, a collaborative effort on the part of Chinese businesses and municipal authorities to present an image of seamless commercial and social integration. This is typified by the Holloway Circus Improvements undertaken by the Birmingham City Council in 1998, an attempt at creating an ethnicized landscape near the Hurst Street "Chinese Quarter." The tropes of connectivity, access, and continuity are very much evident in this kind of spatial project, which consisted primarily of erecting a Chinese pagoda and installing matching decorations such as stone lions in the Holloway circus (Figure 2.1). A commemorative plaque at the base of the pagoda announces that it was "quarried and crafted by hand in Fujian province, China using traditional methods," "donated by Wing Yip and Brothers (Holdings) Ltd., to the

Figure 2.1 Pagoda in Birmingham's Holloway Circus, a symbolic and decentered "gateway" to the city's Chinatown area.

people and city of Birmingham," and "implemented by Birmingham City Council." The pagoda is thus presented as both culturally authentic and respectful of "traditional methods" and materials from the motherland; while at the same time constituting a viable hybrid interface with the adoptive nation. In terms of urban planning, the pagoda is intended (according to the City Council's plaque) "to create a gateway feature" into the city's market quarter (within which Chinatown is located). This ostensibly seamless integration of two cultures is echoed in several of the restaurants in Birmingham's Chinatown, which adopt the name "Chung Ying" (meaning "Chinese-English," or more idiomatically in English, "Anglo-Chinese"; Figure 2.2).

This kind of cultural-commercial will-to-integration is at odds with another kind of discourse about ethnic businesses and enclaves, one that is cognizant of the cultural and physical violence inherent to such spaces. Parker (2000: 76–7) argues that notions of the Chinatown in British cities as "a self-sufficient enclave," where Chinese merchants can engage

Figure 2.2 Awkward hybridity in one of the several "Chung Ying" (Chinese-English, or more idiomatically, "Anglo-Chinese") restaurants in Birmingham's Hurst Street Chinatown area. The mock crenellations and cruciform slits, which gesture as much to a mythic English castle or cathedral architectural form, sit incongruously with the Chinese-themed restaurant, its internal fittings, and menu.

selectively and on their own terms with white British culture, ignores (among other things) the reality of "racial harassment" encountered in such sites. Alexander (2000: 126–9) catalogues the growing perception in the British press during the latter part of the 1990s that "Asian identity" becomes recoded as the "ultra-masculine" activities (rap and ragga music, drug dealing and fights) of gangs of south Asians in "ghettoes." Such images of ethnicity are then carried over into the portrayal of the ethnic district in general: thus Partridge (1999: 31, 33) shows how certain books on Chinatown intended for the popular market, like Gwen Kinkead's *Chinatown: A Portrait of a Closed Society* (1992), foster a readership based on the consumption of a "dangerous and sinister Chinatown," entirely "segregated" from surrounding American society and characterized by gamblers, gangs, illegal immigrants, and the like.

It is difficult to reconcile the polarized images of Chinatown: the model ethnic enclave, fun family zone and site of intercommunal commerce and prosperity on the one hand; and the threatening place of crime and violence on the other. Partridge (1999: 39–41) shows that the "orientalized" perspective of Chinatown is a remainder of older policies of racial segregation in a "Euro-American" model of society, and argues that this has segued into a representation of Chinatown that "seeks to contain and manage the foreign Other," by depicting the other as "lucrative commodity." Yet what disrupts the ideological project of "containment" and "management" is the violent dualism of desire in which the Other is caught up. At one end of this scale, ethnic difference is recoded as a consumable exoticism, immigrant business as commercial vigor, and desire as mainstream commodity culture. However, this sanitized commercial desire is juxtaposed with an opposing form of desire — manifested in the vice industries and the trade in alcohol and drugs, and the condoned degeneration of the urban landscape that this often requires, and which ruptures the managed space of Chinatown.

Thus seen from the reverse approach (coming through the smaller and grimier streets of the Bull Ring and Market area) rather than from the official gateway fronting the larger and busier streets of the city's main shopping area, Birmingham's Chinese Quarter reveals an entirely different and less salubrious face, marked by run-down shops, sex establishments, and nightspots advertising weekly "Flesh"-themed nights (Figure 2.3). In this respect it is hardly unique, and is indeed a more respectable and less spectacular version of the concentration of vice-related businesses found in the backstreets of Chinatowns in London, Melbourne, San Francisco, Amsterdam, and other cities.

The double-faced nature of Chinatowns is thus symptomatic of the duplicity of civic desire and its treatment of ethnic space. Access to the

Figure 2.3 One of several sex-related businesses which confront the pedestrian who approaches the Birmingham Chinatown area from the "opposite" direction from the official, pagoda-marked gateway.

better and more salubrious parts of ethnic business establishments is regulated by symbolic gateways such as Birmingham's pagoda, the typical Chinese archways found in the Chinatowns of San Francisco, Sydney, Melbourne, Chicago, Vancouver, and elsewhere, and by the regulation of flows of traffic (pedestrian ways, vehicular and public transport systems). These gateways thus become an explicit attempt on the part of the civic will to deny more problematic ethnic spaces where the cultural, legal, and economic complexities of the immigrant community are apparent, and yet which are often contiguous with the approved Chinatown. Traversing Chinatowns in a "contrary" fashion (as it were) — moving off the approved main streets and away from the larger and more successful businesses, approaching it through back streets and past smaller establishments whose role is less obvious to the eye of the outsider — is gently and subtly discouraged by the spatial organization and symbolic landscape. Birmingham's politically correct pagoda itself is placed in a small concrete circus surrounded by the heavy traffic of Holloway Circus, presenting a striking visual landmark from some distance, but actually cut off both from the main shopping area and the Chinese shops. Access is possible through underpasses, but once in the garden there is actually nothing to do, nor do the ethnic symbols stand close inspection — while the pagoda advertises its Chinese fabrication, the stone lions are marked "© 1986 Henri Studio Inc." (a well-known landscape decoration firm with branches in the US, Canada, and Europe; Figure 2.4). The garden is also a rather daunting place to be in, especially after dark, with the surrounding noise of traffic, and the dark corners of the underpasses. The function of the pagoda in terms of traffic flows (apart from its symbolic function as an advertisement of commercial-cultural hybridity and harmony) is thus the daylight function of indicating the official entrance to Chinatown, which is not the pagoda garden itself but around it (and around the whole of Holloway Circus) to the pedestrian crossings of Smallbrook, linking the main shopping area with Hurst Street. The location of train stations and expressway exits closer to the official gateways, the concentration of shops and

Figure 2.4 Stone lion in the Holloway Circus, underlining the attempt at a "Chinese" identity in the otherwise nondescript concrete urban site.

restaurants in a central area, the orientation of Chinatowns in relation to the busy city centre from which most of the outside traffic is likely to come, the barricading of "rear" approaches (with fenced trainlines, walled expressways, the no-man's-land of warehouses and deserted buildings), are part of this careful structuring of "right" and "wrong" approaches and aspects of Chinatowns.

The violence of the rear approaches to and areas in Chinatowns is both explicit and implicit, physical and symbolic. Desolate areas, dark and narrow streets, marked by graffiti (whether gang-related or not) and signs of desecrated property (vandalized or abandoned vehicles, broken windows, rubble and debris), strongly suggest threats to the rule of law; such marks of violence to the landscape thus imply a similar threat of violence to persons, whether or not the visitor is unlucky enough actually to be attacked. The congregation in such areas of the city's marginalized population, especially after dark — the homeless, drug users, drunks, and criminal elements (the area just outside Vancouver's Chinatown offers one of the most striking examples of this) — also poses a physical barrier to access, in which quite common minor incidents of verbal abuse and jostling also carry the threat of the greater (if less common) violence of muggings, purse snatchings, and physical assaults. The presence of vice-related businesses in such back areas of Chinatowns poses both the symbols of violence (bouncers in doorways, the depictions of sexual violence and the display of fetish equipment in storefronts), and the actual incidents of verbal and physical violence associated with the lowering or abandoning of inhibitions in such abject spaces.

Thus despite attempts by the civic will to represent parts of Chinatowns as exemplary symbols of racial-commercial harmony, and to map and structure a certain salubrious ordering of such areas, violence is reiterated in alternative mappings and representations. Chinatown, in such alternative maps and discourses, is not the idealized multicultural space, but the space of threats, physical ruptures, and socioeconomic crises that foster violent actions. The internet, quite understandably as a medium enabling a plurality of noninstitutional perspectives and discourses, has also contributed a significant share of such alternative and violent charts of Chinatowns. Thus Stephen Wilson's internet art installation, "Crime-Z-land," is a map-cum-moving image representation of the "Post & Grant/Chinatown crime spot" in San Francisco, chosen as one of several key crime scenes in this art installation (Wilson 2001).

An internet Kung Fu site that calls itself the "Ho-Down Chinatown" school markets its training services by calling attention to the violence constituted by "the challenges of modern city life" (Ho-Down Chinatown 2001). In other websites, "Chinatown" is the symbolic site of violent media texts, the violence and transgression of pornography (especially that dealing explicitly in the depiction of bondage and humiliation of Asian women), and so on.[3]

The spatial organization of Chinatown thus offers a concrete model for the doubleness of desire involved in the construction of ethnic space and identity. It marks the polarized construction of violent and threatening site together with ideal and prosperous ethnic business district. If the Chinatown is the spatial equivalent of the "body without organs," in Deleuze and Guattari's terms (1984: 9) — the creation of a site that presents ethnic identity and its role in the host society as "smooth, slippery, opaque, taut" — the fissures of that construction are revealed in the lapses of civic decorum tolerated (as it were) at the back of Chinatown. Produced by the discourse of multiculturalism and global commercialism, Chinatown is required to repudiate the ubiquitous problems of immigration and cultural contestation, which are then manifested in its schizoid relationship with zones of violence and vice.

VIOLENCE AND VALUES: THE ASIAN "FAMILY" IN DIASPORIC CONDITIONS

This doubleness is required, not only in the spatial cleavage between model ethnic areas (business districts, expensive suburban concentrations of middle-class immigrants) and zones of ethnic violence (back streets, ghettoes, public housing projects), but also in ways of conceiving of human relations in diasporic conditions. The image of the immigrant as family man, as member of an ethnic tribe, is also characterized by a split between integration and repudiation, between assimilation and violence.

At the most obvious and common level, this is the subject matter of popular culture's representation of the Asian patriarch as crime boss. Many contemporary blockbuster movies like *Lethal Weapon Four* and *Kiss of the Dragon* can be read not only as stereotypes of ethnic villainy, but also as immigrant allegories produced by the Western host-culture, and thus as expressions of a characteristic anxiety about Chinese diasporic networks and connectivity. Violence in such texts thus not only reinforces stereotypes of Asian violence and criminality, but also uses such stereotypes to counter the moral weight of (perceived) Asian values of the networked community, filial bonds, and the collective endurance of and struggle against racism.

The Asian crime boss is usually a ruthless and savage Chinese or Japanese man who controls an empire dealing with drugs, prostitution, illegal immigrants, sweat shops, arms, and the like. He exploits his own immigrant community (whether by recruiting them to his criminal activities, or by oppressing them under a regime of violence, terror, and punishment), and this is often highlighted by the mise-en-scène: the massage parlours, seedy bars, run-down warehouses, docks, factories, and restaurants that collectively sketch an extensive ethnic organization whose entry into the host country cannot effectively be policed, and that exists on the borders of legality and morality. Spectacularly violent and powerful, the Asian crime boss is nevertheless strangely proof against the law and the gaze, and can neither be identified nor prosecuted by members of his own ethnic community or by the law — a combination of power and inscrutability that raises the ethnic villain to something of the status of a supervillain. This then requires a particular kind of hero, almost always white, rebellious, and unorthodox — an individual who himself operates outside of the limitations and conventions of the law, and whose penchant for excessive violence matches and even exceeds that of the Asian crime boss.

Thus ethnicity in this narrative archetype is first the mark of violence (in the figure of the crime boss), and consequently the justification of the increased violence that is perpetrated by the "hero" not just on the leader, but also on his associates and often on the ethnic landscape of the Asian enclave as well. Violence in the Asian gang leader is often depicted as gratuitous, pathological, very often related to a sexual dysfunction or fetish, and very often demonized by its opposition to the helplessness of his victims, enough of whom are women, the elderly, or children for this point to be emphasized. Triad boss Joey Tai in the 1985 *Year of the Dragon* (played by John Lone) is typical: inheriting control of the Triad organization in New York, he brings it forward by a ruthless and violent war with the Italian crime families and the New York police. His fate is just as spectacular, and led to this complaint by Maxine Hong Kingston in *Tripmaster Monkey*:

John Lone, who has the most classic face amongst us, will have to have it broken on camera, and his eyes beaten shut. The last third of the movie his expressions are indecipherably covered with blood. He begs to be killed, and his co-star cradles his head, then point-blank shoots it off. (Kingston 1990: 325)

Even more revealingly stereotypical, however, is the Yakuza boss Yoshida (played by Cary-Hiroyuki Tagawa) in the 1991 *Showdown in Little Tokyo*, whose aberrant nature is established early in the film in a scene where he punishes one of his errant (white) "girls" by pretending to let her atone by performing a sex act on him in the presence of his men, only to chop off her head from behind with a samurai sword in lieu of a sexual climax. Once again, this justifies the excessive violence of the hero (Los Angeles detective Chris Kenner, played by Dolph Lundgren), the culmination of which is a brutal bit of poetic justice in which Yoshida is skewered by his own sword to a giant Catherine wheel, which then ignites and spins him screaming on it, before finally blowing him up.

Other versions of the Asian crime boss include the heartless Mr Wei in John Woo's *The Replacement Killers* (1998), whose criminal ambitions are indirectly responsible for the death of his son during a police raid, and who then targets first the son of the offending (white) policeman, and then the friends and family of the scrupulous hitman (John Lee, played by Chow Yun Fat) who refuses to kill the policeman's son. Richard Donner's *Lethal Weapon Four* (1998) sees martial arts star Jet Li playing gang boss and Chinese slave trader Wah Sing Ku, whose ruthless criminal activities are slightly ameliorated by the fact that he seeks the release of his brother and friends from the clutches of an even more ruthless general in China. Perhaps the most eccentric depiction of this archetype is the sorcerer-crimelord David Lo Pan in John Carpenter's *Big Trouble in Little China* (1986), who kidnaps, organizes gang slayings and mass warfare all for the sake of redeeming himself from an ancient curse.

While it is difficult to take this kind of stereotyping popular discourse very seriously, it is curiously echoed by more serious-minded portrayals of immigrant families, including those by the members of the tribe themselves. Interesting in this context is Timothy Mo's 1982 novel *Sour Sweet*, which points to the fundamental parallels between the immigrant family and the Triad organization.[4] The Chen family, struggling to run their small takeaway business in the greater London area while taking care of family members back in Hong Kong, are drawn into the peripheral affairs of the Wo Triad society when Chen is forced to borrow money to pay off gambling and medical debts. A number of parallels between the Chens and the Triad are suggested in the course of the novel's episodic switches: both are diasporic communities and business networks, concerned with adapting cultural knowledge (Kung Fu, cooking, criminal and trade organization) in order to become more profitable. Both use such profits to strengthen community ties, and to bring their compatriots and family members into the country and the business. Both experience a disorienting clash between old ways and the new order in British society, and both change drastically as a result of this.

The Triad's violent competition with its rivals, as well as its own infighting over power and control, leads ultimately to the betrayal and exile of its leader, Red Cudgel. At the same time, Chen (betrayed by a colleague and caught up in the backwash of the Wo family infighting) falls victim to the Triad's harsh justice and is killed; however, as part of its community value-system, the Triad anonymously pays a monthly stipend which allows the Chen family to maintain the fiction that their main breadwinner has "gone to add extra money to our family" (Mo 1982: 272). Tropes of Chinese paternity and paternalism, the rituals and values of paternalistic society, and the sacrifices by and of the father, thus run through these two families in diasporic conditions. As old ways, values, and loyalties are disturbed by migration and contact with British culture, the violent sacrifice of the father figure (of both the Triad and Chen families) is presented as an inevitable part of the process of diasporic change. Both Red Cudgel and Chen are believed to be in Amsterdam, another prominent outpost of the Chinese diasporic network, where they are seen as strengthening organizational and financial links that will enable the growth of the community elsewhere. After these patriarchs leave, both family organizations undergo dramatic changes: the Triad leadership changes to less overtly and anachronistically violent ways, and modernizes to rationalize operations and profits; while the Chen family sees a marriage and a similar modernization and growth in their food business (the opening of a fish and chips restaurant).

Framed by episodes of graphic violence, and interspersed with hints and symbols of violence, *Sour Sweet's* sympathetic portrayal of immigrant dislocation and change insists on the necessity of ruptures and cleavages before life can go on. The sacrifices by, and the sacrifice of, the immigrant paterfamilias in Mo's novel add another dimension to the oft-told story of immigrant thrift and self-sacrifice in service of the extended family "back home." Quite apart from racial harassment and intimidation (and these play a secondary role in the novel), the diasporic network encounters significant internal pressures and conflicts: Chen's financial woes that lead to his fatal involvement with the Triad stem in large part from the demands and arrangements made by his family back in Hong Kong, while the Triad's operations in Britain are both supported and complicated by the rituals, accounting structure, and personalities of its network. White Paper Fan's justification of his betrayal and ousting of Red Cudgel is an acknowledgment of the internal pressures faced by this organizational network:

> Once, family Hung was all-powerful. In Singapore nine-tenths of all Chinese were members of our association. In Hong Kong at least half. ... Now that our influence is slightly less, the actions of family Hung must change to suit the altered times. Here, too, where things are different even from modern Hong Kong, Taiwan, or Singapore, plans of family Hung must change all the more. This is why recent incidents can only undermine our standing. ...
>
> To speak truth: we would have seceded in any case. New societies rise and fall. There is nothing exceptional in this. (Mo 1982: 262)

External change leads to internal pressures which cause violent ruptures before the organism can regroup and proceed. The scapegoat-father — as the main bearer of traditional Chinese authority, the primary breadwinner, and thus the figure most vulnerable in the flux of immigrant conditions — is only the immediate victim of this violence, but not its final consequence.[5] The organizational pressures of the diasporic networks continue after the symbolic deaths of the fathers: the succeeding Triad leaders already begin secret planning to fight for more power and effect greater changes to the society (it is hinted that White Paper Fan himself may be the next figure sacrificed for the good of the family), while the Chen family's bubbles (the illusion that Chen is still alive and will one day return, Lily Chen's conservative and obsessive control over her son) are set to burst in the not-too-distant future.

Mo's novel thus articulates in more serious vein, and with something more of an insider's insight, the immigrant and diasporic anxieties which recur again and again in mass media texts. The pervasiveness of these anxieties, across a range of texts from the exploitatively stereotyping to the more sympathetic and intelligent, suggests the doubleness of the discourse of sacrifice: at one end, it feeds into the lowest common denominator of racial violence, using the caricature of the ethnic villain to justify excessive punishment and mutilation by a white avenger; at the other end, it seems to articulate an anxiety within the tribe itself, a sense that the risks and dangers of cultural attenuation and change that come with diasporic movement must be propitiated and accompanied by the sacrifice of the symbolic father.

With the current rise in international popularity of ethnic Chinese actors and directors like John Woo, Ang Lee, Jackie Chan, Jet Li, Samo Hung, Michelle Yeoh, Lucy Liu, Tony Leung, Chow Yun Fat, and others, and their increasing influence and authority over narratives produced in the West, it becomes increasingly difficult to dismiss symbolic violence as the more or less crude racism of white agents. The double logic of sacrifice relates violence to the anxiety of the tribe itself in this period of global expansion and cultural exportation. Jet Li is an interesting figure in this respect: the subject of an only partially sympathetic treatment in Richard Donner's racialized thriller *Lethal Weapon Four*, Li has more recently enjoyed greater creative input in the Luc Besson thriller *Kiss of the Dragon* (2001), which is based on an idea by Li and co-scripted by him. Li has been quoted as accepting pragmatically his casting as an ethnic villain in *Lethal Weapon Four* ("you play a baddie because, in a new market, not many people know you"; Foong 2001: L4); in this financial exchange, such an image and playing to ethnic stereotyping is accepted as the inevitable price of doing business in and with the West. *Kiss of the Dragon* to a certain extent reverses the logic of racial violence, with the aberrant villain being a corrupt French cop (Jean-Pierre Richard, played by Besson favorite Tcheky Karyo), and the avenging hero a Chinese policeman (Liu Jiuan, played by Li). Yet when French and Chinese clash violently, the end result is a similar symbolic sacrifice of the Chinese father — most significantly the "sleeper" agent who runs a food produce store in which Li hides, and who stands *in loco parentis* to him (he not only offers him a haven, but also shows a touching and not entirely professional concern for his safety). This patriarchal or at least avuncular figure must die violently, it is suggested, not only because the corruption of the French police (a favorite Besson theme) threatens Li and all around him, but also because of the symbolic logic attached to the figure of the immigrant patriarch itself.

Seen in another way, the patriarch dies as the price of the son's success in the West; his *raison d'être* is to run risks on behalf of those who wait to come over from the homeland, and thus the sleeper operates his store in a dangerous part of Paris (prostitutes fight outside his door, and the sleaziness of the district ensures that no help arrives when he is murdered), which provides the appropriate anonymity for his young colleagues. At the same time, the sleeper must die because he counsels a self-interested prudence which is at odds with Li's job and professionalism, and because he also represents older ways inappropriate to new immigrant conditions (for example, his rabid mistrust of white people, even the innocent prostitute played by Bridget Fonda). It is not difficult to see him as a representation of the Chinese patriarch who risks life and limb to establish a diasporic beachhead in the West, yet who also represents the old ways unsuited to this new setting, and who must die in order for succeeding generations to form their own accommodations with their new environment — accommodations which, in the final analysis, are not necessarily wiser or less dangerous.

Read in this way, the new narratives produced by the agents of the current Chinese diaspora encode a deepseated anxiety tantamount to a tribal archetype of ritual sacrifice, abjection, and totemic reproduction. On the one hand, this is the double of Western immigrant anxieties and the articulation of these in not always subtle narratives of racial scapegoating — a repudiation of the racial Other which feeds back into immigrant anxieties about the failure to fit into the host society. On the other hand, this is also an inherent part of diasporic economies, and reflects the violence involved in the struggle to establish a foothold in a new and often hostile environment, in the inevitable loss of certain aspects of one's culture and values, and in the project of immigrant "upgrading" of socioeconomic status in successive generations.

CONCLUSION: TYPES, CULTURAL PRODUCTION, EXCHANGE

Violence is thus the mark of the deep psychocultural anxiety underlying the myth of seamless diasporic networks and immigrant "success stories," as well as the physical irruption which periodically explodes myths of socioeconomic assimilation. This revises the cultural production of the ideology of "western liberal-universalism" (Hall 2000: 228), which produces images of harmony-in-difference and painless assimilation — the ideology of such texts as the television series *Martial Law* and the *Rush Hour* films (with their police coalitions of Chinese and Black Americans), *Shanghai Noon* (a comic Chinese adaptation to and conquest of the American West), and repeated media stories about Asian immigrants "made good" in the West. Violence is itself the repressed Other of diasporic-immigrant scenarios (because of its sensational negative media values, its high human and social costs), relegated to a fringe role by both diasporic peoples and governments of host nations. It might be argued that the easy assumption that ethnic violence is nothing more than the cultural production of stereotyping commercial discourses in the Western media machine is itself a multiculturalist ideological project which seeks to simplify and thus dismiss the true place of violence in diasporic processes. Transnational flows of persons, capital, and culture are a fact of globalization in the present day, but this is not the seamless and celebratory fait accompli narrated by the multicultural state, but rather comes with a processing cost that is more easily ignored and minimalized. To foreground this cost is to confront the physical, emotional, cultural, geographical, and psychological violence that is involved in the notions of global citizenship and global capital structures.

In Europe and America in the 1960s, the violence of civil rights and urban social movements, and their intellectual corollaries of radical theory and the urban sociology of decay and oppression, were required to resist the hegemonizing discourses of post-Fordian production and normative (white, suburban, middle-class, professional) social organization. An analogous situation arises in respect of many aspects of transnational flows and global capital organization in the present era. In this sense the repressed violence of diasporic movements is linked, however distantly, to the violence of recent antiglobalization demonstrations in Seattle, London, and Genoa. While it is probably true that such violent protests lack a clear and unified agenda at the present time (although the same could probably have been said at the time for many social and civil rights movements of the 1960s), the role of violence in fragmenting the false consciousness of the global machine without organs seems to be an unavoidable one.

3

Theorizing Diasporas: Three Types of Consciousness

Regina Lee

This chapter draws upon the current literature on diasporas, in order to advance the field by highlighting the diversity of that community, and by moving beyond conventional models of diaspora that see them as either culturally dislocated or ideologically "fixed" — that is, methods that are culturally essentialist. To begin with, I take my notion of diaspora from Ien Ang, who defines them as "transnational, spatially and temporally sprawling sociocultural formations of people, creating imagined communities whose blurred and fluctuating boundaries are sustained by real and/or symbolic ties to some original 'homeland'" (2001: 25). This chapter seeks to theorize the diasporic community via a taxonomic exercise, examining not diasporic conditions per se, but rather, the different modes of explaining diaspora, by building upon the secondary literature on diaspora studies. I will also be foregrounding the impact/affect of class (or politics of economics and wealth) upon diasporic communities, in terms of economic migration and the creation or further differentiation of levels of privilege and wealth within the diasporic communities. These will have significant bearings on how the diasporic community relates to the diverse groups/groupings *within* itself and also to the wider society at large.

I want to begin with the argument that diasporic communities tend to exhibit, broadly, three main types of psychological states, or forms of consciousness, which are: idealization of homeland, boutique multicultural manifestation, and transitional/transformational identity politics. This chapter, however, does not intend to limit the diasporic experience strictly to these three categories, but rather, to better understand the diasporic condition by way of these categories, which will illuminate concerns that diasporas currently face, thereby pinpointing the bases of theoretical anxieties that surround this field of study. These anxieties are exacerbated by such phenomena as rapid globalization and its accompanying impact on mobility and (homeland) memories.

The characteristic of mobility is closely linked to economic (and historical) materialities of diasporas because it can either facilitate or impair movement or migration. Economic migration, consequently, confers upon the (usually upwardly) mobile diaspora certain levels of privilege, or facilitates such access, upon the crossing of certain borders. This is an important factor on which the decision to migrate is based; in most cases, the move is toward an improvement in one's financial or capital (or other) standing, thereby typifying such phenomena as economic migration. Diasporic relocation to another country, usually an upward movement in the class hierarchy, invariably engenders strong psychological, social, cultural, and political effects for the relocated diaspora.[1] I will briefly describe each of the categories of diasporic consciousness, before entering into a more detailed analysis of each category and how economic migration influences or shapes that consciousness.

Homeland idealism, as a form of diasporic consciousness, is a strong identification with, and idealization of, the homeland by its diaspora. In this conceptualization, the diaspora is defined largely in terms of distance from its homeland, with all the attendant implications of removal or exclusion and geographical, cultural, and psychical dislocation. This way of theorizing the diaspora posits the homeland myth (including the [embedded] myth of return) as a powerful and effective motivator of diasporic experiences.

A second (and popular) conception of diasporas is as exotic, Other communities, whose value for the hostland lies in the fact of their being different. With cultural pluralism fast becoming the norm for most (liberal, democratic) societies, diasporic/ethnic minorities sometimes play up the fact of their difference, highlighting their visibility, to gain recognition and some kind of acceptance into the host society. This, however, involves a *complicit* kind of recognition by which the dominant community has already "read" diaspora in their hegemonic terms, *and which the diaspora recognizes and returns in kind.* In other words, the diaspora knows what the host society wants, and feeds it to them, by self-consciously re-enacting for the dominant community their ethnicity. This reciprocal but superficial recognition is important because, being largely based on a systematic exploitation of the cultural plurality of ethnicities and the economic structuring of those groups into a subclass, it virtually guarantees value-added capital and economic surpluses. Conversely, diasporas that re/present themselves or which get re/presented in this way unveil the extent to which their societies' understanding and practice of multiculturalism are limited to trendy, boutique manifestations (which further entrench them in certain or pre-existing social, cultural, and political relations, thereby replicating hegemonic power structures).

Thirdly, there is the conceptualization of diasporas as being in a transitional or transformational state, representing diasporas as integrating in an informed (if not ambivalent) way with their host societies.[2] The implications for diasporas are that, firstly, they are still evolving (at both personal and community levels) rather than being fully fledged entities; and, secondly, theorizations about their diasporic condition are works in progress that have to be constantly revised. By foregrounding the transitional state of the diaspora, Bhabha's notion of "hybridity" (1994) is highlighted and problematized. Paul Gilroy's influential article, "It Ain't Where You're From, It's Where You're At ..." (1991), emphasizes the transitional social realities that make up diasporic experience and refocuses our attention back onto the irreducible aspects of "roots" and "routes" (Gilroy 1993). His conception of ethnicity considers equally the "doubleness" of diasporic psyche — balancing "where you're from" with "where you're at." Moreover, the present chapter advocates the additional consideration of "where you're going," because, while theorists have tended to foreground the histories of diasporas for significant and primary accounts of how the "here and now" is arrived at and negotiated with, there have been inadequate considerations for the future of diasporic trajectories — thereby intensifying anxieties about the field of diasporic studies. This added notion is an important consideration in the negotiation of diasporic identification, which will have significant impact on the framing/ positioning of diasporic subjects and their narratives.

Before entering into an examination of the categories outlined above, I want to position my notion of diaspora in the context of postcolonialism and the dismantling of classical (and to some extent, modernist) grand narratives, of which the nation-state can be read as an example or manifestation. That is, the nation-state's existence and functioning are built upon the narrative structure of a grand narrative, by way of its address to itself. An easy slippage occurs between nationalist rhetoric[3] and the nation-state itself; both get conflated into the same thing, so that they become (subsequently and consequently) grand narratives. Under scrutiny, however, those grand narratives (and their claims to homogeneity and continuity) are characterized by or as "false consciousness" because the nation-state is deeply divided when it comes to the issue of class and labour; in fact, the state (and its governing apparatus) "constitutes one highly distinctive and important elaboration of the social division of labour" (Gellner 1983: 4).

The phenomenon of globalization further adds to this disjunctive "crisis" by accelerating those processes of fragmentation and causing nation-states (grand narratives) to crumble, even vanish, in its aim to create a "world without borders." Economically motivated processes of globalization divide the classes even more, widening the gulf that already separates "haves" from "have-nots," while creating new levels of privilege based on the emergence of new and different sets of criteria. This "world without borders" favors not only the upper (economic) classes but also, and increasingly, the technologically savvy now emerging as a class of their own. Old(er) distinctions separating the upper from the working classes become less tenable as new forms of criteria, such as technological capital, disrupt the prevailing status quo. The nation-state's balancing act is now complicated by new differentiations of class, in addition to the already existing tensions surrounding racial and cultural differences. Globalization compounds those pressures by challenging and dismantling, even obliterating, its authoritarian narrative.[4] It is therefore timely here to ask exactly what is at stake in the diminishing and disappearance of the nation-state and its narrative.

The grand narrative of the nation-state aimed primarily to convey a sense of "nation-ness," based on shared commonalities (such as culture), while at the same time drawing up boundaries between a perceived unified self and its (foreign) "other." Within those boundaries, "appropriate" members are empowered to imagine themselves as "unified." Outside of those boundaries, the excluded elements constitute a justifiable, distinct basis upon which that unified national self is imagined. As mechanisms of exclusion, boundaries manifest themselves in various ways, one form of which is the act of forgetting. According to Ernest Renan, "forgetting … is a crucial factor in the creation of a nation" (1990: 11). This allows for the construction of a unified narrative that presents the nation as "the culmination of a long past of endeavours, sacrifice and devotion," so as to "have common glories in the past and to have a common will in the present" (Renan 1990: 19). Commonality, of great significance here because it legitimizes the nation-state's claim to homogeneity, leads to the imagination and idealization of a pure, unified self. The Other (impure) voices that make up the nation-state get obscured, forgotten, or silenced — in other words, excluded.

This exclusion exposes an already existing ambivalence and antagonism in the nation-state. For Homi Bhabha, there is "a particular ambivalence that haunts the idea of the nation," that "inscribes a much more transitional social reality" (1990: 1) than most narrative accounts of the nation would have us believe. Discussing the "politics of memory," Andreas Huyssen suggests that "the fault line between mythic past and real past is not always that easy to draw," therefore "[the] real can be mythologized just as the mythic may engender strong reality effects" (2000: 26). The nation-state's self-address therefore reads as an attempt at self-mythologizing, constructing an image of itself that will be effectively and positively motivating. In that act of self-mythologizing, its narrative is necessarily double, because of the need to placate (heterogeneous) "others" coexisting with/in its (imaginary, unified) "self," as well as to alleviate the anxieties of the dominant majority. The resulting ambivalence opens up marginal spaces for cultural and political negotiation, providing avenues for "substantial intervention into those justifications of modernity … that rationalise the authoritarian, 'normalising' tendencies within cultures in the name of the national interest of the ethnic prerogative" (Bhabha 1990: 4).

The "national interest" here would be the construction of a narrative that produces "the fact of sharing" (Renan 1990: 19), so that the nation is conceived of as "a large-scale solidarity" (Renan 1990: 19). It is in the interest of the nation-state to pursue this single and singular interest, therefore many countries have chosen (from force of modernist habits) to obscure the heterogeneous, multiple narratives within. Still, there is no denying that the nation is "an agency of *ambivalent* narration":

> Always itself [in] a process of hybridity, incorporating new "people" in relation to the body politic, generating other sites of meaning and, inevitably, in the political process, producing unmanned sites of political antagonism and unpredictable forces for political representation. (Bhabha 1990: 4)

The unpredictability of those forces means that there is still "incomplete signification." In its narrative address, therefore, the nation-state strives to obfuscate those gaps or "in-between spaces" arising from its hybrid condition, so as to reinforce its message of solidarity. Yet, the excluded multiple narratives cannot be silenced, because "the 'other' is never outside or beyond us; it emerges forcefully, within cultural discourse, when we *think* we speak most intimately and indigenously 'between ourselves'" (Bhabha 1990: 4).

Here, the nation is shown to imagine itself as a unified, consolidated whole — one that it constructs based on a "White Nation" fantasy (Hage 2000). In the nation-state's "intimate" and "indigenous" address to that imagined self, its sense of "nation-ness" is also largely dependent on the exclusion of an "other" from its "self." This is where the ambivalence of the nation-state and its narrative is most marked — because of its need to exclude in order to unify. This ambivalence is further compounded by the fact of its being "hybrid" and transitional, always in negotiation with its multiple selves and its others. This ambivalence reminds the nation-state of its hybrid and transitional state, a fact that it represses by focusing instead on the idea of a homogeneously constituted self. However, the already inscribed transitional social reality returns to haunt the nation-state, along with its other acts of exclusion, destabilizing its linear sense of historicity by dismantling the gestures of grandeur in its modernist, monolithic narrative.[5]

Exclusion is an important point of entry into conceptualizations of the diasporic condition, because the notion of exclusion is always double for the diaspora; first, from the homeland, and second, from the hostland, in different ways and at different levels; physical, psychological, social, cultural, economic, and political. The visibly different and *markedly* excluded diasporic subject is one who carries, or is afflicted by, that "corporeal malediction" (Fanon 1970), and whose difference functions *overtly* as a point of identification. I shall now take up a closer examination of the diasporic categories, beginning with the conceptualization of diasporas in terms of homeland idealism (as it most overtly refers to exclusionary effects of historical, geographical, and cultural dislocation).

HOMELAND IDEALISM

This type of consciousness credits the homeland as being the most powerful motivator of diasporic behaviour, while myths surrounding the homeland and the possibility of return hold great sway over its diasporic community; *consciously* and psychically located in the past and looking back at that past, idealizing it in the form of a "magical belief" so that the past becomes larger than life. The grand narrative of the homeland (and its myths) directed toward some (imagined) unification of the nation are now replicated in the community of its homeland-idealizing diaspora through the narratives that the diaspora tells itself. Often, these are symptomatic of a particular version of social reality that the diaspora wants to inscribe upon its consciousness, resulting in various forms of (perceptual, ideological) parochialism.

Conversely, this kind of diaspora also represents itself as being trapped within an idealized historical space and time, thereby fashioning itself after a "backward-looking conception of diaspora" (Hall 1990: 235). This way of conceptualizing diaspora renders the diasporic community as always *supplementary*. I take "supplement" in Derrida's sense of the term, containing a dual signification: firstly, as "a plenitude enriching another plenitude, the *fullest measure* of presence … it cumulates and accumulates presence" (Derrida 1992: 83), and secondly, it also only "just" supplements, in the sense that it "adds only to replace … it intervenes or insinuates itself *in-the-place-of*; if it fills, it is as one fills a void" (Derrida 1992: 83). For both home and host countries, diasporas represent (a void that is fraught with) ambivalence.[6] Therefore, whether in relation to its homeland or host society, the homeland-idealizing diasporic community is always marginalized because it is physically absent from the homeland (its "center"), and (consequently) socially excluded from the host society and its narrative. Therefore, "whether it adds or substitutes itself, the supplement is *exterior,* outside of the positivity to which it is super-added, alien to that which, in order to be replaced by it, must be other than it" (Derrida 1992: 84). The configuration of diaspora-homeland relations as "other" and "positivity" respectively is insightful because both homeland and hostland, as nation-states, also tend to construct themselves in this way, as "positivities" (and by implication, "truth") via grand narratives that invoke positive images.[7] Diasporic narratives of this kind commonly reveal a genuflection toward the homeland, wherein cultural practices are presented or explained as "alien" and "exotic" — further mystifying their already visible difference.

With the globalization of entire nations and augmentation of a "world without borders," the fragility of national (and class or economic) boundaries is disturbing and disruptive to beliefs in the solidity or solidarity and unity of the nation-state. The inequitable asset distribution and resource re/allocation inherent in globalization means that its impact and effects will be as disparate as they are contingent upon the proximity of access that people have to resources and distribution networks. In other words, the various and particular manifestations of globalization are fundamentally determined by the functionality of economic systems in various places. Consequently, all relations, whether of culture or class, or at the personal, community, or national levels, are economically determined. The excluded position of homeland-idealizing diasporas, now read as negative economic value, explains also the narrative focus on their experiences of exclusion, displacement, dislocation, and so on. These retrospective narratives, in idealizing a historical space and time, reveal a withdrawal from the present, or a denial of their actual current situation. The homeland-idealizing diaspora remains "trapped" in the present because there is a limit to the extent to which their narratives can "recover" those histories. It is a liminal existence that these diasporas inhabit, marginalized by their homeland as well as marginalizing themselves in the new country.

On the other hand, the benefits of physical, geographical relocation (usually derived in terms of economic gain and an upward social or class mobility) are not lost on the diasporic community. While bemoaning the "loss" of homeland, history, and culture, relocated diasporas are often perceived (especially by their homeland counterparts) as gaining access to levels of privilege previously unattainable in the homeland. Because economic migration attaches so closely to, being almost synonymous with, diasporic movement, relocation is considerably influenced by opportunities available in the new country. Those opportunities, however, are not without certain disadvantages — the most common of which would be (perceived and/or real) erosion or loss of the minority group's culture and, sometimes, history.[8] Popular perceptions of relocated diasporas, aided by narratives that attempt to explain their "condition," therefore tend toward normativizations of the diasporic condition as being trapped, or psychologically and culturally located, in historical space and time, regardless of their economic circumstances.

In an attempt at circumventing this kind of normativization, diasporas are sometimes represented as existing in their own right, in terms of an exotic Other community in relation to the more dominant culture of their host society. This type of engagement (albeit limited yet "informed") with its social and material reality re/presents the diaspora as being of value for their host society, especially in an environment of cultural pluralism, known as "boutique multiculturalism."

BOUTIQUE MULTICULTURAL MANIFESTATION

A direct effect of globalization has been the increase in cultural plurality (or pluralism), giving rise to more and more multicultural societies, resulting in debates over the granting of equal recognition and equal worth to minority cultures. The intention is to establish something that is "meant to be universally the same, an identical basket of rights and immunities" (Taylor 1994: 38), which sees the absorption of ethnics into a community, governed, policed, or managed by enforced policies of toleration (Hage 1994). However, this is at odds with "the politics of difference" whereby "what we are asked to [recognize] is the unique identity of this individual or group, their distinctness from everyone else" (Taylor 1994: 38). To assimilate the minority group's distinctness would be to violate the "ideal of authenticity" (Taylor 1994: 38), yet this is what some (or most) multicultural societies, faced with cultural pluralism, are compelled to do: manage and negotiate difference. In this situation, race and ethnicity become the dominant modes of identification as everyone is assigned and "classified" accordingly. The ensuing power relations evolve from racial signifiers, or race markers, now evidently displacing previous older markers of class and status. Race and ethnicity therefore become the new "status symbols" in a racially stratified and hierarchized environment.[9] This is the kind of situation that readily lends itself to and demonstrates popular culture's exploitation of minorities who, when previously disadvantaged because of race and ethnicity, find an avenue for access to cultural capital and credibility vis-à-vis that very same "disadvantage."

Referring to the production (by white, Western discourse) of the minority, or "native," Rey Chow notes that "the 'native' is turned into an absolute entity in the form of an image ... whose silence becomes the occasion for *our* speech" (1993: 34). Yet, "[the] 'authentic' native, like the aura in a kind of *mise-en-abîme*, keeps receding from our grasp" (Chow 1993: 46).[10] The underlying motivation, Chow explains, is that "it is actually the colonizer who feels looked at by the native's gaze" (1993: 51), and therefore has to work at producing (the image of) the native as object, silent and passive. According to her,

> Our fascination with the native, the oppressed, the savage, and all such figures is therefore a desire to hold on to an unchanging certainty somewhere outside our own "fake" experience. It is a desire for being "non-duped," which is a not-too-innocent desire to seize control. (1993: 53)[11]

This passage unveils, to a certain extent, the motivations behind a dominant society's apparent embrace of minorities in a climate of cultural pluralism; basically, to hold on to and replicate existing structures of power that keep minorities in their place.

Another inference from Chow's argument is that, since the "native" is actively gazing, and furthermore, that there is the desire to be "non-duped'" (by an unnamed "us," presumably the dominant social culture), the possibility of "duping" or being duped is very much alive. That is, the "native" can equally possess the same "not-too-innocent" desire for control by complying with the desire of dominant discourse to construct "nativity" in a certain way. Consequently, the "native" who is aware of colonial insecurities and anxieties is *actively* complicit in the production of him/herself as silent object, beneath which is actually an active sense of marginalized subject agency (enabling the "native" to conceal the act of "duping," and to play along with the colonizer's fantasy of "being non-duped"). In multicultural terms, we can say that ethnic/diasporic minorities are consciously playing the multicultural game, by self-consciously re-enacting for the dominant community what the latter expects from them, and by feeding them what they want, in the roles of native as "silent object" or native as "informant."[12]

A native informant, seen in this perspective, personifies ambivalence, standing for all or nothing at once; heavy with signification because of visible ethnicity, and/or simultaneously subverting that mode of signification by knowingly manipulating his/her ethnic visibility. Geoffrey Brennan has noted that people become "culture bearers," deriving value from their visible ethnicity, especially in a multicultural society that "needs representatives of the various cultures to secure that [sense of] betterness" (1993: 172). The ethos of that multicultural society, predicated upon "an extrinsic relation between a White possessor and non-White possessed," exposes a showy form of multiculturalism that is more about "having" — parading its cultural plurality — than about "being" *effectively* multicultural (Hage 2000).

For the dominant community, re-enactments of ethnicity are (commercially) valuable because of diasporic conditions that favor "commoditization by diversion." Value, according to Arjun Appadurai, "is accelerated or enhanced by placing objects and things in unlikely contexts," a situation that he refers to as "the aesthetics of decontextualisation" (1986: 28). In other words, cultural alienation (as a consequence of dislocation and displacement) has its economic advantages. However, the alienated diasporic subject, whether as "object" or as "informant," is *subject* to (exploitative) forms of "self-ethnicization" which is "a confirmation of one's minority status in white, western culture" (Ang 1992: 11). These strategies — of "commoditization by diversion," of "self-ethnicization," in their many guises — are predominantly aimed more at upholding the prevailing status quo than empowering the ethnic minority.

In his book *White Nation: Fantasies of White Supremacy in a Multicultural Society* (2000), Ghassan Hage shows how multicultural societies, underpinned by a largely white majority whose dominance is unchecked, are anxious to preserve that status quo. Whether they are engaged in eradicating the voice of the "ethnic other," or whether they are happily welcoming them under some conditions that the former feel entitled to set (Hage 2000: 17), the two camps are markedly similar in the way that their debates have silenced and constructed the "ethnic other" into passive objects. The shared objective of both white multiculturalism and white racism, therefore, is to contain the activities of the "ethnic other."[13] Containment, however, is eventually rendered futile because later generations of "ethnic others" (the new diaspora) are increasingly participative in the process of governing their new home countries. Unlike first-generation diasporas, new diasporas are usually brought up in the new countries as "assimilated," because locally born. The perception of migrants — commonly typecast as first generation, visibly ethnic, and above all else, Third-World-looking — is that they can "write only of the migrant experience in incompetent English" (Gunew 1993: 50). So the expectation is that they can (and will) "produce only 'plain story-telling' and are incapable of having a playful attitude to language" (Gunew 1993: 50).[14]

Later generations of diaspora, "assimilated" to a certain extent, are consequently less "incompetent" (linguistically), less circumspect, and more assertive — not only socially and culturally, but also creatively and politically. These new diasporas also identify less with concerns of their predecessors — an ideological shift that becomes evident from their literary and film productions. This is not to say that the new diasporas have totally broken away from issues that mattered to the old diaspora. Rather, my point is that the awareness of historical concerns, coupled with an informed sensitivity to the local environment, have enabled the new diaspora to be socially, culturally, and politically aware. Their contemporary concerns are a result of their history of racialization and politicization (experienced by the old diaspora) or a politicized consciousness-raising experience. Having been brought up as "assimilated," the new diaspora now belongs to and identifies with the culture of the new country, at the same time making their presence increasingly felt in local politics. The effect upon the social, cultural, and political landscape is that "white multiculturalism cannot admit to itself that migrants and Aboriginal people are actually eroding that centrality of white people" (Gunew 1993: 50). White supremacy is therefore (becoming more of) a fantasy, at the same time as multiculturalism and racism manifest themselves as simply more sophisticated forms of the same fantasy.

That fantasy is analogized by Gunew, in her image of a dinner table conversation and a telephone communication, to further exemplify the "ethnic" situation (Gunew 1993: 50). Her analogy makes explicit the extent of the host's power. Here, the category of "the host" is synonymous with the dominant group of the host country, complete with the politics of tolerance (Hage 1994) and structuring of power differentials. It becomes animatedly clear who holds the balance of power by their ability to invite and/or tolerate the other, and by the other's ability to play the part of a conformist guest. At the same time, Gunew also demonstrates how opportunistic "host" figures such as "multicultural professionals" and "self-serving academic careerists" have manipulated the logic of (tolerant) multiculturalism to carve niches for themselves. With respect to the "cultural, specifically literary, dimensions of the multicultural debate" (Gunew 1993: 40), I want to highlight the observation that she makes about multicultural writing: "We are accused of concentrating on the same few writers and in the same breath are damned for trying to widen the group by working on bibliography — which comprises 900 writers ... — a no-win situation" (Gunew 1993: 51–2). This statement illuminates the situation that many multicultural writers find themselves in because, in the first place, no matter how assimilated, something about them remains "different" — their visible ethnicity and their names are the first signs of deviation from, hence not belonging to, the mainstream. The writing that they produce is therefore subject to a different set of expectations or perhaps judged by different criteria, and the position of arbiter is best left to someone from within that group. In other words, the belief (by both whites and nonwhites) is that nonwhite bibliographies and anthologies should be worked on by nonwhites themselves because "interference" from any white person can only imply either a white, language-based racist attitude or a white multicultural anxiety about loss of control. Both kinds of attitudes are underpinned by the same white fantasy, which ultimately leaves the "ethnics" in charge of their own cultural affairs, in order to circumvent accusations of racism arising from the dominant white sector.

In an about-turn of events, this practice has met with some degree of success: witness the growing popularity of ethnic-produced cultural events, where, free from any dominating (read: white) influence, there is an increasing tendency toward subverting ethnic norms and expectations. In other words, the act of holding up one's own (minority) culture for critique or for comic ridicule can and perhaps should only be undertaken by minority ethnic persons themselves, and to a lesser extent, by members of other minority groups. This practice, however, is based on a social memory that has reified and stereotyped certain common or popular ethnic practices and traditions. By moving away from normative perceptions about ethnic diasporas, this act of subversion attempts to challenge stereotypes while also highlighting the contingencies upon which those stereotypes are based. In transcending those static categorizations and conceptualizations, new and radical types of diasporic identities and histories can be constructed and narrated into the national space.[15]

From the cultural/creative spheres of writing and performance, the derivation of socioeconomic benefits therefore validates multiculturalism (even if tokenistic) as valuable (as opposed to feelings or anxieties about multiculturalism experienced as "loss").[16] As part of the (then) Australian Labour government's discourse of economic rationalism, Hage demonstrates how multiculturalism, when identified as a source of "economic efficiency" — providing "an economically exploitable resource" — translates into the "marrying of cultural value with economic value" (Hage 2000: 128). This is simply another manifestation of the "multiculturalism of having"; that is, putting a price tag or imposing values on visibly "different" persons, cultural practices, and/or commodities. He goes on to illustrate how multiculturalism can maximize "economic efficiency" by creating conditions that include migrant labor in the national economic space, but at the same time exclude migrant workers from the social space. The migrant worker/person is thus further reified as commodity, whereby surplus value is derived from pure objectification of his/her labor. This inclusion-exclusion dialectic, however, operates only to push those migrants into that marginal space, not totally outside of the national space but also not incorporated in any way into the social space. The main benefit of positioning them in that liminal space is to devalue their labor to such a point that it becomes economically viable for the (usually white) employer. In this way, white multiculturalism demonstrates the Marxist logic of sustaining class boundaries, within a racially or ethnically driven distinction of labor, based on the white supremacist fantasy. Power relations, highly contingent upon race and ethnic markers as status symbols, signify in this case an obvious lack rather than empowerment.

These examples demonstrate the potential capacity for multiculturalism to be manipulated by the socially and culturally skilled, and economically advantaged, to advance their cause or situation, if the game is "read" and interpreted accurately enough. The "authenticity" of one's ethnicity can therefore be "planned," to paraphrase Trinh Minh-Ha (1989), and orchestrated to the requirements of the situation. The variety of cultural stereotypes (made available by dominant culture) means that there is an array of "prescribed" forms of "otherness" (Chow 1991: xvi) for ethnic minorities to inhabit. These absolutist readings of ethnicity become essentialized and adhered to by the same minorities who have no desire to challenge the system under which their migration had been approved. So ethnicity becomes reified and stereotyped, while ethnics remain marginalized in their own minority enclaves, trapped by the dominant culture's perception of them.

The "game" of multiculturalism has shown that it is possible to break out and away from these stereotypical readings of ethnic minorities by subverting dominant expectations and prescriptions of "otherness." This falls precisely into a pattern of "self-ethnicization," which is "self-dramatisation [taking] the route of self-subalternisation, which has increasingly become the assured means to authority and power" (Chow 1993: 13). Ethnicity becomes an enabling trait for opportunistic players of the multicultural game, riding on the short-term benefits that membership of a marginalized group can offer. This involves exploiting institutional handouts and social welfare programs while making overt displays of one's marginalized status — maneuvers that go unchecked by a multicultural society that is possessive and anxious about displaying (while exploiting) its cultural plurality.

This section has thus far accounted for forms of superficial, tokenistic multiculturalism that manifest themselves in different ways, in many places. In opposition to these "gaming" or "boutique" versions of multiculturalism, there exists a strong or critical version of multiculturalism that, as advocated by the Chicago Cultural Studies Group, "minds its proximity to the historical present and its different obligations to the variety of publics in which it circulates" (1992: 553). In other words, strong multiculturalism calls for not only a "double consciousness," but a multiple one that takes into account, firstly, historical and present events; secondly, recognition of other marginalized minority groups apart from one's own; and finally, the responsibility of *proprietary* (rather than temporary and tokenistic) mediation of difference. Stanley Fish's critique of boutique multiculturalism distinguishes it from strong multiculturalism, emphasizing that,

> Whereas the boutique multiculturalist will accord a superficial respect to all cultures other than his own, a respect he will withdraw when he finds the practices of a culture irrational or inhumane, a strong multiculturalist would want to accord a *deep* respect to all cultures at their core, for he believes that each has the right to form its own identity and nourish its own sense of what is rational and humane. (1997: 382)

Strong multiculturalism demands not only unwavering commitment but also sustained engagement and investments over a period of time, making it at odds with machinations of globalization and economic pragmatism.[17] Therefore, it is unlikely that those institutions, genres, and media will ever materialize for strong multiculturalism to gain a foothold. This means that we will now have to contend with the ongoing displays and exploitations of ethnicity in a climate of "commoditization by diversion," where categories of difference can be contained, commodified, and subsumed by an easy generalization (as well as popularization) that maximizes economic efficiency, under superficial multiculturalist rhetoric.

The issue of containing and consuming culture has often been discussed, and I shall now turn, again, to Sneja Gunew and Ghassan Hage for their images of multiculturalism as a "feast" or an enriching fair. By making multiculturalism out to be a form of popular culture, Gunew and Hage show how the commonality of food "has long been the acceptable face of multiculturalism" (Gunew 1993: 41), providing "cultural enrichment" by "migrant cultures" through the "soft" options of food, music, and dance, which are manifestations of popular culture. However, when it comes to the cultural sphere of writing or literary production, the stakes are somewhat different. As this paper has shown earlier, "multicultural writing," or works by nonwhite, ethnic-looking writers, are subject to fluctuating or arbitrary sets of criteria and expectations. Moreover, there has now been a trend toward narrative forms and content that break away from historical-recovery and cultural-recuperation modes of storytelling set by earlier writers.[18] The emerging narrative forms, usually by members of the new diaspora, are not only concerned with race and ethnicity, but are also, and more importantly, attentive to the pressures and demands of their present environment and anxious to represent themselves in a different way. This difference is a variant of the erstwhile theme of ethnic difference that had preoccupied the old diaspora. The writings of the new diaspora are concerned with contemporary issues of the new millennium, while at the same time bearing traces of old diaspora concerns such as racial or ethnic consciousness and forms of racism, or simply illustrating the effects of racialization (as part of their upbringing and consciousness).

Amidst the celebration and consumption of (intertextual) "difference," these new diaspora writers — whether as ethnic minority "natives," or as "silent object" and "informant" — play a crucial role in the perpetuation of existing power relations within dominantly white hegemonic structures of racial categorization. Ethnicity is still being commodified, although in different forms and sometimes by different groups, thereby presenting to the dominant culture an image of the ethnic or native as exotic, as Other. The difference is that the new (assimilated) diaspora now has the cultural, sometimes economic and political, capital as well as *agency* to present itself as "different" in a progressive and multidimensional way. The new direction is a result of what I shall be referring to as a transitional and transformational consciousness.

TRANSITIONAL DIASPORIC ETHNICITIES/IDENTITIES

This type of diasporic consciousness is a highly politicized one, which enables the diasporic subject to be "critically aware of the 'hyphen,' of its rootedness in more than one history, its location in the present as well as in the past" (Radhakrishnan 1996: 354). The doubleness of diasporic identity is highlighted in the hyphen that locates the diasporic subject, spatially and temporally, as existing in between two cultures (for instance Chinese-Canadian, Chinese-Australian). The former term usually denotes a place and time from which they came — an idealized homeland, usually of the first-generation diasporas — while the latter term signifies their (problematic) location in a different present. The hyphen that simultaneously separates while joining both terms therefore performs a double function, which I shall be referring to as a "disconjunction": constituting and identifying a break (disjunction), while also connecting two disparate cultural entities (conjunction). From this double function, an interstitial space is created, in which the dialectics of separation and unification are played out and against each other, giving rise to another equally significant consideration — the future of diasporic trajectories, or the matter of "where you're going."[19]

The "disconjunctive" hyphen, as a middle term, not only encapsulates the double aspect of diasporic subject identity, it also stands for the liminal space and time that diasporic subjects inhabit, forming the basis upon which "diasporicity" is experientially negotiated, and from which its future trajectories can be charted. Homi Bhabha has referred to this as the "third space," an "unrepresentable" space "which constitutes the discursive conditions of enunciation that ensure that the meaning and symbols of culture have no primordial unity or fixity; that even the same signs can be appropriated, translated, rehistoricised and read anew" (Bhabha 1994: 37). In other words, this third space is or represents the site in which discursive practices can be disrupted, where history and culture can be reinterpreted. These possibilities mean that the space is charged with "the potential to unsettle static, essentialist and totalitarian conceptions of 'national culture' or 'national identity' with origins firmly rooted in fixed geography and common history" (Ang 1992: 13). Like Bhabha, Ien Ang attributes to this space subversive and destabilizing potential, while reading into it unlimited creative possibilities, in terms of the trajectories along which diasporicity may unfold. Ang points out that "diasporic imagination is steeped in continuous ambivalence," and this is an ambivalence that "highlights the fundamental *precariousness* of diasporic identity construction, its positive *indeterminacy*" (Ang 1992: 4). The implications of that "precariousness" and "indeterminacy" manifest themselves in a "changeability of the meaning of Chineseness [or diasporicity] as a marker of and for 'identity'" (Ang 1992: 10). Constant shifts in markers of identity (and also race and class) point to the arbitrariness of meaning (and meaning-making), and the inherent transitionality of diasporic experience, imagination and identification. The productive potential and "disconjunctive" capacity represented by this transitional space is a result of it being "in between," as Bhabha reminds us, "it is the 'inter' — the cutting edge of translation and negotiation, the *in-between* space — that carries the burden of the meaning of culture" (1994: 38). From this hybrid space, "culture bearers" (Brennan 1990) are enabled and empowered to articulate cultural difference "as a *hybridity* acknowledging that all cultural specificity is belated, *different unto itself*" (Bhabha 1994: 58). In other words, (arbitrary and highly contingent) cultural differences contribute to the hybridity of that space, providing it with productive and "positive *indeterminacy*" (Ang 1992: 4).

This is a space fraught with tension (hence, the "disjunctive" aspect) because the significance of historical past and the immediate present are at stake in the charting of diasporic futures. Moreover, the transitionality of this space, always in progress, demands the striking of a balance between "where you're from" and "where you're at," in order to move on and beyond the present moment, to seek out "where you're going." The envisioning of the future as an idealized space and time in which "progress" (or being "in progress") means that diasporic experience and identity constructions are constantly being rewritten and reinterpreted, in a foreseeable, positive, and productive (or conjunctive) manner.

While all these concepts denote a positive sense of empowerment, they transpire as a result of the ambivalence that latently inheres within the notion of hybridity. The hybrid "third" space, whether as nation or notion, harbors within itself indeterminate and syncretic elements that contribute to its productive dynamism. That is to say, indeterminacy accounts for much of the (disjunctive) instability within concepts, which enables their affirmative potential. Indeterminacy, however, is not always or necessarily a source of empowerment. As it has been noted in the consciousness of multicultural game players, the instability and ambivalence that gives rise to indeterminacy can also mean that "culture bearers," as personifiers of ambivalence, may signify (in postmodernist fashion) all or nothing at once. The duality integral to this notion or concept also works to its detriment, rendering it inert because of the demand for equal representation from both sides.

Therefore, culture bearers, because of "prescribed otherness," carry the "burden of the meaning of culture" when the collective consciousness and social memory of the dominant and minority groups adhere to previously set paths of homeland idealization, leading to marginalization of minorities and preservation of the dominant group's power. The situation is no better when both dominant and marginal groups engage in reciprocal forms of cultural and economic exploitation in a climate of tokenistic multiculturalism. All of these demonstrate that those aspects of hybridity and indeterminacy that are charged or associated with being positive and productive are not always and equally accessible to different members of diasporic groups — such as first-generation diasporas, or/ especially those in refugee circumstances. Put in another way, diasporas do not derive empowerment from the same sources, partly (and simply) because diasporic peoples, even within the same community, do not have equal access to those sources. For some, disjunction may be more representative of diasporic experience than for others.

Because the potential empowerment associated with hybridity and indeterminacy is not equally accessible to all members of diasporic groups, the onus is therefore upon those already or adequately empowered (such as later generation, or new, diasporas) to make sense of the ambivalence inherent in a transitional social reality. In other words, the logic of (ambivalent) transitionality is predisposed toward those (diasporic subjects) already in a position of privilege and access. These members of the diaspora are better equipped with the skills and capital necessary for the task of harnessing those indeterminate elements for new and productive readings of culture and history, so that collective normativizations can be destabilized, and differences interpreted anew. For instance, the sense of exclusion commonly associated with diasporic experience and narratives can be drawn upon, in creative ways and in an empowering and enabling manner, to highlight historical contingencies that in turn expose certain prejudicial assumptions or conceptualizations underlying particular cultural normativizations and stereotyping practices. Therefore, in this "disconjunctive" and transitional space, where cultures and their perceived norms are destabilized and stripped of claims to authenticity and purity, "in this hybrid gap, which produces no relief" (Bhabha 1994: 76), cultural essentialism and hierarchy become non-issues, and the diasporic subject *"takes place."* As R. Radhakrishnan illustrates, "the diasporic location is the space of the hyphen that tries to coordinate, within an evolving relationship, the identity politics of one's place of origin with that of one's present home" (1996: xiii). This hybrid space, highly unstable and uncomfortable or discomforting, even alienating, is also where the subject's transitional consciousness evolves. This is the space in which traces of "where you're from" are constantly framed by "where you're at," an evolving process that displaces fixed notions and memories, and which challenges easy resolutions and reconciliations.

The diasporic subject's "willingness to descend into that alien space" (Bhabha 1994: 38) makes this transitional consciousness a positively charged one (like Ien Ang's "productive *indeterminacy*"). As Radhakrishnan articulates it, this is also a form of consciousness that would "insist on a fundamental difference between hybridity as a comfortably genuine state of being and hybridity as an excruciating act of self-production by and through multiple traces" (1996: 159). Two forms of hybridity are distinguished here, which now significantly illuminate that transitional and "disconjunctive" space. Theorizations of hybridity that often revolve around the first type, and that assume a comfortable state of being, usually stand as abstract concepts upon which notions of empowerment can be constructed. These (re)conciliatory notions (idealistic and imaginary) also have implications and manifestations — real and actual material effects — on diasporic subjects, who possess varying levels of agency, privilege, and capital. That is to say, the other aspect of hybridity, as "expressions of extreme pain and agonizing dislocations" (Radhakrishnan 1996: 159), is often depoliticized by the smooth machinations of the former (the unrepresentability of hybrid space becomes a convenient diversion).

This hybrid space (also a liminal space constituted by indeterminacy and transitionality) poses a difficulty firstly because it is "unrepresentable" (like concepts of indeterminacy, and so on). While it functions mainly at a conceptual (hence, abstract) level, the transitional space nonetheless affects and influences perceptions, as well as conditions, of diasporas. On the one hand, it offers an active way of being that is coextensively reconciled to the many differences around, while on the other hand, it remains constantly and critically reflexive of the differentiated minutiae of everyday, diasporic life. Consequently, diasporic selfhood or subjectivity is necessarily double; on the one hand, broken down into its multiple components and various trajectories, while on the other hand having also to maintain a certain "coherence" to enable the ongoing questioning, challenging, and revising of its consciousness. That is, in Radhakrishnan's words, "acknowledging the imperatives of an earlier 'elsewhere' in an active and critical relationship with the cultural politics of one's present home, all within the figurality of a reciprocal displacement" (1996: xiii). The double consciousness of being diasporic has been articulated by Paul Gilroy in his theorization of what he calls the "Black Atlantic," a "rhizomorphic, fractal structure of [a] transcultural, international formation" (1993: 4). He explores W. E. B. Du Bois's concept of "double consciousness" as a way of approaching and conveying "the special difficulties arising from black internalization of an American identity" (Gilroy 1993: 126). Extending that consciousness to this essay's discussion of diasporas in general, the difficulties facing most diasporas is the continual *internalization* (whether voluntary or not) of an *external, imputed* identity that is often alien to their racial ethnicities.

Contemporary diasporic experience has seen the addition of another aspect to diasporic consciousness that takes it a level above the double; that is, diasporic experience and consciousness is now multiple. The pressures facing diasporas are not only those of having to make sense of a past in order to reconcile with the immediate present, but also a future that will be significantly influenced by how negotiations between past and present are performed. The proliferation of hybridities means that theorizations of diasporas will (necessarily and constantly) be destabilized; its indeterminacies will therefore have to be pushed or harnessed in increasingly productive and creative ways. In other words, it is important to maintain "a critical cultural politics of diaspora [that] should privilege neither host country nor (real or imaginary) homeland, but precisely keep a creative tension between 'where you're from' and 'where you're at'" (Ang 1992: 13). That tension is an important factor in the determining of diasporic futures, which is highly dependent on "where you're from" and "where you're at." The way diasporic experience is constituted — around notions and concepts of doubleness, ambivalence, indeterminacy, and so on — shows not only the heterogeneity and diversity within diasporas but also the constantly changing experience of being in diaspora, crucial to the transitional consciousness that diasporas inhabit.

Although diasporic consciousness is transitional and multiple, there is a danger in homogenizing diasporas based on those characteristics. Radhakrishnan points out that "the politics of solidarity with other minorities and diasporic ethnicities is as important and primary as the politics of 'representations of origins' [and that] diasporic communities do not want to be rendered discrete or separate from other diasporic communities, for that way lies co-optation and depoliticization" (1996: 177). However, what needs also to be expanded is that "relational space" for the "heterogeneously but relationally diverse subaltern/oppressed/minority subject positions in their attempts to seek justice and reparation for centuries of unevenness and inequality" (Radhakrishnan 1996: 177). As Avtar Brah reminds us, while "the politics of solidarity with another group is one thing ... the self-organising political mobilisation of the group itself is quite another" (1996: 8). Herein lies the importance of keeping minority groups distinct, if not differentiated, because it would be (again) a violation of their unique identity by homogenizing and collapsing their different politics, political causes, and particular histories into the one category (manageable and sometimes all-encompassing, but a generalized *singularity* nevertheless). Concurrently, "the politics of solidarity" must also be maintained, so that diasporic communities do not lose the numbers that constitute the force, the impetus behind collective political action. It has to be noted that even in politicized situations, the possibility of exploiting the diasporic condition remains at large (rather than attenuated). Aligning oneself with the political causes of disenfranchised diasporic groups for empowerment can lead to the misrepresentation, or manipulation, of subject constitution as being impaired, and which attributes its cause to the diasporic condition as its cause. In other words, political consciousness-raising within the diaspora can lead to an invalidation of the conditions of diaspora (as terms of oppression), reducing those terms and then robbing them from the real diasporic groups seeking justification and redress.

This is where effective planning of future trajectories is needed to circumvent those opportunistic maneuvers. Drawing upon Gayatri Spivak's "strategic essentialism," that planning involves "the *strategic* use of a positivist essentialism in a scrupulously visible political interest" (Spivak 1993: 3–6). To put it to use as a "mobilizing slogan or masterword," the strategic use of essentialism activates certain subject positions out of theorizations that have been (or are easily) rendered static. This is significant where theorizations about the future of diasporas are concerned. The transitional diasporic consciousness, because racialized and politicized and aware of its similarities and differences with other diasporic groups, can draw upon diasporic identifications and representations to strategically present its political causes for greater effectivity and more equitable representation, not only in the social and cultural aspects of the nation, but also at the economic and political levels.

This brings us back to the anxieties invoked by the transitional space of diasporic consciousness: being dialogic and in process, it is also transient. However, because it is dialectically constituted and multiple, the transformations enabled by and from this space can be empowering to the diasporic community/ies. While this kind of theorization may seem to fall into a pattern of idealizing certain spaces and/or discursive practices, I want to emphasize that levels of mobility and of access to capital resources and other privileges are not equal for all members of the diaspora.[20] Therefore, when diasporic hybridity is referred to, under exactly which hybrid condition is the diasporic subject constituted and located? That is, when more than one hybridity presents itself, "which hybridity are we talking about?" (Radhakrishnan 1996: 160). Consequently, when the hybrid subject speaks, "who is being spoken for?" (Radhakrishnan 1996: 161). The vicissitudes of diasporic consciousness have to be seen as specifically derived from historical contingencies of being positioned in particular configurations of race and class ideologies. The diasporic subject of such a hybrid and evolving (even alienating) space is continually displaced, as social and cultural formations are constantly destabilized. This defamiliarization is but the result of the creative tensions that constitute "hyphenated" diasporic identity and its conditions of existence.

From the three types of consciousness outlined in this chapter, no one particular "model" of diaspora emerges that will sufficiently account for the range of contemporary diasporic experiences. While transitional diasporic consciousness is mindful of the dangers of reductionism implicit in the homeland idealizing consciousness and the exploitative manipulations available to superficial multiculturalism, homeland idealism and multiculturalism are not without their merits. Firstly, it is crucial to see homeland idealism as an invaluable reminder of cultural history and historicity, as well as a powerful and useful mechanism in the form of collective social memory (and memory making). Secondly, in a climate of tokenistic multiculturalism, diasporic communities that choose to engage themselves in this way with their host society are also making a point (even if inadvertently) about the type of active agency that they have; as "free"-ly displaced subjects in liberal, humanist, and culturally plural societies. What is important about these categories is how they have alluded to and articulated underlying concerns and issues facing diasporas, problems that have been exacerbated by the phenomena of globalization, made more urgent in an environment of cultural dislocation where homeland memories are tenaciously held on to.

4

Cultural Citizenship in Diaspora: A Study of Chinese Australia

Wenche Ommundsen

I have my passport, and no doubt soon I shall have my identity card. I have done jury service. I am sent my voting card at election time, and my tax demand once a year. These rights and obligations confirm my status as a member of the state. What more do I want to know? What's the problem?

The problem, of course, is that this legal status as citizen does not feel as though it has anything much to do with my sense of self. It tells me what I am, not who I am. (James Donald, "The Citizen and the Man About Town")

My dear in the beginning there was the Word! And there was me. And the Word was CHINAMAN. And there was me ... I lived the Word! The Word is my heritage ... I am the natural born ragmouth speaking the motherless bloody tongue. No real language of my own to make sense with, so out comes everybody else's trash that don't conceive.... Born? No! Crashed! Not born. Stamped! Not born! Created! ... No more born than nylon or acrylic. For I am a Chinaman! A miracle synthetic! Drip dry and machine washable. (Frank Chin, *The Chickencoop Chinaman*)

The two volumes of Eric Rolls's history of the Chinese in Australia are entitled *Sojourners* and *Citizens* (Rolls 1992 and 1996). The first volume concludes in 1888, the year the Anti-Chinese League forced an almost total ban on Chinese immigration and four ships carrying Chinese immigrants were refused entry to Sydney. "The day of the sojourners was almost over," writes Rolls, "the aim of the Chinese in Australia from 1888 on was to become whatever citizens society would allow" (Rolls 1992: 508). His sojourner/citizen distinction is potentially misleading, however. Measures to restrict Chinese immigration had been enforced by the Australian colonies from the very beginning of European settlement, and particularly in the wake of the massive influx of Chinese during the 1850s gold rush. At the same time, it was possible for some early Chinese settlers to become citizens of the British colonies, whereas access to citizenship was virtually barred during the period of the White Australia policy, which remained in place from 1901 until 1973.[1] What sort of citizen did nineteenth-century Australia allow a Chinese to become, how did the diminishing numbers of Chinese in Australia negotiate citizenship at a time of legislated discrimination in the first half of the twentieth century, and what is the position of Chinese-Australians today, after thirty years of color-blind immigration policies but in a climate of social disquiet over levels of Asian immigration, a climate in which boatloads of nonwhite immigrants are once again being turned away from Australian waters?[2] In order to tease out the implications of some of these questions, this chapter examines the concept of cultural citizenship, asking what sort of fit, if any, between the "what" of citizenship and the "who" of identity is conceivable, achievable, and desirable in a world of complex cultural allegiances.

Mei Quong Tart, who came to Australia from Canton as a young boy during the gold rush in the 1850s, rose to prominence as a businessman and spokesman for his community. He became an Australian citizen in 1871, and his standing within white colonial society was, by all reports, high. It is clear, however, that Quong Tart's status as a "good" colonial citizen was granted *in spite of*, not *because of*, his Chineseness. He was complimented in the *Mail* as being "the whitest Chinaman we know," and the *Bulletin* wrote that

> Quong Tart's Mongolian qualities are only skin deep. He is a native of Australia and a loyal subject of Her Most Gracious Majesty the Queen ... and a true Briton, expert at manly sports. (Cited in Broinowski 2001: 14)

In a country in which a *good* citizen meant a *white* citizen, Chinese and other minorities were tolerated only to the extent that they made themselves inconspicuous, either through segregation or through assimilation. Not surprisingly, many of the values they had to adopt in order to survive were internalized, becoming part of their personal and cultural makeup, in Australia as elsewhere in the Chinese diaspora. Shen Yuanfang, in her recent book on Chinese-Australian autobiographies, notes examples of writers trying to "prove" their worth by pointing to characteristics they share with white Australians. Their Chineseness had to be unspoken, in fact only became available as a cultural identity in Australia after the introduction of multiculturalism in the 1970s (Shen 2001: 146). But what was the nature of this Chineseness after decades of suppression; did it seriously challenge what is sometimes referred to as the "banana" culture of assimilated Chinese Australia?[3] A number of new models for cultural belonging emerged almost simultaneously, both from inside the established community and from the outside. Within the Chinese-Australian community, efforts were made to reclaim the silenced past, resulting in renewed interest and pride in their cultural origins and heritage. At the same time, new waves of Chinese immigration from Singapore, Hong Kong, Taiwan, and the People's Republic of China, as well as from the Southeast Asian diaspora, brought with them alternative versions of Chinese identity. Many argue, with justice, that the differences between the various groups of Chinese-Australians are such that it is impossible to speak in terms of a "cultural identity" common to them all (Ang 2001). On the other hand, the mainstream culture is rarely capable of making such distinctions: in the eyes of most Australians, there is little difference between an ABC (Australian-born Chinese), an ethnic Chinese from Vietnam, or a mainlander. Cultural identity, one is reminded, is not just a measure of one's own complex perceptions and preferences, but also of crude exercises of pigeonholing over which individuals and groups have little control.

Australian Chinese today find themselves negotiating a number of models for cultural belonging, some inherited, some thrust upon them, and others evolving through contact with the wider Australian community. The relationship between "culture" and "citizenship" was perhaps never simple, but while it has traditionally tended to be taken for granted, this is no longer possible: the category of the nation has become culturally complex and contradictory while at the same time other "imagined communities" (the homeland, real or imaginary, the wider diaspora, and other global formations) make competing claims for cultural allegiance. The contemporary diasporic subject is culturally "polyglossic," and it is precisely this complexity that makes the Chinese diaspora an ideal site for testing notions of cultural citizenship in a globalizing world, a world in which the simple equation of culture and citizenship is becoming increasingly redundant.

Theories of citizenship have evolved within the disciplines of politics and sociology, and the concept's recent migration into cultural studies has not occurred without a measure of disciplinary tension. If it is nevertheless my chosen place of departure, it is because much of the cultural negotiation I am interested in can be traced back to notions of inclusion and exclusion, belonging and not belonging, and the most potent symbol of social and cultural belonging remains the passport. Citizenship in the most general sense is about group membership, but as Gerard Delanty has pointed out, "no account of citizenship can evade the fact that it was originally constructed in order to exclude and subordinate people" (Delanty 2000: 9, 11). We have all experienced the moment when, on entering a country, we are channeled into two lines, one marked Citizens, the other Aliens, and, if stuck in the Alien line, will face a much longer wait, a careful scrutiny of our credentials, and a feeling of rejection, and dejection, as we watch those blessed with the correctly colored booklet sail through passport control and customs. Most countries these days choose more euphemistic terms for some groups of aliens ("visitors," "noncitizens," "other passports"), and much less polite words for others ("illegal immigrants," "boat people," "queue-jumpers"). Indeed, recent Australian history offers telling examples of how the vocabularies of immigration have the capacity to differentiate between different categories of noncitizens.[4] My argument here, however, is that there is more than one way to be alienated, and that the little blue book (in the case of Australia) does not necessarily offer full franchise to the rights and privileges of *cultural* belonging. Indeed, to go by recent trends in Australian immigration history, the migrants who are *least* likely to feel a sense of cultural belonging are generally the first to seek full legal citizenship.[5]

"Cultural citizenship" is only one of a great many models for "personhood" developed within the disciplines concerned with what Nikolas Rose (1996) calls "regimes of subjectification," or languages for human self-definition. For the purpose of the kind of cultural analysis I am interested in, it sits conveniently at the crossroads between discourses of multiculturalism and "cultural identity." Like multiculturalism, it is defined by official state policies, but has a dimension of lived experience that cannot be captured at the level of policy. Like "identity," it defines notions of group belonging and participation as well as individual self-perception. Unlike either, it goes beyond the state, the group and the individual to name cultural *rights* and cultural *responsibilities* in a world of shifting allegiances, a world in which mass migration, multinational capital, and global communication have destabilized traditional sites of authority such as the nation-state. A definition of citizenship based on passive rights and privileges bestowed by the nation-state is becoming increasingly redundant in a globalizing world composed of a number of overlapping imagined communities, communities with new sets of criteria for inclusion and exclusion that have opened up new possibilities for cultural enrichment, but also for cultural abuse. At the same time, the question of how *much* difference can be accommodated within multicultural nations before the political, legal, and social fabrics of the state become intolerably strained crop up with monotonous regularity at all levels of national and international debate.

Theorists of citizenship refer to a "cultural turn" in citizenship studies in the last decade, arguing that one of the main innovations has been to add *cultural rights* to the list of rights to which citizens can claim entitlement. According to the influential model established by T. H. Marshall, citizen rights were previously defined as belonging to the civil, political, and social spheres (Delanty 2000: 18; Stevenson 2001: 7). However, despite the emphasis on the intimate relationship between citizenship and culture, Bryan Turner has recently argued that "cultural citizenship and the cultural underpinnings of modern citizenship remain neglected aspects of contemporary studies of citizenship" (2001: 12).

What exactly do we mean by "cultural citizenship" and what are the issues that make the concept problematic? Globalization and the fragmentation of homogeneous national cultures have made it increasingly difficult to define cultural citizenship simply as the capacity to participate in the reproduction of a national culture (Stevenson 2001: 7), but exactly what kinds of cultural capital, rights, responsibilities, and competencies should be called upon to replace it remains uncertain. The very term *culture*, with its different inflections depending on disciplinary contexts, is problematic: should it be confined to the aesthetic dimensions of human experience, to the domain of cultural consumption, or instead be opened up to include the multiple structures and experiences of everyday life? Depending on which part of the compound is emphasized, culture or citizenship, the phrase can be taken to mean *either* a type of national or civic belonging predicated on cultural characteristics *or* the cultural attributes without which the full meaning of citizenship cannot be realized. Notions of "global," "cosmopolitan," or "postnational" citizenship have frequently been evoked in these debates, as have tensions between the traditional notion of citizenship as the pursuit of equality and the current emphasis on the recognition of difference. In the context of diasporic or other minority cultures, a frequent issue of debate is also the contrast between a static or "museum" version of culture as preserved heritage and the fluid, dynamic, and plural cultural reality of these populations.

Jan Pakulski's definition of cultural citizenship puts the emphasis on rights in relation to cultural difference: "a new domain of cultural rights that involve the right to symbolic presence, dignifying representation, propagation of identity and maintenance of lifestyles" (Pakulski 1997: 73). Nick Stevenson, in his introduction to the recent book *Culture and Citizenship*, similarly stresses the "right to be different," but "difference" here means an ability to range across diverse cultural registers: "A cultural citizen is a polyglot who is able to move comfortably within multiple and diverse communities while resisting the temptation to search for a purer and less complex identity" (Stevenson 2001: 2). In an earlier definition, Stevenson has also argued that "cultural citizenship" must include dimensions that go beyond the mere recognition of difference: "Cultural citizenship can be said to have been fulfilled to the extent to which society makes commonly available the semiotic and material cultures necessary in order to make social life meaningful, critique practices of domination, and allow for the recognition of difference under conditions of tolerance and mutual respect" (1997: 42). Bryan Turner argues that the citizen is both the *subject* and the *object* of cultural life, and a definition of cultural citizenship should also include notions of cultural *agency* or empowerment (2001: 12). "To have access to cultural citizenship," writes Stevenson, "therefore is to be able to make an intervention into the public sphere at the local, national or global level" (1997: 5). Turner, optimistically, suggests that it may be possible to assess the yardsticks for cultural citizenship in any given society: "It should be possible to create indices which could be constructed to measure to what extent location, education, social class, gender, race and linguistic knowledge stand in the way of full access to and participation in either the high or low cultural spheres of any particular state or society" (2001: 27). The difficulty is that no such indices can be created as absolute: indeed, in times of rapid social change the most outstanding feature of cultural citizenship is its dynamism. Yardsticks not only change over time, but also vary within different sections of an increasingly fragmented society — nowhere more dynamic or more fragmented than in the relationship between diasporic populations and the different imagined communities to which they claim a sense of belonging.

The close relationship between the concepts of cultural citizenship and cultural identity is stressed by most definitions and theories, but therein also lies its most problematic dimension. For while cultural citizenship is generally evoked in the context of culturally complex and inclusive communities, the concept has the capacity to become a prescriptive category, defining the "ideal" cultural attributes of the citizenry and by extension marking others as less desirable or even unacceptable. In the context of the recent backlash against multiculturalism in Australia and other Western nations, the view that cultural diversity is incompatible with a stable and harmonious citizenry is becoming increasingly common in populist and neoconservative discourse. A polarization of opinion is taking place: on the one hand, an enthusiastic endorsement of multiculturalism and antiracism, but simultaneously, a strengthening of xenophobic attitudes in some sections of society, arguing that more traditional notions of cultural identity are under threat from "prescriptive" multiculturalism. This should remind us that it is not only definitions of citizenship that have taken a "cultural turn" in recent times; so has racism. Neoracist discourse, as Etienne Balibar has argued, is more likely to cite insurmountable cultural differences than biological heredity as a justification for discriminating against individuals and ethnic groups (1991: 21). Both sides of these debates use some notion of cultural identity to define their ideal imagined community, and both accuse the other of wanting to impose an unacceptable model on the citizenry. Based on such considerations, James Donald, quoted in the first epigraph to this chapter, concludes that the discourse of cultural citizenship "conflates different questions of citizenship which are better kept apart" (1996: 172). Arguing against Habermas's attempt to give the legal status of citizenship a "post-traditional" cultural identity, he prefers to regard the citizen as "an empty place," a "what" rather than a "who" (Donald 1996: 173). The problem with his line of argument, as a number of feminists and other theorists have pointed out, is that the "universal" subject of liberal democracy can never be empty, but is always already culturally inscribed, and so potentially exclusive. The concept of cultural citizenship may at least have the advantage of enabling us to name these inscriptions and exclusions, thus making possible a challenge to its prescribed cultural contents.

Another objection to the discourse of cultural citizenship, or rather, to the "cultural turn" in citizenship thinking and practice, is raised by Jan Pakulski, who links the emergence of *cultural rights* with the shrinking of *social rights* in contemporary liberal democracies. If cultural rights such as the right to symbolic representation and tolerance of previously marginalized lifestyles are used to somehow compensate for a crisis in the welfare system, they may represent shallow victories. As Pakulski writes, "the new claims to cultural rights are embraced by state apparatuses eager to prop up their declining legitimacy yet unable to extend further the expensive welfare rights" (1997: 83). In the worst cases, granting rights to cultural difference may serve as a mask for the *removal* of rights to social and economic equality. I would argue that such a strategy has been used by the current Australian government in relation to both Aboriginal and immigrant communities in recent years. The problem with such political strategies, as Aboriginal Australians know only too well, is that *real* cultural rights do not come cheap: a serious commitment to the protection of cultural heritage and the maintenance of cultural difference can never be an alternative to social rights, but on the contrary builds on them, confirming the interpenetration of the social and the cultural. Pakulski's objection highlights an unresolved tension within current theories of cultural citizenship, between what we might call a postnational, generally multicultural conception, operating at the level of transnational or cosmopolitan social spheres and emphasizing representation and cultural consumption, and the more basic kinds of cultural competence required to function effectively within particular, more circumscribed social environments.

How does one "measure" cultural citizenship, when the criteria and indices are yet to be created, and the nature and scope of the concept itself a subject of debate? The most obvious answer is that one cannot, and that it is highly unlikely that objective and universally accepted measurements will emerge. What is possible, however, is an assessment (subjective, culturally contingent) of individual and group self-evaluation against community standards, set alongside the legal, political, and social frameworks of any given nation or other cultural group. Currently available information about culture and citizenship in Australia is abundant, but still insufficient for the purpose of assessing the cultural climate for Chinese-Australians. A number of large-scale surveys of community attitudes and standards exist (see, for example, Ip et al. 1994), as do excellent analyses of Australian cultural relations in the last decade (see Hage 1998, Stratton 1998, Docker and Fischer 2000). Surveys based specifically on Chinese-Australian communities and recording the perspectives of Chinese-Australians are less complete. In addition to histories like that of Eric Rolls (1992 and 1996), a number of oral history projects have been recorded and published, of which one might mention Diana Giese's *Astronauts, Lost Souls and Dragons* (1996), Sang Ye's *The Year the Dragon Came* (1996), and most recently, Chek Ling's *Plantings in a New Land* (2001). The problem with these collections is not just that they are incomplete, but that they tend to reflect the views of particular groups of Chinese-Australians, and so can create a misleading picture of the community as a whole. They are also strongly colored by the cultural and political perspective of their editors. For example, Diana Giese and Sang Ye present almost diametrically opposite views on the social and cultural integration of their interviewees. As Tseen Khoo has recently argued, Giese portrays her informants as "good citizens" (Khoo 2001), and while the conclusion that Sang Ye's interviewees by contrast are "bad citizens" grossly oversimplifies their portrayal, this is nevertheless how the collection has been received by parts of the Australian readership (see in particular Sheehan 1998). These differences are primarily due to the fact that Giese concentrates on established and integrated members of the Chinese community, whereas Sang Ye's informants are for the most part recent immigrants from mainland China.[6] What these collections reveal, then, is the danger of generalizing about a widely divergent community. Another source of direct, though highly subjective, information about Chinese-Australians is their rapidly growing body of literary writing, in both English and Chinese. This new but thriving diasporic literature, which frequently takes for its theme the question of cultural negotiation, has also recently become the subject of critical analysis from a cultural perspective (see, for example, Ommundsen 2001).

Apart from these printed sources, the current survey is based on a series of semistructured interviews specifically formulated to address questions of culture and citizenship. In 2000 and 2001, my research fellow Dr Ouyang Yu conducted 27 interviews with members of the Chinese-Australian community. While we were careful to select subjects who would represent a wide range of Chinese-Australians in terms of age, cultural background, and time of residence in Australia, our selection does not, statistically speaking, claim to be fully representative of the community. Our concern was rather to choose people who, because of their personal or professional background, were particularly well placed to speak on matters of cultural competence and affiliation. The following observations are in the main based on these interviews, supplemented by information available from a range of printed sources.[7]

A set of research questions, however carefully targeted, constitutes a blunt instrument for measuring cultural citizenship; as our interviewees kept reminded us, the relationship between culture and citizenship is too complex and too fraught to be reduced to simple answers. Most of them were, however, prepared to risk generalizations, as I shall have to be in my summary of their responses. To start with, the survey testifies to the simultaneous inevitability and impossibility that citizens of the contemporary world will be identified in terms of their cultural attributes. The "what" of citizenship, to use James Donald's terms, is indelibly linked to the "who" of identity and, one suspects, always has been; but the contemporary world, with its greater complexity of cultural belonging and weakening of unitary and unquestioned cultural categories, makes the question of identity at the same time more difficult and more significant. In terms of both theory and practice, it has become impossible to divorce culture and identity from any notion of citizens' rights and responsibilities. At the same time, the danger of conflating citizenship and culture is greater than ever. The link between culture and ethnicity in the Chinese diaspora, as Ien Ang (2001) and others have pointed out, is tenuous. What does a Malaysian business migrant have in common with a mainland refugee, apart from the "Chineseness" forced on them both by a mainstream society incapable of making cultural as distinct from ethnic distinctions? Our research indicates that while notions of

"Chineseness" are frequently cited as categories of cultural belonging, there is little sense of a common community in diaspora, and even less agreement about what this ethnic identity actually means. There is also a strong sense, enforced by recent developments in Australian mainstream culture, that the neoracist discourse of "culturalism" (Stratton 1998) is surviving, even strengthening, despite official endorsement of the antiracist rhetoric of multiculturalism.

Is ethnicity, or more crudely, race, in itself an important enough marker of identity in today's Australia to serve as a major indicator of cultural citizenship or lack thereof? At one level, this is undoubtedly true. To be a member of a visible minority in a society in which elements of racism survive means being issued with frequent enough reminders of one's "outsider" status to question one's position as a fully franchised citizen. Interestingly, few of our interviewees reported being subjected to direct and malicious racist behavior, or to suffer personally from its consequences, though they agreed that racism was a reality of Australian life and might more indirectly have influenced their personal attitudes and circumstances. More important, it would seem, is the fact that racial identity is often the *only* common denominator in an otherwise widely divergent diasporic community; the category of *Chineseness*, in other words, is constructed on the basis of race rather than culture. The Chinese-American critic David Leiwei Li in a recent paper discusses the shifting meaning of Chineseness in diaspora. Initially composed of three dimensions of meaning, national, cultural and racial, it is soon reduced to a single aspect, that of race:

> Unlike class and culture, race appears not something that can easily assimilate. It is what you cannot leave home without, and it is not exactly your American Express. (Li 2001)

Diasporic subjects whose identity has previously had to remain unacknowledged find themselves in a situation of having to "re-ethnicize" themselves, looking to a repressed and forgotten history for the cultural content to "fill" the empty, but visible, signifier of difference (Ang 2001). The paradigmatic illustration of this dilemma is offered in the very first novel published by a Chinese-Australian writer, Brian Castro's *Birds of Passage* (1983). Castro's character Seamus O'Young is an Australian-born orphan of Chinese origin who knows nothing of his own background and so has to invent a personal history and ancestry based on what is known about the history of Chinese immigration to Australia. Unlike Castro's Seamus, however, most Chinese-Australians do not have a blank slate where their personal and cultural history should be, but on the contrary bring with them a complex and varied cultural inscription, including their own versions of Chineseness.

On the basis of the interviews as well as other sources, I would argue that sociocultural background, rather than race, is the most important indicator of a person's ability to function as a fully franchised cultural citizen of Australia. Our survey revealed a sharp differentiation between on the one hand, immigrants from the People's Republic of China, and on the other, Australian-born Chinese or immigrants from Hong Kong, Singapore, and Southeast Asia. This is hardly surprising. PRC migrants are initially less proficient in English; they have grown up under a social, political, and economic system fundamentally different from Western liberal democracy and capitalism; and they are mostly poor: many had to borrow money to come to Australia.[8] The other categories of Chinese migrants have generally grown up under Western, or Westernized, systems of government, they are fluent in English, and, in most cases, relatively affluent (many entered Australia as part of the "business migration" scheme). Levels of education tend to be high among all these groups, but PRC migrants, for the reasons given above, have greater difficulty in getting their educational qualifications recognized in Australia and finding employment in the professions for which they trained in their home country. Interestingly, those PRC migrants who had met with professional success in Australia (the artist Guan Wei and the opera singer Du Jigang were the most obvious examples among our interviewees) reported a much weaker sense of cultural alienation than did less successful mainlanders. What these differences indicate, I would argue, is that the categories of "cultural identity" and "ethnicity" are in themselves insufficient markers of capacity for cultural integration if they do not take into account differences in education, class, age, and socioeconomic mobility. On the other hand, Bryan Turner's "indices" of cultural citizenship cited above, which are based on such sociological categories, are too static to allow for the constant evolution of community standards and citizen attributes that have been characteristic of Australia, and of Australia's migrant communities, in the last decades. It would appear, for example, that the upward social mobility of Chinese migrants is greater and more rapid than in most other migrant groups. Levels of educational attainment, in particular, are outstanding. While the percentage of university-age Australians engaged in courses of higher education is only 27 percent for the general population, that percentage rises to over 60 in the Asian-Australian population. Not surprisingly, then, diaspora Chinese, in Australia as well as in countries like the US and Canada, are sometimes jokingly referred to as the "new Jews."

In the context of this research, we have found it useful to distinguish between what one might call compulsory and optional cultural attributes. A compulsory cultural attribute is one over which the individual has little power, at least in the short term. This may refer to particular skills or educational attainments, or to deeply embedded cultural conditioning of which one may not even be fully aware. Compulsory attributes define the limits of one's cultural mobility and may exclude individuals or groups from full cultural citizenship. By contrast, "optional" aspects of culture are those that can be adopted or discarded at will. While often important to an individual's sense of cultural identity, they rarely work to exclude him or her from a particular community, but on the contrary serve as an instrument of inclusion, a cultural passport, so to speak, to a number of different cultural groupings. Not surprisingly, individuals affected by a mismatch between their own compulsory cultural attributes and those of their society tend to speak of their situation in terms of loss, whereas those who are free to concentrate on optional attributes speak of cultural gain. The contrast between the "Tiananmen Square" migrants on the one hand and the business migrants and established Australian Chinese on the other was constantly expressed in such terms. To the recent mainland migrants, cultural identity was experienced as an impediment to effective participation in Australian society, whereas most others regarded their Chinese heritage as an enrichment, not only in their own lives, but also to Australian culture. Interestingly, aspects of such optional markers of identity can be transferred to non-Chinese individuals, most commonly to white spouses. One of our interviewees reported that his search for a lost Chinese identity was prompted by his Australian wife, and in Diana Giese's *Astronauts, Lost Souls and Dragons* it is the Anglo-Australian husband of a Chinese-Australian woman who speaks most enthusiastically of his cultural enrichment through the recovery of his wife's cultural heritage: "it adds to our own identity, to the richness of our lives" (Giese 1997: 260).

A telling illustration of this contrast between compulsory and optional cultural attributes can be found in the difference between the two most commonly named signifiers of cultural belonging, language and food. Insufficient language skills constitute a major handicap for PRC migrants in their attempt to gain employment relevant to their professional training, also in their participation in the social and cultural life of their new country. "Language workers" such as journalists, writers, and academics are particularly handicapped in this respect, and often find themselves with precarious careers, working in Australia but publishing in Chinese-speaking countries, or in the Chinese-language press in Australia. While their levels of English proficiency tend to be higher than for other professions, they still lack the "deep" linguistic and cultural literacy required to perform language work in the mainstream Australian context. Some are scornful of Australian culture, arguing that the predominance of English, and the lack of understanding produced by a monolingual tradition, prevent Australia from being multicultural in anything but the most superficial manner. Others simply accept their own social demotion as an inevitable consequence of migration and put their hopes in the next generation. Proficiency in the Chinese language is generally lost in the second or third generation after migration. Individuals with little or no knowledge of a Chinese language report a desire to learn Chinese, and their sense of exclusion from a community of Chinese speakers, but also their sense that it is possible to participate in some aspects of Chinese culture in diaspora without this linguistic competence. It would seem, then, that knowledge of English is a compulsory cultural attribute for Chinese Australians, whereas the Chinese language becomes optional, a desirable but not essential signifier of cultural heritage.

Food comes a close second to language as the most immediately recognizable signifier of culture. Almost all ethnic Chinese in Australia report eating more Chinese than "Western" food, and those who have a wide culinary repertoire are more likely to choose other Asian foods, and Mediterranean foods, in preference to what they called "Australian." Significantly, the time of migration seemed of minor importance: a fifth-generation ABC is as likely to prefer Chinese food as a recent immigrant, and recent PRC migrants are the only who express (or admit to) a taste for Western delicacies of the fast food variety. The cultural "weight" of food differs, however: while recent migrants prefer a particular food because it "tastes good," established diasporic subjects attach greater importance to food as a signifier of tradition and are more likely to cite culinary diversity as proof of Australia's cosmopolitan sophistication. This differentiation between compulsory and optional markers of culture lends weight to Stevenson's notion of the competent cultural citizen as the polyglot who can move effortlessly between cultural registers, provided, of course, he/she is equipped with the cultural capital necessary for basic functionality in the social world.

When asked directly what cultural characteristics they attached to "Chineseness," the interviewees gave a range of different answers, confirming Ien Ang's notion of Chinese cultural identity as an "open signifier" (Ang 2001). While many agreed that this identity varies according to historical contexts, it was also clear that, to *them*, Chineseness was not an empty signifier but one that carried a specific, though complex, cultural content. Those who tried to name traits considered to be typically Chinese regardless of time and place would come up with a list similar to the one recently offered by Shen Yuanfang: "perseverance, hard work, resignation, scholastic achievement, respect for the elderly and filial piety" (Shen 2001: xix). Some also mentioned the weight of a 5,000-year-old history, and a philosophical tradition: a "mixture of Confucianism and Taoism," the "middle way." More named historically contingent versions of Chineseness. Because of their precarious social status in diaspora, overseas Chinese were said to tend toward self-preservation and caution. As the mother of one ABC (born in 1915) is reported to have told her son: "work hard, don't make a lot of noise, and blend in" (Ling 2001: 71). Today, as the community, especially its younger members, are getting more confident in their cultural positioning, this conditioning is the mold they are trying to break.

The impact of half a century of Communism in China, and especially their experience of the Cultural Revolution, for many overshadow more traditional notions of cultural heritage. Recent migrants who have grown up in Mao's China have spent much of their time in Australia coming to grips with its effects on their personal and cultural makeup. Many report an intense hatred for China but also a need, once out of the country, to reassess a Chineseness they had attempted to leave behind. Confusion is a prominent sentiment among PRC migrants, and a growing sense of not belonging anywhere. On return visits to China, they also note rapid changes in the social, economic, and cultural climate of their homeland,

and feel increasingly alienated and foreign. One of our informants told us he thinks China has changed more than he has in the six years since he left the country. The realization that being Chinese means different things in different places is generally brought home to all migrants when they return to their countries of origin, where most feel they no longer belong. The migrant's dilemma of trying to fit in everywhere and ending up belonging nowhere is clearly in evidence, but so is the sense that different cultural qualities, by some named as part of an "Australianness" or at least an "Australian Chineseness," are making an impact on their outlook, self-perception, and patterns of behavior. Australianness, however, seemed even harder to define than Chineseness. Some referred to Australians as innocent, naive even, but generally honest, open, and friendly. Others talked of an innate conservatism in Australian culture, a suspicion of outsiders. Life in Australia was seen as relaxed and comfortable, verging on laziness. Significantly, when asked about the characteristics of Australianness, most spoke as outsiders: they were describing mainstream Australians, not themselves. Only when the matter came up indirectly in relation to other questions did they identify the Australian traits they had themselves taken on board. Comparing Australia to other parts of the world (for example, the US or the UK), they were more likely to stress the positive points of the national culture, and to include themselves in the category "Australian."

There was no uniform response to Australian multiculturalism: some regarded it as the cornerstone of Australian society; others found it superficial, potentially divisive, or even an impediment to social integration. Similarly, when asked about the importance of preserving a Chinese cultural tradition in diaspora, views varied greatly: from those who regarded the recovery and celebration of the Chinese past as a personal vindication and proof of their franchise as cultural citizens of Australia to those who dismissed cultural preservation as nostalgic, backward-looking, and irrelevant. The problem with cultural traditions, many pointed out, is that when "preserved" they end up as static museum pieces, whereas culture is "a living, changing thing." Some called for a greater exposure to contemporary Chinese cultural production, but complained that mainstream Australian society, as well as local Chinese community organizations, were stuck on Chinese culture of the dragon dance or "Chinatown" variety and less open to contemporary forms.

Our survey confirms tensions also identified in the theoretical literature on cultural citizenship: between the basic cultural competencies needed to function effectively within a particular society and the surplus or value-adding attributes that enable social and cultural mobility. These competing versions of cultural citizenship may both be legitimate, but they should not be confused or conflated, and one might argue that some of the problems afflicting multicultural societies, including Australia, stem precisely from the fact they have been. Similarly, there is a need to distinguish between the regime of representation and the regime of action, and to acknowledge that cultural rights must of necessity partake of both: dignified representation is an important first step, but counts for little if one remains the *object* of representation, never the *subject*. Full cultural franchise must also encompass intervention, including intervention into the processes of representation.

Is it possible for notions of cultural citizenship to be extended to even wider imagined communities, to postnational, postethnic, or global formations? Are diaspora populations and their hybridized cultures, as some theorists have argued, the very models for the postmodern ethnicities and identities of a future globalized world? The potential is certainly there, cogently argued by theorists such as Ien Ang and Homi Bhabha. The pull of more circumscribed cultural formations is still strong, however, just as the nation-state remains the predominant category of citizenship. We may all aspire to be world citizens but, as David Parker has recently pointed out, the world does not issue passports (Parker 2003: 173). Stuart Cunningham and John Sinclair argue in a recent book on media usage among Asian-Australians that the tendency to celebrate diaspora as "a universal metaphor for the deterritorialized, decentred, postmodern or postcolonial subject" (2000: 13) can also be seen as the product of a "romantic conceit" homogenizing the diaspora experience, and by so doing submerging not only the issue of class (Morley 1996) but also the still powerful cultural space of the nation-state. The effect of globalization on cultural identity in diaspora communities is experienced differently depending on cultural and social status, and the very notion of globalization is perceived as a profoundly contradictory phenomenon. Chinese-Australians often report feeling that they are both the beneficiaries and the victims of globalizing forces. Many welcome a globalized economy and flow of information, but are strongly opposed to cultural globalization. Others welcome opportunities for cultural exchange and interaction, but are suspicious of the social and economic consequence of globalization, especially for non-Western countries and cultures. They regard the domination of Western culture as both cause and effect of globalization and are ambivalent about its long-term consequences. The oft-touted possibility of a "Chinese world system" to rival Western-dominated globalization is met with skepticism. It is true, one of our interviewees conceded wryly, that Chinese medicine and Chinese movies are now popular around the world, but only because they were first "discovered" and marketed by the Americans. Another interviewee, a mainland migrant, summed up his attitude in the following terms: "To put it simply, 'globalization' is not only seen in the transformation of identity of many individuals but also … in a dilemma in which some people have to change their identity but cannot completely change it." His words point to a conflict experienced by individuals and communities across the world as they move from a relatively stable sense of cultural belonging to more complex notions of citizenship predicated on cultural mobility but frequently experienced as personal and cultural loss.

5

Mimics without Menace: Interrogating Hybridity in Bharati Mukherjee's Fiction

Rebecca Sultana

Bharati Mukherjee's attempt to become an American writer plays a significant part in securing her place in the American literary canon (Mukherjee 1992: xv). Writing about this acculturation process, Mukherjee says: "I have learned that in this era of massive diasporic movements, honorable survival requires resilience, curiosity, and compassion, a letting go of rigid ideals about the purity of inherited culture" (1997: 30). Mukherjee, therefore, distinguishes between two kinds of immigrants in terms of their assimilation into the Western metropolitan center and according to their resistance to adaptation or assimilation into such culture. Mukherjee's characters, diasporic or not, appropriate the metropolitan culture by replicating and becoming hybridized or what Homi Bhabha terms "authorized versions of otherness" (1994: 88).

In the colonial context, hybridity involves "a dialectical relationship between European ontology and epistemology and the impulse to create or recreate independent local identity" (Ashcroft, Griffiths, and Tiffin 1989: 95). In postcolonial societies, Ashcroft, Griffiths, and Tiffin (1989: 95) see hybridity occurring as a result of the "conscious affiliation of the indigenous peoples with the new social patterns as defined by the colonizers or when settler-invaders force the indigenous to assimilate to their ways." Bhabha (1994: 88) describes hybridity as a near duplication that produces a reform by appropriating the "Other."

I will discuss Mukherjee's first novel *The Tiger's Daughter* as foreshadowing the subsequent development of the writer's conception of hybridity. Her characters' colonial education, class, and economic positions facilitate their hybridization into a Western culture, yet their social construction, as shaped by hybridity, subvert the concept's positive objectives as defined by Bhabha.

The Tiger's Daughter describes Calcutta-born Tara Banerjee Cartwright, who is educated in the US and married to an American, David Cartwright. Tara returns to India after seven years to find the city of her childhood altered beyond recognition. Against the backdrop of the riot-torn city, Tara once again establishes contact with her old friends, all members of Calcutta's Westernized upper class. In the idle chatter of these young people, in their melodramatic references to the "troubled times," she notices a frightening naivety. Being educated at progressive institutions in the West, Tara alone seems to possess a deep understanding of the remorseless processes changing their world. In a rewriting of the patriarchal imperialist discourse that had cast the white man as savior, Mukherjee's novel brings the educated, emancipated Indian woman back from the West as the only remaining symbol of cultural progress in a moribund, tradition-bound society and, therefore, as the possible redeemer of the East. Tara, too, is drawn into the effete, indolent climate and can neither communicate her knowledge nor effect positive change. Such ineffectiveness also becomes the text's ideological judgment on the political climate of the 1970s, in which Tara can see only the end of all order and the onset of total anarchy.

The society to which Tara returns preserves traces of Calcutta's colonial aristocratic culture. Tara's childhood home still displays the eclectic meeting of two worlds, from the Italian tables in the entrance halls and the tiger skin decorating one wall, the heavy imported furniture in the living room, and the deep canvas chairs on the balcony, reflecting "the order and ease of the British days," up to the marble prayer room on the third floor where the array of Hindu gods and goddesses are the objects of Tara's mother's constant preoccupation (1972: 30–4). In the city at large, the few remaining colonial institutions — the Rotary Club, the British Council, and of course, the Catelli Continental Hotel — are the last social sites of this cultural encounter. The violence of colonialism is carefully written throughout the text, which celebrates, instead, the exuberance of cultural interchange. While Tara and her friends participate in intellectual debates at the British Council, their city is torn apart by peasant riots. If there is a critique of this society at all, it is merely a censorious eyebrow raised at an anachronistic world that still lives "by Victorian rules, changed decisively by the exuberance of the Hindu imagination" (Mukherjee 1972: 34).

The novel highlights tragically the decline of the Bengali elite by providing a flashback to the upheavals of social and political change over the last century. Significantly, even before the narrator introduces Tara, the novel recalls the murder, nearly a hundred years before, of Tara's great-grandfather Harilal Banerjee, the renowned *zaminder* (landowner) of Pachpara. Harilal's death signaled the end of an epoch, and the rise of the "Jute Mill" Roy Chowdhurys, representatives of a rising mercantile elite. The surviving members of the landed aristocracy, such as Tara's grandfather, were easily absorbed into the ranks of the rising mercantile and professional classes, and Bengal's cultural and economic prominence was uninterrupted for another century. Yet the text implies that the murder of a nineteenth-century *zaminder* by unknown assailants signals the start of a degenerative process whose final, fatal form is the riot-torn Calcutta of 1970.

Situated at a significant moment in the history of contemporary India, the novel foregrounds the Naxalite uprising of the 1970s, which shook the eastern and southeastern sections of India. Originating from a part of west Bengal, the organization consisted of and was led by tribal cultivators and the landless lower classes, rather than by an urban leadership, against feudal oppression. Largely supported by leftist intellectuals, the Naxalbari rebellion was responsible for starting other similar agrarian reform movements across the state.[1] Mukherjee not only alludes to the Naxal movement but also locates her text at a sensitive crossroad of historical change; yet without the presence of contesting perspectives, which could have provided a historical background to this insurgency, the riot deteriorates into mere anarchy. Mukherjee can possibly plead ignorance of the "Other," but this misreading of history can only emphasize the destruction of properties while the Naxalites are belittled or euphemistically referred to as hooligans or as "left of left politicians" (Mukherjee 1972: 44). The positive charges of the social revolution that rocked Calcutta in the early seventies are completely erased from her representation and, therefore, the dominant classes implicated in oppression seem to emerge as the victims of random violence. A revolutionary movement that marks an important juncture in the history of class struggle in the postcolonial nation-state through what Gayatri Spivak calls the "peculiar coalition of peasant and intellectual" (1985: 181) comes across as widespread vandalism in the novel. Instead, Mukherjee foregrounds the nostalgia of the upper classes, their collective yearnings for "the peaceful times" in "the real Calcutta" (1972: 39). This group's acquiescence to neocolonial oppression is most evident in the portrayal of Tara's father, known as the Bengal Tiger.

In order to valorize figures like the Bengal Tiger, Mukherjee creates a binary of the good entrepreneur versus the bad entrepreneur. The Bengal Tiger's depicted benevolence does not highlight his association in the industrial proletariat's oppression of the working class, which has allowed him to afford an opulent house with "imported furniture" (1972: 31) and a retinue of servants in an upscale neighborhood of Calcutta. The text is also silent about his possible participation in systems of exploitation. Frantz Fanon had predicted similar bourgeois repression, in "The Pitfalls of National Consciousness": In fact, the landed proprietors will insist that the state should give them a hundred times more facilities and privileges than were enjoyed by the foreign settlers in former times. The exploitation of agricultural workers will be intensified and made legitimate (Fanon 1990: 126).

The oppressive production relations under feudalism and later under mercantile and industrial capitalism that periodically led to peasant militancy and labor unrest in India are left unexamined in the novel. Instead, the sociopolitical history of Bengal for the last hundred years is narrated as the elegiac tale of the privileged class.

Tara's father continues this heritage of strength and vision. Ideology as presented in the novel idealizes the benevolent, paternal employer who, impervious to the pressure of the times, performs his duties, "working out medical and disability insurance for his workers, night classes in the factory for those who could not write or read" (Mukherjee 1972: 9). Social protest of the workers is decontextualized so that we merely hear of "angry, fanatical faces," "unreasonable murders," "suspicious drownings," "bloody and mutilated bodies," without any reconstruction of the socioeconomic causes that provoked such acts of violence. From the safety of the hotel balcony, the rioters appear to Tara as "rebellious children rather than political militants," an impression that succeeds in trivializing the ominous slogan "Blood bath! Blood bath!"

Ignoring the socioeconomic forces that erupted into the revolutionary situation of the 1970s, Tara looks for answers in the psychological makeup of the upper-class Bengalis. In the young men of her circle, Tara notices a regrettable lack of the entrepreneurial energy that characterized empire builders of the past generation such as the Bengal Tiger. Their present descendants, the young people who had "inherited, not earned, their wealth" (1972: 45), are equipped neither to extend their empires nor to protect their world against the agents of destruction, figured in the novel by the riotous mob on the one hand, and on the other, the crude Tuntunwalla, representative of a new race of unprincipled capitalists. The nostalgic narrative of the immigrant's return also precipitates the fear surrounding the loss of class privileges, the tragic implications of their imminent dispossession and the destruction of their Calcutta. The insularity of the bourgeois classes is rationalized through Tara's and her friends' perspectives. Their apathy for change is sustained by their skepticism.

In his essay on celebratory writers, Brennan (1989) attributes to Mukherjee the virtues of democracy and freedom. However, these two virtues lose some of their potency by Mukherjee's own admission that she enters the new world already endowed with considerable privilege. Likewise, Tara is privileged with a Western education, class standing, and wealth. Privileges, whatever they may be in terms of race, class, nationality, and gender can work as impediments, which block certain kinds of knowledge. Striving to recognize these limitations and overcoming them is one of the most powerful tasks set by Gayatri Spivak (Bhatnagar, Chatterjee, and Rajan 1990: 69). To unlearn our privilege entails, on the one hand, working hard at gaining some knowledge of the others who occupy those spaces closed to our privileged views. On the other hand, it means attempting to speak to those others in such a way that they might take us seriously and be able to answer back.

CLASS DIVIDE AMONG WOMEN

An interesting aspect of the Naxalite movement was its ability to mobilize women both in the rural and urban areas. But Mukherjee does not perceive gender politics as a possible segue into the exploitation of the revolutionary struggle. Women's participation in political movements is belittled when, toward the end of the novel, a female revolutionary has her bottom pinched during a demonstration while Tara sits unseeing, locked in a car, wondering whether she would get out of Calcutta (Mukherjee 1972: 210). Clearly, women who are involved in active resistance movements are imprisoned within degrading stereotypes of harassment as they make a spectacle of themselves. The text does not persuade us to look for the elements of subversion that frame this moment. Nor does it offer us images of female subaltern agency.[2] Yet again, in an ideologically significant formulation, the novel brings the West back into the life of the East with a new "civilizing" mission, but this time without the darker imperialist agenda. The two Western characters in the novel, the student civil rights activist and the social worker, are both in India "because India needs help. The third world has to be roused to help itself" (Mukherjee 1972: 166). These latest representatives of the West, however, with their liberal-humanist agenda, are largely incomprehensible to a native population that still lives by Victorian rules. Therefore, in the "new" Bengali woman, with roots in both worlds, the text attempts to construct the ideal cultural ambassador.

Not surprisingly, then, Tara alone possesses an acute understanding of the changing times. It is Tara who sees in her father, the Bengal Tiger, a lonely "pillar supporting a balcony that had long outlived its beauty and its function" (1972: 29). Armed with a liberal education and Western notions of sexual emancipation, she alone notes, with exasperated pity, her friend's uncritical submission to a traditional marriage with a "foreign educated and very brilliant boy" (1972: 127). And it is she again, who recognizes in the *Marwari* the real enemy of the elite. But Tara can only suffer her vision by sinking into the same apathy and, despite her progressive Western ideals, she can neither save herself nor communicate her understanding. Although Bhabha perceives mimicry as a presence that is partial, incomplete, and virtual, and so able to disturb the power and its difference, Tara becomes ineffectual at transforming anything, reminding us of Thomas Macaulay's "class of interpreters."[3]

Tara thus places Calcutta outside of the discourse of historical change. Calcutta in Tara's vision is always entrapped within a quagmire of political impasse, its political exigencies are naturalized, and, in a sense, it is denuded of history. The problem is not only that Tara cannot connect in meaningful ways with the nation whose history is being reconstructed through her; she does not even engage at discursive levels with the forces that anchor the histories. Tara never questions how the history of the postcolonial state is inextricably bound up with the ideology of class privilege.

Finally, in a calculated distortion of history, the novel's concluding scene presents an unexpected alliance of two savage forces. Between them, the bloodthirsty mob and the henchmen of the *Marwari* attack old Joyonto Roy Chowdhury, that human caricature of Bengal's elite colonial culture. The book ends with the death of Pronob, the most prominent member of Tara's circle, in a desperate act of martyrdom to save the old man. By granting Pronob this final, albeit futile, moment of heroism, the text manifests its ideological stance on the sociopolitical situation of the time. Within the terms of the novel, the decline of the Bengali elite — admittedly now effete and sterile — also signals the death of a grand humanist code of honor, decency, and chivalry. But the poignancy is undercut by the knowledge that the Bengali upper class owes its present fate to its own spiritual sterility, its inability to produce in the current generation such men of vision and action as the Bengal Tiger.

Colonial representation of Third World subjects were long inculcated through an educational system, which replicated stereotyped images among the colonized themselves. In her book *Masks of Conquest* (1989), Gauri Viswanathan affirms the mutually reinforcing relationship between literary studies and British rule in India. She claims that the British administration in India used English literature strategically to suppress the anticipated threat of native insubordination: "A discipline that was originally introduced in India primarily to convey the mechanics of language was thus transformed into an instrument for ensuring industriousness, efficiency, trustworthiness, and compliance in native subjects" (Viswanathan 1989: 93). The successful inauguration of this discipline in the colonized world is said to mark the juncture at which native populations came to internalize the ideological procedures of the colonial civilizing mission. In *The Empire Writes Back* (1989), Ashcroft et al. develop this thesis in terms of textual invasion, or "interpellation" of colonized subjectivities. Thus the assimilated text is shown to spread the subtle influence of colonialist imperatives within the unsuspecting native body. Urged to memorize choice passages from English literary masters, the colonial child submits to the secret logic of spiritual and political indoctrination. The very "recitation of literary texts," these critics argue, "becomes a ritual act of obedience" (Ashcroft et al. 1989: 426).

Tara is, in part, such a product of a colonial education, the rationale for which was the creation of a group of "insiders" who became outsiders to fellow Indians. Tara muses about her sense of estrangement from her family and surroundings. She realizes that while an American husband and a passport can create a new distance between herself and her old home, the distance had its seeds in her anglicized education in Calcutta:

> How does the foreignness of the spirit begin? Tara wondered. Does it begin right in the center of Calcutta, with forty ruddy Belgian women, fat foreheads swelling under starched white headdresses, long black habits intensifying the hostility of the Indian sun? The nuns had taught her to inject the right degree of venom into words like "common" and "vulgar." They had taught her *The Pirates of Penzance* in singing class, and "If I should die, think only this of me ..." for elocution. (Mukherjee 1972: 37)

Metropolitan culture, therefore, exerts its influence on her even prior to her migration.

MONOLITHIC PORTRAYALS: WOMEN AS HELPLESS VICTIMS

R. Radhakrishnan accounts for the dissimilarities within the Indian diaspora in the United States by noting that these diasporics have to negotiate, for themselves, between not only "subnational spaces such as the ethnic, the communal and the tribal" but also "the deracinating imperatives of internationalists and multinational modern and postmodern trajectories" (1992: 106). Mukherjee, though, perceives the immigrant's response only in gender-differentiated ways. She claims that while men remain content with material prosperity, "they have locked their hearts against mainstream culture." The women, on the other hand, are "exhilarated by that change" and find such change to be empowering in contrast to the Indian experience (cited in Connell, Grearson, and Grimes 1990: 6). Tara escapes to the US, and what leads to her empowerment is her easy affiliation with the metropolitan social patterns. Colonial and neocolonial glamorization of the West finds fertile soil in this affiliation to nourish the longing for a liberating journey to the West, what Homi Bhabha calls "the displacement or escape motif, the moving away from where you are to somewhere else where the problem will be solved" (1990: 80).

The West offers an escape from the constraints of "traditionalism" particularly attractive to Mukherjee's female characters. They escape the oppressive confines of traditional Hindu widowhood and wifely duties for the anonymity and mobility of the American dream. All her stories of Indian women in the US trace various stages of a trajectory proceeding from docility, dependence, and modesty to assertiveness, independence, and sensuality. A recurring pattern in Mukherjee's fiction makes the Indian woman's emergence coincide with her arrival in the US or with crucial experience in that country. Thus, an ostensibly feminist narrative of emerging selfhood underwrites the construction of the US as the land of freedom and fulfillment.

Mukherjee's Indian women, on the other hand, are oppressed and unfulfilled because they are being recreated through the discourse of Western liberal feminism.[4] Chandra Mohanty (1991) argues that Western feminist representations of oppressed Third World women are usually contrasted to the implicit Western feminist self-representation as independent and sexually liberated. Mohanty comments: "These distinctions are based on the privileging of a particular group as the norm or referent ... Western feminists who sometimes cast Third World women in terms of 'ourselves undressed' all construct themselves as the referent in such a binary analytic" (1990: 337). Lata Mani (1987), in her essay on the practice of *sati*, writes how colonial discourse had represented colonized women in two mutually exclusive ways — either as heroines or as pathetic victims. But such depictions can, as Mani (1987) writes, preclude the possibility of female subjectivity that is shifting, contradictory, inconsistent. Such a constrained and reductive notion of agency discursively positions women as objects to be saved — never as subjects who act, even if within extremely constraining social conditions. This representation of Indian women has been fertile ground for the elaboration of discourse of salvation, in context of colonialism, nationalism, and more recently, Western feminism.

IMPACT OF MUKHERJEE'S WRITING ON THE IMMIGRANT GENRE

Fredric Jameson, assuming nationalism to be the valorized ideology in Third World literature, posits that "all Third World texts are necessarily ... to be read as ... national allegories" (1986: 69).[5] If *The Tiger's Daughter* is to be read as an allegory of Third World culture, the Third World becomes a repressive location for women by perpetuating such representations. I share Aijaz Ahmad's (1992: 263) concerns about Jameson's presumptuousness in producing an overarching and all-embracing theory of a Third World literature. Because orientalist readings depend on a Jameson-like neglect of the political questions of intellectual labor, language, translation, and other issues of publication, similar reading of Mukherjee's novel will highlight her monolithic descriptions of the Third World. The problem is that Mukherjee has been elevated to one of those writers who, as Spivak has observed, "speak for all immigrants: in terms of funding, and in terms of the dissemination of their work," etc. (Gunew 1990: 60). The concern with such tokenism is that "you don't hear about the rest, because ... those few token figures function as a very secure alibi" (Gunew 1990: 60). Trinh T. Minh-ha expresses similar concerns about the perception of Third World among Western academics:

> Now, I am not only given the permission to open up and talk, I am also encouraged to express my difference. My audience expects and demands it; otherwise people would feel as it they have been cheated: we did not come to hear a Third World member speak about the First (?) World, we came to listen to that voice of difference likely to bring us what we can't have and to divert us from the monotony of sameness ... eager not to disappoint, I try my best to offer my benefactors and benefactresses what they most anxiously yearn for. (1989: 65)

In light of the "transaction" detailed in Trinh's description, Mukherjee's attempts to give voice to her subaltern characters cater to the expectations of what Spivak calls "cardcarrying listeners" (Gunew 1990: 60). While Timothy Brennan praises Mukherjee for her cosmopolitanism and her "defiant challenge to traditional ways of conceiving the 'national'" (1989: 7), he ignores the ways in which she reconceives nationalism and recuperates the experience of diverse constituencies into a new hegemony. In her wish to write about the immigrant experience, Mukherjee claims all kinds of experiences as her expertise — "Chameleon-skinned, I discover my material over and across the country " — and ends up portraying all ethnic minorities as identical (1988: 28).

Mukherjee's use of pluralism can also disguise potent power struggles. Pluralism can give the impression of an acceptance of the culturally marginal, yet such universal acceptance also presupposes the erasure of the culturally others' heterogeneity. Because the retrieval of history and identity has informed much of oppositional postcolonial and diasporic writing, to lose such differences, especially ones that incorporate the history of a language, class, or gender, is to give in to the hegemonic ideology of the metropolitan center.

The question is not whether Mukherjee is authentically representing the people that she portrays in her books but, as Spivak writes, "What one has to tease out is what is not there" (Gunew 1990: 63). The indigenous will attempt to speak through the intellectual only "if you make it your task not only to learn what is going on there through language, through specific programs of study, but also at the same time through a historical critique of your position as the investigating person, then you will see that you have earned the right to criticize, and you will be heard" (Spivak, cited in Gunew 1990: 63).

Mukherjee's unambivalent affiliation to the US becomes a problem in the context of her continuing to use postcolonial material in her work, which is published and mostly read in Western metropolitan centers. Her work exhibits no awareness of the global configurations of power that operate within the complexity of colonial histories and neocolonial forces.

In analyzing Mukherjee's cosmopolitan modernity, Inderpal Grewal (1995) finds the author's elitist nationalism to be responsible for this particular ideology. Nationalism as such, Grewal finds, engenders degrading notions of the minority, the poor, people of lower caste, and the working class (1995: 62). Ranajit Guha, a historian in the Subaltern Studies group, also criticizes such "bourgeois-nationalist elitism" that disassociates one from any involvement with the mass population or the subalterns (1982: 1). These intellectuals, then, become nothing more than "native informants," for the benefit of the First World intellectuals (Guha 1982: 2).

Timothy Brennan's comments on the postcolonial writer's commodification of national identities for international currency are significant in regard to Mukherjee. For many immigrant writers, geographic and cultural affiliations have become uncertain because of conflicting locations of "home." Mukherjee herself minimizes her immigrant status when it entails having to maintain dual identities. But she also justifies her stance by pointing out the "artificial retentions of 'pure race' and 'pure culture' as dangerous and reactionary illusions fostered by the Eurocentric and the ethnocentric empire" (Mukherjee 1988: 28). Her fictional characters follow a similar trajectory where they "have all shed past lives and languages, and traveled half the world in every direction to come here and begin again" (1988: 28). Those who do not follow Mukherjee's migrant trajectory are derogatorily portrayed. For example, the Indian immigrants in Flushing, in her novel *Jasmine* (1989), are nothing but ethnic caricatures.[6]

Mukherjee's "strategies of survival" or assimilative strategies have already achieved for her a celebrity status within American literature. On the other hand, texts that challenge the models of representation of the dominant culture can become more inaudible than ever within mainstream culture. Mukherjee achieves her success by sidetracking such challenges, but the question remains — at what price?

6

The Shadow of Diasporic (Auto) Biography: The Traveling-Self in Michael Ondaatje's *Running in the Family*

Carol E. Leon

In postcolonial and postmodern discourses, diaspora comes to signal the liberating aspects of interrelationships and a resistance to the monologic thought and oppression that colonialism represents (Childs and Williams 1997: 210). Works by Homi Bhabha and Vijay Mishra, for instance, celebrate this social formation of displacement. Diasporic spaces are often likened to border zones or borderlines, indicating overlaps of histories and narratives. For Bhabha, the "interstitial passage" opposes hierarchy by opening up possibilities for negation and hybridity (1994: 4). Mishra highlights the "vibrant kinds of interaction" that take place within diasporic communities (1995: 147). It could be said that the diasporic experience provides the new postcolonial subjects. However, because diasporas are complex sites or communities, they are not unproblematic, particularly in negotiating home. In "Mourning Becomes Diaspora," for instance, Mishra explores the role of memory and melancholia in the lives of diasporic peoples, triggered by the traumatic moment of the loss of the homeland (1999). Stuart Hall, an important commentator and analyst of the diasporic condition, highlights the processes of history that impact on the search for identity. He believes that the "shifting divisions and vicissitudes of . . . actual history" (1993: 393) negate the possibility of a stable, shared identity. Cultural identity, he says, has "its histories — and histories have their real, material and symbolic effects" (1993: 395).

Hall's observations on identity and history illuminate my study of the search for self in *Running in the Family*. Michael Ondaatje is a diasporic writer and his background of mobility and hybridity informs his travel memoir *Running in the Family*, first published in 1982. The book is a result of two return journeys made by Ondaatje to Sri Lanka in 1978 and 1980. Some of the journeying was done alone and some of it with his family. In the opening pages of *Running in the Family*, Ondaatje writes that the purpose of the narrative is "to touch . . . into words" his family "who stood in [his] memory like frozen opera" (1993: 22). At the same time the book also delicately depicts the uncertainties of the traveler Ondaatje returning to his homeland after an absence of 25 years.

Philip Michael Ondaatje was born in 1943 on a tea estate in Kegalle, Ceylon, now Sri Lanka. When he was 11, soon after his parents' divorce, he left to study in England. In 1962 he emigrated to Canada, where he still resides. Though his ancestry is a mixture of Dutch, Sinhalese, and Tamil, the family "was solidly British colonial in outlook" (Jewinski 1994: 23). Ondaatje's Ceylonese and English educational background formed the British streak in him. In Canada, however, he awoke to a new, robust literary tradition. Ed Jewinski, a biographer of Ondaatje, writes: "For the young poet there was now a sense of a new tradition being formed, a new, vigorous, and vital outlook on the world, one that linked to, but significantly differed from, the British tradition in which he had been educated in Sri Lanka and England" (1994: 31). The ambivalence and confusion that usually emerge from a diasporic background translate easily and fully into the textual mapping of *Running in the Family*.

Apart from the fact that his personal history is inscribed by multiple spaces, Ondaatje grew up in a volatile household in which the father, who contributed to much of the uncertainty, was, at the same time, a fascinating and compelling figure. Mervyn Ondaatje's absence created a void in his son. In *Rat Jelly*, a collection of poems published in 1973, Ondaatje's moving elegy to his father is called "Letters & Other Worlds." The poem resonates with the writer's sadness that he could not and could never know the man who was his father:

> My father's body was a globe of fear
> His body was a town we never knew
> He hid that he had been where we were going

His letters were a room he seldom lived in
In them the logic of his love could grow. (1980: 44)

The yearning to capture some of the essence of Mervyn permeates
Ondaatje's travel book; in *Running in the Family* Ondaatje is "searching
for [his] father" (Ondaatje 1993: 158).

In *Running in the Family*, Ondaatje uses different genres to negotiate
a divided subjectivity. The narrative is a combination of travelogue,
autobiography, biography, poetry, photography, eyewitness accounts,
and journal entries. The blurb of the 1993 Vintage edition of the book
describes it as "an inspired marriage of travel narrative and family
memoir." Other reviews in the edition extol the way in which "memory
and legend are woven together" in the text, creating tales of "romance
and intrigue" which lift the reader "into soaring flights of fantasy." Bharati
Mukherjee describes the book as "part family saga, part the typical North
American roots search, part travel account and part social history,
delivered with the conciseness and intensity of poetry" (1982: 30). The
general concurrence that *Running in the Family* seems to destabilize
generic expectations makes it an engrossing text. The narrative textualizes
the sensibilities and struggles of the diasporic writer as he tries to locate
himself within his new surrounding which is also his homespace. The
network of personal, cultural, social, and national identities that forms
the locus of home for Ondaatje also unsettles, considerably, his own sense
of identity. This study looks at the (auto)biographical strategies employed
in the text that work to relinquish static, fixed identities in favor of flux
and plurality. These strategies create the dynamic "critical space" that
Virilio (1998: 58) talks about and which is essential in recreating diasporic
identities.

FICTIONAL AUTOBIOGRAPHIES

Running in the Family is often discussed and analyzed as a postmodern
narrative. Indeed its themes and approaches actively engage with
important features of this movement. Postmodern strategies employed
in *Running in the Family* intersect with and powerfully structure the
autobiographical dimension of the text. The genre of autobiography raises
important questions concerning the nature of identity, and highly self-

reflexive forms in postmodern approaches emphasize the autobiographical subject as an agent in discourse. Through the lens of postmodernism, autobiography becomes "a site of identity production," one of those "texts that both resist and produce cultural identities" (Gilmore 1994: 4). Susanna Egan's *Mirror Talk: Genres of Crisis in Contemporary Autobiography* (1997) foregrounds the notion that postmodern selves are relational selves constructed from the acute need to find identity through collaboration with others. The "mirror" of her title is more constructive than reflective, involving interaction between people and among genres. This kind of process of identity formation is implicit in the autobiographical (as well as the biographical) narrative in *Running in the Family*. Indeed, Ondaatje's quest for self-identity is superimposed on his search for his father.

It is Mervyn Ondaatje who inspires this trip to Ceylon. "What began it all was the bright bone of a dream I could hardly hold onto" (Ondaatje 1993: 21). In this dream, Ondaatje's father, "chaotic" and surrounded by dogs, looks into the tropical landscape (1993: 21). The nightmare is later confirmed by Arthur, a friend of Mervyn's, who tells Ondaatje a story about his father with which the writer cannot come to terms:

> My father is walking towards him, huge and naked. In one hand he holds five ropes, and dangling on the end of each of them is a black dog. . . . Terrible noises are coming from him and from the dogs as if there is a conversation between them that is subterranean, volcanic. (1993: 181)

This disturbing image of Mervyn seems to bring to the surface the man's inner demons and also hints at the writer's own fears about himself because underlying the search for the father is Ondaatje's own need to recover self. At the time of his travels to Ceylon and the writing of the book, Ondaatje was undergoing a personal crisis. His marriage to his first wife was crumbling and in 1980, the year he made the second trip to Ceylon, they were legally separated. Another woman was implicated in the proceedings. The painful disintegration of their marriage and his anguish and guilt are articulated in the poems he wrote between the years 1979 and 1980, most of which were published in the collection *Secular Love* in 1984. This was a time of great displacement and longing. "He was increasingly haunted by Ceylon, at least by his separation from it, and, of course, by his separation from his father, his wife, his son, and his daughter" (Jewinski 1994: 112).

Mervyn had also separated from his wife, Doris (Ondaatje's mother). In the chapter "Thanikama" or "Aloneness," Ondaatje tries to evoke the feelings that his father would have felt after his divorce (his parents divorced in 1945 when Ondaatje was two). He recreates a scene in which Mervyn waits in a hotel terrace, hoping to see Doris, who works in the hotel:

> At five he got into the white Ford. She had not come down to him. And he drove to F. X. Pereira. . . .Then he parked near the Galle Face Hotel, old haunt, and crossed the street to the bar. . . . Did not mention Doris. Drank and laughed and listened, till eleven at night at which time they all went home to their wives. He walked down to Galle Road and ate a meal . . . sitting alone. . . . This was 1947. (1993: 186)

The scene, imaginatively reconstructed, is informed not only by Ondaatje's impressions of his father and hearsay, but also, very likely, his own feelings of loneliness. There is a strong suggestion that Ondaatje needed to appease his own sense of betrayal and uncertainty by reliving the feelings his father must have had at his own failed marriage. The desolation that emerges from this scene also gestures toward Ondaatje's sense of dissonance, his own fragmented self. He hopes that by coming to terms with his father, he will shed some light on his own situation.

Mervyn had gone down a path unknown to most of the people in his life (1993: 149). For Ondaatje, one of the greatest regrets of his life was not knowing his father and in *Running in the Family* he proceeds to depict this little-known father within a "fascinating mixture of fiction and wish fulfillment" (Jewinski 1994: 13). The figure of Mervyn that emerges in the narrative does not reconcile completely with the real person. Ondaatje's brother, Christopher, in *The Man-Eater of Punanai*, addresses tensions between fact and imagination in *Running in the Family*. Although Ondaatje talks about his father's frequent drunken bouts, they are mostly seen in a funny, lighthearted context. The mysterious man, so full of vigor, was, in reality, an alcoholic who created havoc in the family. Christopher writes that he had been "deeply involved with the man, and had had to grapple with [his] demons, which never seemed either romantic or amusing" (cited in Jewinski 1994: 116). Christopher calls *Running in the Family* "Michael's . . . love letter to the father he never knew, a large and glamorous man away in the distance" (cited in Jewinski 1994: 14). In an interview with Linda Hutcheon, however, Ondaatje justifies his preoccupation with myth in his writings: "When characters in books are 'lesser' than the writer, there seems to be a great loss in the subtleties and truths being discovered or discussed" (cited in Jewinski 1994: 115). By moving away from fixed, remembered images of his father and creating a "supple" portrait that embraces both fact and fiction, Ondaatje hopes that some truths, perhaps even other truths, about Mervyn might emerge. Ondaatje's larger-than-life portrait of his father is, as Jewinski suggests, one that evokes "a distinct impression of realism" (1994: 118).

Coupled with exaggerated accounts about Mervyn are snippets that project different sides of the man. This is especially evident in the chapter "Dialogues" in which a medley of voices string together a narrative about Mervyn which also contains the darker, more vulnerable side of the man. Ondaatje discards the use of monologue and its reductive strategies of assuming other voices and experiences for "the diverse possibilities of dialogue" (Chambers 1990: 104) so as to evoke a multifaceted, ever-changing identity for his father. Another example of the "dialogical element" (Pesch 1997: 68) appears in an incident when Mervyn, on his way home, offers a lift to a cinnamon peeler. Mervyn enjoys talking to the man, and as the cinnamon peeler's "smell filled the car, he did not want to stop, wanted to take him all the way past the spice gardens to Kegalle rather than letting him out a mile up the road" (1993: 187). This incident has its echoes in the poem "The Cinnamon Peeler" in which Ondaatje slips into the role of the cinnamon peeler. Here one situation seems to talk to another, and in Ondaatje's imagination, he is the man whom Mervyn "enjoys talking to," the cinnamon peeler the writer yearns to be in the poem. In this way Ondaatje, who knew so little about Mervyn, opens a space for communication and "engages his dead father in a dialogue" (Giltrow and Stouck 1992: 167).

Nonetheless, in *Running in the Family* Ondaatje does more than create a fluid image of his father. He sees Mervyn as reflecting fragments of his own being, and in trying to establish an imaginary relationship with his father, Ondaatje is effectively reinventing links to a dimly remembered past. In one section of "Thanikama," there is complete identification between father and son. Describing his father drinking alone in his room, Ondaatje recreates an emotional experience which he "shares" with Mervyn. Here, as Hutcheon (1988: 88) states, there is "one telling sequence in which 'he' reaches for a whisky bottle and the 'I' drinks from it": "The bottle top in my mouth as I sit on the bed like a lost ship on a white sea" (1993: 188). But the "I" converts to the third-person pronoun as the father's biography merges into the autobiography of the son:

> The bottle was half empty beside him. … He wanted to look at his face, though the mirror was stained. … In the bathroom ants had attacked the novel thrown on the floor by the commode. A whole battalion was carrying one page away from its source. … It was page 189. (1993: 189)

In this scene, the son "becomes" the father. In trying to recover aspects of his "emotional inheritance" (Snelling 1997: 29), Ondaatje is reconstructing a sense of identity for himself. This is a highly self-reflexive description and the page that the ants carry away is the very page that Ondaatje is writing and we are reading, page 189. The identities of father and son are formed in the process of writing. For Ondaatje, facts were "more valuable as clues, beginnings to truth" (cited in Jewinski 1994: 98). The truths of his father's and his own life had to be imagined. So too the encounter between them. The chapter "Blind Faith," particularly, depicts the need for reconciliation between father and son. Ondaatje alludes to *King Lear*: "I long for the moment in the play where Edgar reveals himself to Gloucester" but "it never happens" (1993: 180). At the close of the book, many questions about Mervyn are left unanswered:

> There is so much to know and we can only guess. Guess around him. …
> We are still unwise. (Ondaatje 1993: 200)

Ondaatje endows his father with the qualities and emotions that he wants to believe the latter had and which he himself shares. By doing so, one could say that he Others Mervyn in the narrative. This, Kamboureli asserts, is "perhaps Ondaatje's ultimate autobiographical act" (1988: 88). She adds that while the early section of the book seems to suggest that the narrative will chart an interior journey as well, this generic expectation is not fulfilled. The text flows from one genre to another and this deconstructs "the sovereignty of self-referentiality that autobiography demands as a genre" (Kamboureli 1988: 81), i.e., the privileging of the subject's voice. Indeed, Ondaatje does seem an elliptical figure in the text. But while Kamboureli's comments are valid, the autobiographical practice in the text does inform and strengthen the travel discourse in *Running in the Family*. Mervyn Ondaatje is Othered but that Other is not the symmetrical opposite of Ondaatje. It does not lie within the binary of difference between self and Other. Ondaatje does not attempt to define this ambiguous, unknown entity — the recurrent motif of deferral in the narrative testifies to this point.

The sense of a reporting self is played down in *Running in the Family*. The fact that the self is destabilized as a point of reference reinforces the travel motif and authenticates the travel experience in the book. Identity is constructed through the act of traveling and writing about travel. Though Ondaatje is recounting his trip to Ceylon, we find that the "I" in the narrative is not validated as the source of prevailing knowledge. When Ondaatje visits his father's army colleague, the ex-Prime Minister John Kotelawala, to find out about his father, he prompts Sir John as the latter tells his story: "I've heard it from three or four other points of view and can remind him of certain bones — the pots of curd, etc." (1993: 158). This conversation, however, comes directly after Ondaatje's own description of this incident, i.e., Mervyn's bizarre train ride. In this version, John Kotelawala is unconscious for the most part of the journey: "[Mervyn] rushed back time and again into the train and brought out the pots of curd that passengers had been carrying. They were carefully loaded into the jeep alongside the prone body of the future Prime Minister" (1993: 155). Here we have divergent versions of a story. Sir John's "inaccurate" version is one of the "many, still growing, stories of Mervyn Ondaatje's last train ride" (Snelling 1997: 28). Indeed, this episode also undermines Ondaatje's versions of the story; they could equally be inaccurate. Ondaatje is just one of the interpreters in the text and he does not have authority over a verifiable past. Another good example of this fact appears in the chapter "Dialogues," when a voice, probably his sister, Gillian, tells Ondaatje:

> The sections you sent me made me very sad, remembering him and all those times. . . . I showed what you had written to someone and they laughed and said what a wonderful childhood we must have had, and I said it was a nightmare. (Ondaatje 1993: 178)

This conversation testifies to the changing nature of memory. Ondaatje's memories of his father do not coincide with his sister's, and the writer becomes one of the many voices in the narrative trying to piece together a history. In *Running in the Family*, the centrifugal pattern of movement reflects the traveler's desire to embrace what lies beyond the self.

Ondaatje's autobiographical narrative in the travel book underlines his sense of dislocation. Though his inherited displacement is apparent in his sketches of family members, it is most intensely felt in his search for his father. The absent parent comes to represent aspects of Ondaatje's self which in turn underscore the fragmentary nature of that self. However, by destabilizing the self as an authorizing figure, Ondaatje is able to reconstruct a personal identity (or identities). Through the act of writing, he narrates the self and creates a space for reinvention and definition of identity. Iain Chambers, when discussing the notion of home, refers to spaces like this which, he contends, forever defer the homecoming. We can never return to the moment of our beginnings and "authenticity," he says, "for there is always something else in between" (1990: 104). In *Running in the Family*, the mode of travel is fluid. Historical information weaves through chimerical events and portraits. In the interplay between fact and fiction, in the confusion, in what is said, in a gesture or action, in the movement between genres, the writer hopes a glimmer of understanding will emerge. Ondaatje says:

> I go to writing to discover as many aspects of myself and the world around me as I can. I go to discover, to explore, not to state the case I already know. (Cited in Jewinski 1994: 120)

Towards the end of his travelogue-memoir, Ondaatje writes: "I think all of our lives have been terribly shaped by what went on before us" (1993: 179). He feels that by going back to Ceylon everything will change. The homecoming does indeed challenge common conceptions of home for Ondaatje with his mobile background. Though not all the conflicts are resolved at the end of the text, there is certainly a deeper consciousness of self. Ondaatje finds his father and a sense of self within what could be called a mythical space. In "Thanikama," as discussed earlier, there is complete identification between father and son when the person of Ondaatje is superimposed on that of Mervyn. Mervyn's life — and by extension Ondaatje's and the life of the whole Ondaatje clan — is pictured as a mid-summer dream. All of them had moved at times with an ass's head, Titania Dorothy Hilden Lysander de Saram, a mongrel collection part Sinhalese part Dutch part Tamil part ass moving slowly in the forests with foolish and serious obsessions (1993: 188–9).

The absence of commas in the line suggests a continuum and a histrionic blending of histories; the merging of past and present that constitutes both personal and public stories. Mervyn Ondaatje, whom the writer portrays as alone and isolated, "always separate until he died" (1993: 172), reappears after his death in the form of a grey cobra to protect his family. The autobiographical and biographical projects in *Running in the Family* create spaces wherein Ondaatje reclaims his long-lost father and also a sense of his own self. By denying the self its usual position as a center of authority, Ondaatje's auto(biographical) practice in the narrative moves away from a fixed point of definition and reference. In doing so, *Running in the Family* demonstrates that fluidity is the one viable mode towards a sense of identity and, in the case of the traveler returning to his homeland, a feeling of belonging.

7

Translating Indian Culture from Diaspora

Alessandro Monti and Rajeshwar Mittapalli

National archives are the sites in which communal identities are defined and discourses of resistance negotiated. This definition highlights the possibility of considering alternative viewpoints, external foci that modify the meaning of the archive itself. However, one should not forget what Ahmad (1999) writes apropos of the institutional archive, considered to be the product of a process of cultural and hegemonic globalization. According to him, the archive shifts and moves values from periphery to center and endorses authenticity by including "non-European immigrant intelligentsia in structures of metropolitan hegemony" (Ahmad 1999: 92). Given such premises, one should argue the notion of the archive itself in overt terms of power and simultaneously of disseminative strategies of textual production.

These practices point to a further analytical agency, whose conceptual agenda concerns enunciation and the crucial issues of "distance" between the agent and the discursive product. As Stuart Hall puts it, one has to deal with "dialogue, an investigation, on the subject of cultural identity and representation" (Hall 1997: 110). The point is that the very definition of "cultural identity" implies not only a shared belonging, but also a "position" within the locating structure of the archive. In other words, one is provided with individualized codes of reference that integrate and modify the category of "oneness," out of which the notion of the unique archive is shaped. The claim for such a select belonging foregrounds an inverted procedure of self-identification, so as to seek a condition of staying "in between" the interstices rather than aiming at straight continuity in the discursive techniques of narrative representation.

We should consider the case of the expatriate Indian writers, who are spread across the Western world and who have been reunified in the "imagined" archive of globalizing postcolonial literature. These writers attain the dubious bliss of vicarious communal identity, notwithstanding their fragmented dispersal, through imposed coherence and enforced conformity to nativized type. They are represented by means of lasting connections with a dehybridized heritage that reconstructs similarity where difference reigns. This *modus operandi* suggests a differentiated movement of postcolonial representation, one that is grounded respectively in a narrative of distancing and in its theoretical relocation within a hegemonic frame of consensus.

It is well known that the French literary critic Genette has analyzed "distance" as the intratextual relationship of a narrative discourse with its enunciative agent (or "voice"). One might think of this careful positioning of textual responsibilities and hierarchies as a mere "exercise of cultural power and normalization" (Hall 1997: 113). In other words, the "distant" viewpoint expressed by the expatriate writer slowly percolates into the demarginalizing construction of a stereotyped mode. This strategic move figures the discursive presence of the expatriate writer in the national archive of culture as a positioned landmark of identification. He becomes the problematic "native" through a mediated return to origin — the Eastern type who must be included in the Western canon, but only after considering difference as a high consequence of hybridization. Hybridity (or hybridization) is thought here to be a postcolonial form of disavowal, one that introduces continuity and authorizes revaluating patterns of identification (Flundernik 1998: 126).

Hybridity acts primarily as a defusing signifier of refusal and simultaneously enacts an exercise of authority. By doing thus, it challenges fixities and reconstitutes difference by yielding an integrating behavior of cultural assimilation. The expatriate and Americanized Bengali writer Bharati Mukherjee constitutes a valuable case in point. A perfect backdrop of the so-called Bengali Renaissance (an early instance of colonial hybridization, in which the parodic "Babu," or "Baboo," adopted mimicry so as to appropriate Western identities), she shapes a symbolic discursive strategy of representation that highlights the migrating experience of the expatriate intellectual in dissociated (and eventually dissociating) conditions of cognitive and cultural estrangement (Göbel 1998: 62). Her narrative discourse represents the failure of the Indian elite to accommodate the "native" masses into the liberated archive, one that has been disciplined after Independence by the newfangled ruling class.

The unsettled events that lay bare the underlying scenario for such a problematic "return of the hegemonic native" emphasize again social and cultural differentiation as the factors that inscribe hybridized consciousness in the semantic field of intentional representation, an issue first explored by Bakhtin (Stilz 1998: 86–7). This double "intention in language" devises something more complex and seminal than a double articulation of semantic values and perspectives. It also details the "double inscription" that we are able to detect in the narrative of Bharati Mukherjee, a path of migration *à rebours* from the West to the East again, after a previous stage of assimilating colonial hybridization. One should compare the implied act of representative mimicry operated by Bharati Mukherjee with the return to the unmixed Hindu identity that one finds in Raja Rao, a migrant writer of the first contemporary generation.

It is quite significant to our purpose how in *Kanthapura* (1936) the writer loads the rising Gandhian myth of a Sanskritized Hindu nationhood, minus the castes. To impress ideological force to the "nativist" message of resistance against the English advocated by Gandhi, Raja Rao claims regional belonging, either in the linear genealogy of the fictional text (which the author himself discloses to us in terms of *sthala purana*, that is, of local chronicle) or through the rehearsal of southern devotionalism and the refusal of mimicry. As a matter of fact, his response to the cultural influence of the West introduces an insidious discourse of the "subaltern studies" type, with all its attached paraphernalia, including what in Bhabhaian language I could define as "agentical displacement." Thus the Brahmin villagers of Kanthapura are "displaced" from their caste and from their native place, in order to resist the English. Here the conceptual framing of the national archive is rooted in a representative strategy of counterhegemony, a procedure that we have to understand in qualifying terms of control and reassessment of communal values. By exalting Gandhism for its regenerative power, Raja Rao eludes the permanency of casteism "in the distribution of powers and privileges in Indian society" (Ahmad 1997: 287–9).

The too-rapid realignment of the rustic Brahmin elite to the denial of castes displaces the national paradigm of antagonistic discrimination between classes, so as to privilege the "affective discourse" of which Bhabha speaks (Ahmad 1997: 287).[1] Such a treatment concerning the conflicts out of which independent India has been generated calls forth the question of the advantaged point of observation. One might fit Raja Rao (who wrote *Kanthapura* in France) into the role of the distant onlooker, whose comprehensive survey is notably free of the tensions caused by actual instances of marginalized belonging *within* the shifting society of which he writes. This view anticipates the nostalgic stance assumed by more recent expatriate writers, such as Bharati Mukherjee. This individualized and sharp sense of displacing nostalgia posits a consciousness of power and confirmed hegemony, in terms either of money, social position, or gender.

However, one should locate this feeling of select belonging in an erstwhile dimension of achieved identity: it constitutes an imagined regret rather than reflecting an expanded notion of shared values. This collapse is focused quite sharply in the astute short story "Nostalgia," by Bharati Mukherjee, in which a successful medical expatriate tries to retranslate his prestigious metropolitan self into the archaic and timeless figure both of the domestic *pati* and of the feudal landlord (Mukherjee 1990; 1985). The impossibility of coming back to type in the context of migration confirms the basic notion of endurance, across and notwithstanding cultural miscegenation and hybridity. Our forceful claim for permanence, alongside the inclusive relocation of the self, denies the globalized figure of the migrant intellectual, such as it has been repeatedly evoked by Bhabha. Needless to say, we would substitute a more problematic idea of fragmentation for the issue of transnational (or globalized) hybridity, so as to be able to negotiate the textual strategies that refuse spatial and national homogenization.

Viewed from this angle, our repudiation of the teleology of the migrant figure foregrounds diaspora (that is, a metaphor of dispersal) against the notion of interactive affiliation among different cultures. Better than migration, the term diaspora takes account of loss and disaffiliation, of actual distancing and reconstructed proximity. Our position shifts the conflict from the antagonism of the migrant with the host country to the intercommunity clash in the homeland. It is easy to outline this procedure in Rohinton Mistry, say from such a "nostalgic" short story of failed cultural integration as "Squatters" to his "political" novel *A Fine Balance* (1995). The nameless city, in which most of the narrative representation in the novel takes place, illustrates this double pattern of familiarity and estrangement, of threatened identities and transitional movements inside embryonic possibilities of social development.

The discursive exploration of the interactive spaces that saturate and occupy the interstices within the notion of a shared community leads to effects of displacement, rather than dissemination. In Mistry, this denial of viability does not consolidate the identity of the migrant through Bhabhaian subverting procedures of mimicry and hybridity, but postulates an interrupted capacity of movement inside the blocking borders, or internal frontiers, that are set against the possibility of social exorbitance. One should replace the transgression of exorbiting (that is, of flowing over one's fixed position) for the more ambitious prescriptions that seem to surround the maieutic figure of the migrant. Mistry unfolds a textual representation of the national archive that emphasizes the disjunctive violence of the state and the oppressive practices against the subaltern strata of population. The issues that are roused by *A Fine Balance* deploy in a unique sequence casteism and the feudal power of the landed *thakurs*, the crushing politics of "reforms" and modernization enacted by the Gandhi dynasty, with particular reference to the two most notorious campaigns of *garibi hatao* and of enforced sterilization.

This regressive network grounds lines of deconstructive juxtaposition and simultaneously enforces the backward predominance of casteism. It erases through coercion the freedom of movement in space: pavement dwellers and professional beggars are transported out of the city. The postcolonial and modernized project of the "nation-state" seems to be inextricably linked to issues of social stratification and imposed casteism. The permanence of fragmentation constitutes the institutional counterpart of the imagined "national allegory" of which Peter Morey (2000) speaks. In particular, the split topography of social belonging represented by Mistry provides the clue for the critical revision of the idealized and utopian-like allegory of the village, viewed in *Kanthapura* as a perfect example of resistance through the reconfiguration of the colonial space in terms of a "self-sufficient" rural community, "operating along pre-industrial lines" (Morey 2000: 164). In Raja Rao, the vision of a Hindu (more than Indian) *oikumene* enhances the inchoative idea of nationhood and shared belonging through the semantic fullness of *deshi*, a specific Indian-English term of Sanskrit derivation that may indicate both the village (that is, the small native center) and the whole nation as well.

However, *deshi* can be used colloquially to indicate a product made in India and presumably of inferior quality. One should read the semantically nuanced word *deshi* as a striking countermetaphor of national unity and intercommunality. Its all too derogatory quality, one that argues inferior belonging and peripheral identity, could as well indicate contiguous effects of blocked and failed social passage in the unnegotiable disciplinary stricture that antagonizes the two different calls for homogeneity, either in the village (the localized *deshi*) or in the metropolitan center (one likened to the notion of *deshi* as homeland). The unyielding dichotomy blocks the chances that the internal migrants (that is, the untouchables that leave the discriminating *deshi* of the village for the imagined freedom of the city) nurture of reinscription in the national archive. Such intimations of inclusive belonging are seen through the *phoren* eyes of the expatriate, in a sour reversal of the institutional procedures of social "beautification" that expel the poor and the maimed from the city, making "invisible" beings of them. The expatriate writer seems to share an analogous condition of "invisibility" and distanced power of vision from the outside. His detached belonging, as it were, constitutes a source of subversion and rupture within the canon governing the modernization of the national image: his representations of terrorism and violence in the handling of the dissonant conflict of interests construe "uglification" rather than the proposed "beautification" of the country. One should confront these practices of expulsion from a shared community with the "epistemic violence involved in constituting the (post)colonial subject," of which critics like Gayatri Spivak and Bart Moore-Gilbert speak (Moore-Gilbert 1997: 86).[2]

The issue concerns how the centralizing power views "identities" and how it constructs categories of belonging and origins. One should argue that the use of violence constitutes continuity in exclusion and perpetuates marginalization in the control of the subaltern classes and castes. Given that, one should not dissociate such unidyllic representations of rural everyday life from the destructive raids operated by the police, in the great city or elsewhere. For instance, the habitual use of violence in resolving social conflicts is made clear throughout Chapter 3, "In a Village by the River":

> The news was of the same type that Dukahi had heard evening after evening during his childhood; only the names were different. For walking on the upper-caste side of the street, Sita was stoned, though not to death — the stones had ceased at first blood. Gambhir was less fortunate; he had molten lead poured into his ears because he ventured within hearing range of the temple while prayers were in progress. Dayram, reneging on an agreement to plough a landlord's field, had been forced to eat the landlord's excrement in the village square. Dhiraj tried to negotiate in advance with Pandit Ghanshyam the wages for chopping wood, instead of settling for the few sticks he could expect at the end of the day; the Pandit got upset, accused Dhiraj of poisoning his cows, and had him hanged. (Mistry 1996: 132)

Such a nasty catalog of punishing activities parallels the careful listing of the duties that constitute the daily routine of a police sergeant during the campaign of "beautification" (Chapter 8):

> But demolishing hutment colonies, vendors' stalls, jhopadpattis was playing havoc with his peace of mind. And prior to his superiors formulating this progressive new strategy for the beggary problem, he had had to dump pavement-dwellers in waste land outside the city. He used to return miserable from those assignments, get drunk, abuse his wife, beat his children. (Mistry 1996: 395)

By underlining the aggrieved consequences represented in these "chirurgical" operations of removal and social sanitation, we are trying to negotiate the dislocating passage from the selective and closely knit sense of community expressed by the archive to the fully inclusive dimension of the collectivity. Our shift should include social mobility (across class and caste lines) as the comprehensive notion that indicates the specific margin within and through which corporate identities could be defined and illustrated. To us, *A Fine Balance* refuses whatever available dichotomy in classifying the reactive strategies against flexibility and simultaneously denies any premised assumption in favor of procedures that bind the subaltern to marginality. Mistry does not seek legitimization in his hybridized experience as an expatriate writer; his position greatly differs from the reactive attitude of resistance to renativization stubbornly adopted by Bharati Mukherjee, who disclaims or discards her Indian origin on the grounds of such different issues as the practices of gender discrimination adopted by the Hindus (these meaning Manu, *stridharma. et similia*) and the progressive decadence of the Bengali elite into which she was born. Indeed, she accomplishes a sort of personal "beautification" against the confirmed social and cultural evils of India, to which she adds the insurgent spirit of the working class and the vulgarity of the encroaching *Marwaris*, who are slowly dispossessing the *bhadralok* of their hegemony and prestigious heritage. Bharati Mukherjee still belongs to a corporate identity, whose roots are typically and specifically Indian, in a way that is somewhat reminiscent of the behavioral return to regressive type shown by the protagonist of her short story "Nostalgia." Her attitude of qualified regret and excessive contempt, both of them rendered in the discriminating lexicon of regional belonging, saturates any possible perception of hybridity viewed as a multicultural response.

This full excision of integrationist values and communal purposes, in terms of social and cultural cooptation, is articulated back by Mistry with a vengeance. *A Fine Balance* is a novel of resistant critique, one that glosses over the modes of internalized rejection against the dispossessed and exposes the cannibalizing refurbishment of the Indian metropolises activated by the Gandhis. The use of such countercategories in the historical representation of nationhood expresses and reveals a radical crisis in the narrative representation of fragmentation and regional belonging, of hegemony and alternative response in the making of the new Indian society. This bitter exploration of the conflicts engendered by inequality should be confronted advantageously with the mawkish dramatization of the recent history of India, through the intermingling of different and more or less romantic life stories. *A Suitable Boy* (1993) by Vikram Seth makes a good case in point, apropos of the subdued tension that sometimes emerges in the narrative of the expatriates.

In Seth, the birth of the new Indian nation, with its tearing dissent among the different communities and the decline of the prebourgeois elites, takes the benign aspect of a sophisticated sequence of highly suggestive and implied quotations that regulate the construction of the text in reassuring terms of reinscription within an already fixed narrative canon. Thus, one should pay qualified attention to such issues of social, cultural, and political fragmentation as the economical decadence of the feudal nawabs, the split between Hindus and Muslims, the unsolved inflexibility of coexistence between modernity and tradition in customs and ways of life, the rise of savage and unregulated modes of industrial production. These powerful agents of crisis and disorder are not depicted in their whole and tragic rawness, as they are by Mistry, but are toned down and actually bowdlerized into a tamed rhetoric of narrative discourse, one that draws its significance and anticontestatory strength from its highly negotiable conformity to pacifying regulations of style and dramatic plot.

It is possible to trace the "sentimental" genesis of *A Suitable Boy* to clever and backdrop echoes of Ahmed Ali's *Ocean of Night* (1964), or even to the skillfully manipulated rehandling of the traditional literary theme of the *nashtar*, with the added pun on the metaphorical and real knives that in the novel act as agents of thwarted passion and sad failure.[3] These and further intimations of preordained script indicate practices of *deshi* stylistic affiliation, irrespective of any ongoing process of social change and struggle. As a novel that deals purposely with feelings and interpersonal relations, *A Suitable Boy* mimics the traditional nineteenth-century chronicle of bourgeois life. However, it also touches upon regionalism (particularly in the long sections devoted to the representation of the *bhadralok* bourgeoisie) and finally substitutes "beautified ethnicity" (such as represented by the romantic themes of sentimental loss and separation, owing to the clash of difference in communal belonging) for the Western mimetic discourse of social ascent through the power of money and individual enterprise. By structuring his novel around the multiple small "partitions" that divided and still split the multicultural "hybridity" of the Indian subcontinent, Seth correlates its narrative with indigenous themes of dispersal and fragmentation.

Indeed, it seems to us that the fiction of the more recent expatriate writers *does* mainly concern the strictures and the forbidding regulations (or "dharmic rules," to adopt an easy semantic shortcut) that continue to harness the lives of the Hindus. These dissonant cries for autonomy and visibility assume a wide range of representations. For instance, in *In an Antique Land* (1992), Amitav Ghosh constructs a utopian-like vision of a precolonial globalized Eastern world, whose shaping symbol is aptly constituted by the hazy figure of an Indian "Slave," so as to contrive a redeeming rhetoric of disappearance and reappearance, a deliberate revindication of cosmopolitan and communicative belonging (Dayal 1998). This obvious plea for a regulated movement across homogeneous boundaries represents a premodern vision of the migrant, not seen as a figure destined to glorious marginality and refurbished presence, but viewed as a fully integrated co-agent of shared belonging and free circulation of cultures and identities.

This myth of yielding availability to distanced representation deploys a soothing range of metonymic and implied figurations, whose terminal point of reference might be aptly recognized in the persona of the expatriate writer. In our view, Ghosh theorizes an extended ideal of shared belonging and uncompetitive intercommunalism, whose position is located beyond the borders and the excluding margins of the modern quest for nation-states. It is not casual that in *In an Antique Land* the founding quest revolves around a lost and forgotten archive: a transnational site enclosing distanced memories of a shared past and the unchronicled lives of the subaltern people. This reorientation of the national discourse toward a "migrant text," devoid both of apologetic overtones and stylized regret (or of its defused version, in the wake of the sentimentalizing script devised by Seth), finds its more significant outlet in *A Fine Balance*. Here the strategic movement across borders and the reconciliation of detached identities emphasize the difficult, and finally impossible, survival of small and comfortable groups of lonely individuals; for instance, those that are constituted by the Muslim tailor and the *chamar* boys, or again the self-contained tiny groups of mixed people who live together in the crumbling urban flat, or even the poor communities that inhabit the slums.

All these characters share an uncertain and precarious point of arrival, one that commits them to marginality and reduces their identities to a catachrestical disclaim concerning belonging. Mistry does not vindicate a nostalgic stance for them, on the basis of negotiable ethnicity and the regretful memory of a happy life prior to loss (as Arundhaty Roy does astutely in her pathetic *The God of Small Things*, 1997). Nor does he abandon his commitment to the unpalatable representation of Indian reality, in favor of an unchanneled stylistic surplus, Salman Rushdie-like. Instead of soothing his hurt sense of national belonging, Mistry explores the intricate network of relations constituted by the rehearsal of hegemony and power in the processes that maintain stifling pressures of select communalism in the reshaping of national identity.

Mistry re-migrates his bitter text from the quite safe and prestigious shores of the globalized postcolonial script to the more compromised issue of the internal debate concerning process and change. The class-differentiated scenario depicted by him transcends marginality, or even the effects of marginalization, to concentrate instead on the construction of the frail "other" inside the national archive.

By doing thus, he discounts hybridity from the narrative agenda of the expatriate writer and simultaneously elaborates on the monologic quality concerning the national project. The distancing gaze adopted by Mistry reveals ostensibly the links between the subaltern groups and the new national (or postnational) elite. It also lays bare to what extent the identity of the subaltern is defined by the hegemony of the dominant (Moore-Gilbert 1997: 87). However this full disavowal of any procedure regarding the "rational" consolidation in the making of identities restores a will to power that is unidirectional and unintentional. The compulsory flattening of diversity and social "otherness" could be aptly recognized as "dehybridization." Of course, this deprivation of status deconstructs the strategy of plural alliances that is highly seminal to the notion of hybridity. Instead of focusing on issues of cross-culture (or culture-across), Mistry lays a grim claim on the wholly structural relation that connects the life of the destitute subaltern with the strategy of power enacted by the postcolonial elite. This account generates a portentous movement from the native "other" (as such, a staple object of radical representation) to the more ethical "other," whose constitution as part of a consolidated system denies the economy of change and assimilation. Hence, the necessity of filling the intermediate space between hopeless subalternity and domineering hegemony: such a move could restore to uncompromized meaning the interstitial position assumed by the expatriate writer, otherwise a mere "informant" on the subject of nativism or exoticism.

By discarding any explicative mediation between the subaltern and the curious gaze of the West, Mistry distances himself from the persona of the "benevolent outsider." Thus, he provides a penetrating critique concerning the discourse of power in the formation of the nation-state and simultaneously emphasizes resistance against the "pastoral strategies of reform," advocated by Gandhi and embodied by the fictional discourse of such novels of independence as *Kanthapura*. *A Fine Balance* highlights the passage from colonial dominance to postcolonial hegemony and attests to the challenge of unmitigated representation, against the sense of nostalgia and the excitement of hybridization that we usually associate with the figure of the expatriate.

It would be possible to claim migration as a crucial passage towards composite identities, set more or less dangerously on the edge of multiple locations. Such a perception of the diasporic movements in conflictual terms of disorder and corrupting *métissage* does require a safe agency that would discriminate and restore a monoglossic order, inside (rather than against) the miscegenation caused by heteroglossia. Thus it would be possible to constitute archives, in the sense suggested by Ahmad, but simultaneously to deconstruct or deregulate them, in the wake of Bakhtin and Bhabha. We can discuss the notion of the archive with reference to the dialogic construct deployed by Bakhtin or connect its structure with Bhabha's formulation of an interstitial space that constitutes the identity of the diasporic migrant. Perhaps, as a further step, one should read Bhabha in the perspective of the "carnival" strategy of resistance and appropriation against a hegemonic power. As a matter of fact, the discourse is now bordering on the Gramscian analysis of "cultural hegemony," whose subtler procedures of control move beyond the use of raw violence. Of course, one should be able to detect the heritage of hegemony in the colonial construction of "hybridity," considered by Bhabha to be complementary to the military conquest and possession of an alien territory.

Although a few postcolonial writers refocus the issue of diaspora in terms of updated marginalization within the select files of the archive and inside the "domestic" rules and norms that construe a modernized version of "native" nationhood, the postcolonial text at large has failed, in the long run, in its attempt to cope with the interstitial dimension of being advocated by Bhabha. Instead, its discursive strategies emphasize private-oriented narratives of deranged life stories, as if the postcolonial writer (particularly of Indian origin) would catch up with the traditional novel of formation written by Western bourgeoisie. This withdrawal from a wider external world has induced the postcolonial writer (and the critic as well, to some extent) to ignore the momentous changes within the migrant universe, from its previous interstitial location to patterns of temporary exile. The migrant tends to be someone who still belongs elsewhere and consequently acts on behalf of a true "distant" native and superior culture.

Instead of the "accommodated" migrant, postcolonial globalization must face a secretive militant figure whose uncompromising antagonism reintroduces military conflict (through terrorism) in the multiple network of cultural, social, economic relations. This crucial splitting operates well inside the disturbed postcolonial nation (Ram vs. Babar, to adopt a shortened and simplifying image), but also migrates inside the hegemonic texture of the Western world, as a belligerent refusal of hybridization. Diaspora may also mean a diffusive dispersal of violence — a counterglobalizing plea against the splintering of identities and finally a return to compulsory unification. Indeed, we are a long step beyond the defused chronicle (in terms of eulogy) of post-independent India contrived by Mistry: the notion of the archive itself has been darkened and changed into something muted and invisible.

8

Claiming Diaspora in Shirley Geok-lin Lim's
Joss & Gold

Jeffrey F. L. Partridge

In our desire to find definite breaks between the territorially bounded and the deterritorialized, the oppressive and the progressive, and the stable and the unstable, we sometimes overlook complicated accommodations, alliances, and creative tensions between … diaspora and nationalism. (Aihwa Ong, *Flexible Citizenship*)

CLAIMING AMERICA AND CLAIMING DIASPORA

At a recent conference in Singapore, an Australian scholar challenged my approach to Shirley Geok-lin Lim's novel *Joss & Gold* on the basis that my Asian-American framework might be inappropriate for a "diasporic" author such as Lim. Reading Lim as diasporic rather than American is, in many respects, a more "natural" position. Though a citizen of the United States, Lim aligns herself closely in her creative and academic writing with a diasporic identity. Lim is a Malaysian-born academic and creative writer committed personally and professionally to retaining and fostering ties with Southeast Asia. Much of her poetry and short stories and her recent novel have been published jointly by Times Books International in Singapore and by US presses such as the

Feminist Press in New York. She returns regularly to Malaysia and Singapore for readings and conferences, and she has visited for extended periods under fellowships to the Centre of Advanced Studies and the National Institute of Education in Singapore. Most recently, she served for two years as the chair of the English department at the University of Hong Kong. Shirley Lim is by no means a writer who has severed ties with her Southeast Asian homeland and adopted an American authorial identity. Thus, for me to read Lim as Asian-American appears to be a case of cultural appropriation, or, to put it sinisterly, yet another case of American imperialism.

What my Australian colleague wanted to know was why so much of the literature coming out of US academia seems preoccupied with notions of American identity. The question is astute, and gets right at the heart of an unresolved issue that has been debated in Asian-American scholarship for the last decade — the issue that I am describing as a rift between "claiming America" and "claiming diaspora." This chapter is concerned with the problem of an either/or confrontation between claiming America and claiming diaspora in discussions of contemporary Asian-American literature. Through a preliminary reading of a new novel by Shirley Lim, this chapter explores what is at stake when we read a diasporic writer as only diasporic, and suggests that it is possible to understand such a text as *both* diasporic *and* Asian-American.

Asian-American scholars largely agree that "claiming America" has been a central tenet in Asian-American cultural politics since the 1960s. The trope of "claiming America" developed out of the longstanding exclusion of Asian-Americans from US citizenship,[1] or from the full rights of their citizenship.[2] These legalized exclusions inscribed institutionally the popular belief that America was a society of European immigrants in which Asians had no place — even though Asian immigrants were instrumental in the development of the United States from as far back as the gold rush and the construction of the transcontinental railroad in the nineteenth century. Claiming America, according to Sau-ling Wong, refers to the strategy of "establishing the Asian-American presence in the context of the United States' national cultural legacy and contemporary cultural production" (1995: 6). Maxine Hong Kingston, who uses the phrase to describe the aims of her first two books *The Woman Warrior* (1976) and *China Men* (1980), describes claiming America as "a response to the legislation and racism that says we of Chinese origin do not belong here in America" (Skenazy and Martin 1998: 25).

In recent years, Asian-American scholars have questioned the appropriateness of the claiming America model to the realities of the twenty-first century, and some have turned instead to the notion of diaspora as an organizing principle for Asian-American cultural politics and cultural production. For Asian-American critics such as Lisa Lowe and Shirley Lim, "diaspora" rather than "claiming America" more accurately represents the demographic exigencies of Asian-Americans in the new millennium. Due largely to changes in immigration laws and to US interventions in Asian conflicts, the Asian-American population is larger and comprised of more recent immigrants than ever before; it is also more diverse in terms of ethnic group, national origin, class, education level, and income. Due to rapid advances in communication, travel, and information technologies, the Asian-American population is more fluid and more closely linked to communities in Asia than in the past when immigration from Asia to the United States was likely to be an irreversible enterprise. Shirley Lim describes the relationship between recent Asian immigration trends and shifts in Asian-American notions of identity as follows:

> The 1970s' critique of the conflation of Asian American with Asian and Asian immigrant identity, and the enunciation of a U.S. identity not composed of Asian cultural elements, had severely delimited the terms for cultural belonging for smaller and more recent immigrant groups such as South and Southeast Asians and Filipinos ... The historical specificities in the experiences of heterogeneous Asian immigrant groups inevitably call into question and destabilize the construction of a monolithic U.S.-identified Asian-American identity. (1997: 303)

Lisa Lowe argues in her seminal 1991 article for a diasporic vision of Asian-American identity. Echoing the rhetoric of Bhabha, Bakhtin, and Deleuze and Guattari, Lowe writes, "we might conceive of the making and practice of Asian-American culture as nomadic, unsettled, taking place in the travel between cultural sites and in the multivocality of heterogeneous and conflicting positions" (1991: 39). Lowe's argument seeks to undermine ethnic nationalism as an organizing structure in the concept of Asian-American identity by claiming a "fluid" and diasporic perspective. Largely in response to Lowe's article, Sau-ling Wong (1995) argues that claiming America is still a valid and necessary strategy in

Asian-American cultural politics. In her view, ethnic nationalism is essential to effective political struggle in America because it fosters solidarity and unity of purpose:

> if claiming America becomes a minor task for Asian-American cultural criticism and espousal of denationalization becomes wholesale, certain segments of the Asian-American population may be left without a viable discursive space. . . . the loosely held and fluctuating collectivity called "Asian-Americans" will dissolve back into its descent-defined constituents as soon as one leaves American national borders behind. (Wong 1995: 16–7)

David Leiwei Li is similarly cautious about moving away from the nationalist conception of Asian-American literature. Like Wong, he cautions against a hasty and uncritical embrace of diaspora. In his reading of Amy Tan's *The Joy Luck Club*, for instance, Li criticizes the book's conclusion, which he describes as performing the "voluntary removal of Asians from the United States" (1998: 116). In the conclusion of his book, Li writes, "although ethnic nationalist strategies are likely to ignore the dialogic voices within Asian America and are inadequate for dealing with a plurality of interests, their insights about the hierarchy of social division and the necessity for broad social transformation are perhaps too easily dismissed in contemporary revisionist critique" (1998: 192).

The "revisionist critique" of claiming America differs from multiculturalism in its de-emphasis of US national identity. "The concept of the Asian diaspora," according to Li, "was introduced [in Asian-American Studies] to argue against a single national identity with one destiny in favor of a shared history that recognizes different origins and multiple transformations" (1998: 196). While the claim about a diasporic perspective in this statement appears identical to the aims of multiculturalism (i.e., a revision of the "melting pot" theory; an expansion of the tent stakes of "America" to allow and appreciate ethnic difference), proponents of the diasporic view distinguish between the two approaches on the grounds that multiculturalists still argue within a "single national identity" and a "shared destiny." Shirley Lim, a sharp critic of the claiming America stance, argues that

> Many U.S. feminist and ethnic critics question the patriarchal, Eurocentric interpretations of texts, but they seldom interrogate the national-identity parameters in these interpretations. Instead, they attempt to enlarge that

American identity, appropriating myths and characteristics that construct
more permeable, flexible, and plurally enclosing borders. (1997: 289)

Lim's critique of Maxine Hong Kingston reveals what she sees as a two-pronged problem with the claiming America model: namely, that claiming America often means "disclaiming" diaspora on the one hand, and remaining complicit with US hegemonic nationalism on the other. In her 1992 essay on the novels of Timothy Mo, Lim sets up Kingston as the negative to Mo's positive embrace of diasporic roots. Kingston is, in Lim's view, a "diasporic writer" whose work is "overtly non-diasporic" because of "its insistence on a United States site" (1992: 92–3). She argues that "United States identity in Kingston's writing is continuously claimed, while the political and state elements of a China identity are disclaimed" (1992: 92–3).

In "Immigration and Diaspora," the essay in which Lim most clearly defines her position on these issues, she again returns to a critique of Kingston's notion of claiming America. Lim writes, "Kingston repeatedly asserts that in her books she is claiming America for Chinese-Americans, a proposition that can be restated to mean claiming Chinese-Americans for America" (1997: 302). In other words, in asserting that her ethnic group belongs to America, Kingston may be contesting the prescribed borders of the nation, but she is also complicit with the broad concept of US nationalism. She is, Lim suggests, appropriated by "the" nationalist cause.

> The double movement of appropriation is marked in the critical reception
> of her [Kingston's] work, chiefly praised for making accessible to American
> readers the strange world of Chinese living in the United States. The
> accessibility works more in one direction than the other. Americans of
> Chinese ancestry, or even Chinese living in the United States, do not find
> that *The Woman Warrior* has made the United States more accessible to
> them, or that the book helps them to negotiate the dominant culture and
> to appropriate it for their needs. The book's popular reception in the
> universities suggests that it is the dominant culture which is incorporating
> Kingston's version of the Chinese into its transcultural psyche. (Lim 1997:
> 302)

Lim's argument about the power of US nationalism to appropriate immigrant and minority literature to its own ends points to a blind spot in the multiculturalism movement.

At the same time, Lim's argument fails to portray "US nationalism" as anything but monolithic, static, and perennially evil. What is missing in the debate outlined above, and particularly in Lim's critique of Kingston, is an attempt to define nationalism as "nationalisms" — to understand the nationalist sentiments as heterogeneous and fluid.[3] While Lim may have in mind ultra-right forms of US nationalism that could be described as fundamentalist, essentialist, or white supremacist, Sau-ling Wong may have in mind a nationalism based on a sense of shared space within prescribed national borders and political realities that must be faced collectively. Moreover, in positing such a staunch antinationalist stance, Lim leans toward rejecting outright American identity and embracing instead a universal, exilic, or transnational aesthetic. It may be true that she privileges texts that do not treat Asia as "void," or as Other to US identity, but it seems to me that Lim is not advocating the embrace of a global fantasy. She seems skeptical of writers who posit themselves as cosmopolitan nomads in a borderless world, calling them "elites" (1997: 290). She is also critical of the tendency for US academic and cultural critics to view diasporic writings as "falling outside U.S. canonical work" (Lim 1997: 290). Lim holds to a tenuous middle position between birthplace and the "intaking state" (1997: 296), as expressed in the following statement: "The discourse of diaspora is that of disarticulation of identity from natal and national resources and includes the exilic imagination but is not restricted to it" (1997: 297). She asserts the need to view American race relations from an international position (1997: 291).

Congruent with her theoretical stance, Lim's recent novel, *Joss & Gold*, can be read as an internationalization of Asian-American literature. The novel can be seen as a fictional participant in the conversation about what Aihwa Ong calls "the creative tensions between ... nationalism and diaspora" (1999: 16). By exploring issues of language, literature, identity, race, and gender in a largely Malaysian/Singaporean context with intersections with America, the novel presents American identity as an important but peripheral concern to the Southeast Asian characters of the novel. America's marginality in the text (even though one-third of the book is set in the US) furthermore raises important questions regarding approaches to, and categorization of, the novel. Is it justifiable to read the novel as an Asian-American text? Does reading it as such automatically appropriate, or recuperate, the book and its author under a US nationalist "agenda"? On the other hand, is it justifiable to read the book as only diasporic? In removing the novel from an Asian-American context, do we miss the opportunity to understand US nationalism and Asian-American literature in new ways? Is it possible to read *Joss & Gold* as an Asian-American *diasporic* text?

US IMMIGRATION PLOT DEFERRED

In its embrace of diaspora, *Joss & Gold* departs from the "claiming America" strategy within Asian-American literature and discourse. One point of departure is the novel's refusal to fully plant its feet in the US despite indications in its plot development that it will. The first few chapters of *Joss & Gold* raise the reader's expectations of a classic Asian-American immigrant story, only to thwart those expectations. Li An, the novel's Asian protagonist, is a Chinese Malaysian first-year English literature teacher in a university in Kuala Lumpur who is defined as "Western" in her habits, attitudes, and dress. Li An is represented as an independent woman despite her recent marriage to Henry, a PhD student in biology who comes from a rich and traditional Chinese family. We learn on the first page of the novel, for instance, that "she had insisted on keeping her motorbike after they married" (Lim 2001: 7). The motorbike is a symbol of freedom and singlehood — not only is it a holdover from Li An's life as a single, but the very nature of a single-seat vehicle makes it an emblem of individuality. The fact that she "insisted" upon keeping the motorbike further reveals her attitude toward her new life as a woman married to a man from a traditional Chinese family with its hierarchy and patriarchal center. She is determined to retain her identity as an individual woman.

Thus, from the beginning, Li An stands in contrast to the book's portrayal of the Malaysian culture of 1968, and she seems to be a likely candidate for immigration to America. Her love of classical English literature, Leavisite literary critique, and the language of British poetry all seem to align her with England, and there are hints early on that Li An will gravitate toward America. Henry notes, for instance, that "she was like a Western girl—bold, loud, and unconcerned about her reputation" (2001: 15). It is little surprise, then, to find that Li An has been contemplating the idea of moving to America after graduation —

though why she would choose the US over the UK is not made clear in the novel. When Henry asks in exasperation, "America? Why America?" Li An responds,

> Why not America? Isn't that where everything is happening? It's so boring here. Nothing ever changes. No one is doing anything, no one is writing poetry, no one is painting, no one is singing, no one is going anywhere. So why not go to America? (Lim 2001: 15–6)

In a classically orientalist (or occidentalist?) construction, Li An sees Asia as the unchanging, inert contrast to the vibrant, liberating energies of the West, with "the West" clearly defined as the United States of America. This East/West dichotomy is especially apparent in Li An's identification of the West as a place of liberation from the traditions of patriarchy. In Malaysia, she feels stifled by the assigned role for women and envious of Henry. At one point, Li An complains to Henry,

> You know where you're going and where you belong. I wish I were a man and a scientist. Then there would be a place for me here. (2001: 17)

It would seem, then, that the entrance of Chester Brookfield, an American Peace Corps volunteer, sets the stage for Li An's Asian exodus. Despite her marriage to Henry, Li An grows close to Chester and eventually sleeps with him on the night of the Kuala Lumpur race riots. Yet Chester is not the orientalist white knight saving the Asian woman from patriarchy. In the novel, he functions to stir up in Li An a sense of meaning and belonging for Malaysia, as is evident from the early days in their relationship when Henry and Li An invite Chester over for dinner. At the dinner, Chester mocks Li An's love for English literature and declares, "You've got your own culture ... that's what you should be teaching" (2001: 42). Chester's pronouncement against the English literature that Li An so cherishes propels her to examine her own presuppositions about language, literature, and national identity.[4] More important, Chester's assumptions about Malaysian race politics challenge Li An's views of allegiance and belonging. Chester, under the influence of his Malay roommates, argues that "Malay is the only real culture in this country" (2001: 43). He moreover raises the issue of the Chinese diaspora in terms that echo the sentiments of his Malay friends:

The Chinese aren't really Malaysian, are they? ... They're here for the money. They speak Chinese and live among themselves. They could as easily be in Hong Kong or even in New York's Chinatown. (2001: 44)

Henry's enraged reply gives Li An a feeling of solidarity with her husband. Holding Henry's hand, Li An expresses for the first time in her life a vision of a united and peaceful Malaysia:

You sound just like the ultra-Malay politicians who want to kick the Chinese out of the country. My mother's family has been in this country for five or six generations, and some of the Malays are really immigrants who have just arrived from Indonesia in the last few years. You can't make any judgments based on who or what is "original." Sure, the Chinese traditions came from China, but Islam came from Saudi Arabia, didn't it? And no one says it's not original. Everything in Malaysia is chompor-chompor, mixed, rojak. A little Malay, a little Chinese, a little Indian, a little English. Malaysian means rojak, and if mixed right, it will be delicious ... Chinese and Indian are also Malaysians here. What matters is what you know you are, inside ... Give us a few more years and we'll be a totally new nation. No more Malay, Chinese, Indian, but all one people. (2001: 44–5)

What is striking about Li An's speech is the way it connects with American racial and identity politics, and the way it confuses such politics. Chester's comment "you almost sound like an American" (2001: 45) verifies what was implicit in her speech: the position of the Chinese in Malaysia is similar to, and analogous to, the position of the Chinese in America. Li An's solution and her hopeful sentiment are marked by Chester as "American," but the politics are decidedly Malaysian and unconnected with the US.

The text undermines both the solution and the sentiment in Li An's speech in at least two significant ways. First, Li An's metaphors conflate two dominant racial theories prevalent in the United States, creating a contradiction that marks the impotency of the theories for Malaysian and for American racial politics. Her "rojak" metaphor is an Asian equivalent to the popular "salad" metaphor in the United States: the idea that the nation is a place where all races live harmoniously without loosing their individual and cultural markers. Oddly, Li An conflates this metaphor with the one it is meant to displace, that is, the "melting pot" metaphor. Her concept of "a new nation" signifies the disappearance of race as a marker of difference: "no more Malay, Chinese, Indian, but all one people" (2001: 45). Suddenly the rojak has become a melting pot, at which point Chester "beams" and exclaims that she "almost sound[s] like an American." While both Chester and Li An seem to have missed the leap in logic that Li An's speech performs, the text seems to suggest that the hopeful American solution to the dilemma is a similar quagmire of muddy reasoning. Second, the failure of the rojak metaphor is prefigured by the historic setting of the conversation: less than a year later, in May 1969, Malaysia is rocked by racial riots. These riots signify the failure of Chinese, Indian, and Malay Malaysians to see themselves as a united nation with equal share in the governance and direction of the nation.

If we are to read Li An's daughter Suyin as a symbolic reference to a differently configured future than that offered by Li An above, then the novel does suggest an alternate vision of race relations. Suyin was conceived, significantly, on the night of the riots as Li An and Chester found themselves stranded at his home after the police declared a city-wide curfew. This child of the race riots is therefore biracial, a fact so obviously written upon her face that Henry refuses to accept her and Li An home from the hospital and soon after files for divorce. Bearing the stigma of adultery and divorce in a traditional Asian community, Li An finds she must leave Malaysia in order to make a home for herself and her daughter. The obvious solution would be America. America usually stands in Asian immigrant novels as the site of freedom and tolerance. Moreover, Li An has a legal right to citizenship because of Chester's legal and moral obligation to his child. Professor Kingston, the only person Chester confides in back in the United States, makes this assumption when he says, "she's putting the screws on you to get them into the United States" (184). Yet Li An never contacts Chester. She refuses to chase after him, preferring instead to migrate to Singapore to make it on her own.

What Lim offers the reader in the first part of her novel is an interruption of the hermeneutic circle — a disruption that must be adjusted when the whole of the novel is comprehended. Once readers learn that Li An is never going to leave Asia, they recognize that the genre of the American immigrant novel has been broken. According to Hans-Georg Gadamer, "the anticipation of meaning in which the whole is envisaged becomes explicit understanding in that the parts, that are determined by the whole, themselves also determine this whole" (1989: 259). Hence, the parts that seemed to suggest a particular and recognizable whole (the "envisaged whole") must be re-interpreted once the envisaged whole has been disrupted, and this re-interpretation produces a new whole. My point is that Lim's novel disrupts both the fictional circumstances or plot expectations and the genre and tradition that were signified from the beginning. When viewed from within Asian-American literary studies, this generic break challenges our notions of Asian-American literature and deliberately positions the novel in a transnational space.

SINGAPORE AS SUBSTITUTE, OR "A NEW WOMAN IN THE FRESH NEW ASIAN CITY"

In the novel, Singapore replaces America as the site of freedom and tolerance; and, as with many Asian immigrant novels, the "promised land" turns out to be less tolerant and free than expected. We are told, for instance, "even after moving to Singapore, where a woman could be husbandless, a child must have a father's name" (Lim 2001: 199). Suyin does face prejudice in school at being mixed,[5] but more so at being fatherless. It is not until Henry decides to be her father that her schoolmates stop teasing her, after which "no one in Cho Kang called her 'Sin-ner'" (2001: 297). But husbandlessness has not limited Li An to a lesser share of the Singapore capitalist pie: as their Indian friend Paroo puts it, "She's happy, got money, got condo, got car, got big-time job" (2001: 195). Chester thinks of her as "a new woman in the fresh new Asian city" (2001: 280), a description that registers his admiration for her success as well as the success of Singapore. Li An is an independent Asian woman with a tenacious will to provide for her daughter on her own terms. For her, there is no desperate desire to claim America, despite her legitimate right to make that claim. Singapore, a nation that is home to a large Chinese diasporic community, is the preferred site of migration.

The freedom and tolerance fostered in Singapore contrasts not only with Kuala Lumpur in the novel, but also with New York. Asian feminism, as exemplified in Li An, contrasts sharply with the feminism of Chester's wife Meryl in the New York section of the book. Meryl is portrayed as a woman who places her rights to a fulfilling career above the needs of her husband and the good of her marriage. She insists, for instance, that Chester go for a vasectomy since they have decided not to have children. When Chester asks her if they have really agreed not to have children, Meryl says,

> We've looked at our priorities over and over again. I'm coming up for the deputy commissioner's position next year, and if the federal grant comes through, I'll have my own project in the New York Parks to administer. Dan said I could be commissioner in a few years, the first woman commissioner in the history of the Parks Department. (2001: 121)

Clearly (perhaps too clearly) the priorities Meryl lists as "ours" are in fact her own. Her insistence on not having children, and her persistent hounding of Chester to be the one to undergo surgery, suggests that her brand of feminism is self-serving ambition by another name. Li An, on the other hand, is driven by necessity to succeed as a woman in a male-dominated society for the good of her child. She furthermore forms a nurturing home for Suyin by assembling a "family" of females — made up of herself, her good friend Ellen, and Suyin's grandmother.

Thus, to say that Singapore is the novel's substitute for America should not suggest that it is either a better or a worse substitute. For Singapore resembles but does not replicate America. In moving to Singapore rather than the US, Li An trades in her idealism for pragmatism and her poetry for security. She literally throws away her poetry books — which early in the novel marked her for immigration to the United States. In Paroo's words, "No more poetry, no more literature. She's trying to make a buck." Singapore life, as constructed in the novel, is writing with the poetry sucked out of it. Li An's love of the English language and of British literature inspired her as a young student and teacher to deep feelings for renewal and change. But in pragmatic Singapore, this kind of idealism becomes petty and useless. As her friend Abdullah says,

> What is the purpose of all the literature they're still teaching in the university? Malay literature, Chinese literature, English literature — no practical use. Better to teach communications, public relations, like you are doing now. (2001: 208)

BioSynergy's news bulletin, of which Li An is editor-in-chief, fits Abdullah's definition of useful literature. The weekly bulletin is not only a constantly updated information sheet on business activities, but it is a much used document in Singapore business society: "it was a hot document studied by investors, shareholders, and the Monetary Authority of Singapore for clues to the company's health and future" (2001: 206). In short, Li An's work feeds the capitalist machine rather than humanistic ideals.

The kind of language Li An must use in the newsletter comes to characterize her changed approach to life. In her youth she was outspoken, passionate, and almost wild in comparison to her classmates; as editor-in-chief of *BioSyn-Sign*, Li An is as levelheaded and composed as her business writing. When Chester shows up in her office eleven years after his departure from Malaysia, Li An keeps her emotion in check by invoking a business-writing style in her speech: "Li An kept her voice low, feeling for the steadiness of business writing, the clear agenda of the memorandum" (2001: 244). The novel constructs business writing as writing without poetry; it is steady, emotionless, and secure. For Li An, the pragmatism of business life in Singapore and in the language of her weekly stock articles marks the hard fact of growing up to a life of single motherhood. She had learned "to embrace the empty depth in the glittering surface of things" (2001: 210).

The Singapore of *Joss & Gold* seems at first glance to be America without a spirit. The country embraces capitalism and the minimal freedoms required to make it run, but it shines on the surface like a façade or an empty shell. However, although pragmatic capitalism is signified through business language, there is a difference in this particular business language that reveals a uniquely Asian quality. As BioSynergy's executive chief explains to a British visitor, "It doesn't matter that BioSynergy is a wholly research-oriented company, staffed by some of the best-trained scientists that money and top facilities can attract … We Singaporeans invest our Sing-dollars cautiously, and every good omen and sign is needed to keep us loyal to the company" (2001: 207). In the West, the strength of the company is reflected in the quality of its business plan and in its performance, but in Singapore investors look also at omens and signs. Singaporeans, the novel suggests, do not make business decisions on strictly pragmatic evidence; they may, for example, buy more stock in the year of the rooster because it is considered an auspicious year, or take good care of their ancestors to enhance "auspicious conditions" (2001: 207–8). In terms of language, there is a distinctively Asian poetic even in business writing. As one character puts it, "no Singaporean believes that there is such a thing as unintentionality in language, especially once your language becomes fixed in print!" (2001: 207).

While on the one hand the novel suggests that Li An loses her soul (or at least her poetry) in her business transaction with Singapore, it suggests on the other hand that the language she writes in pragmatic, business-minded Singapore is far more nuanced than an outsider might imagine. Li An succeeds at her job because of her unique understanding of both local culture and the potentials of language. Unlike her American-trained predecessor, who was fired for printing a slightly critical article by a prestigious writer (he chose personality over language) that sent the company stocks plummeting, Li An knows her audience is driven by what she calls "the Singapore reflex" — "an advanced version of the desire to be superior" (2001: 211). Although not labeled as such in the novel, this "reflex" is known in Singapore as "kiasuism" — *kiasu* being a *Hokkien* dialect word meaning the fear of losing out. This concept, which is closely associated with the Asian concept of "face," is Li An's guiding principle as editor-in-chief: publish facts, but only those that present "the company in its most positive light" (2001: 211). In a rewrite of Christ's words about losing one's soul, Ellen says that "even if you conquer the world and lose face, you lose everything" (2001: 211).

The novel does not present a strong case for cultural resistance to Western and global forces through the process of localization, but Li An's adaptation of business language to local customs can perhaps be understood in these terms. According to Rob Wilson, "in Asia/Pacific interzones of heightened globalization and localization, 'global cities' like Taipei, Hong Kong, and Singapore have sprung up — cities that unevenly fuse transnational technologies to local customs" (1996: 313). Aihwa Ong remarks, "despite the widespread dissemination of the trappings of globalization — world markets, mass media, rapid travel, and modern communications — cultural forms have not become homogenized across the world," but have in fact "increased cultural diversity because of the ways in which they … acquire new meanings in local reception" (1999: 10). Li An's job is to linguistically do just that: to create new meanings for local reception, to "fuse" BioSynergies transnational technologies to local sensibilities. She coined the newssheet's title "BioSyn-Sign" in order to suggest to its local Asian (mainly Chinese) readers "a doubling of the values of shares" (Lim 2001: 209) due to the double sound in the title. The newssheet functions as a giver of signs that the executive chief likens to "fortune almanacs" that some Singaporeans use to interpret dreams and events as lucky horse racing picks and lotto numbers (2001: 206). Such local vitality existing within and transforming global capitalist structures instantiates Wilson and Dissanayake's claim that "within these spaces of uneven modernity, we are witnessing not so much the death and burial of 'local cultural originality,' as Fanon once feared within residually colonial structures of national modernity, as their rehabilitation, affirmation, and renewal in disjunctive phases and local reassertions" (1996: 3). Li An's negotiation of the global and the local is not as clearly drawn in the novel as is her negotiation of the poetical and the pragmatic. The global/local element, however weak, does in fact provide a more complex view of Singapore. Singapore, from this view, is not a soulless America, but has a vitality and agency of its own. There is an indication in the final pages of the novel that Li An will regain her poetic sensibilities and her "soul" in Singapore, without needing to emigrate to the United States. In Singapore, Li An finally regains her feeling, her "inner-ear," for poetry and its "rhythms" (2001: 306).

CONCLUSION

While Li An's individualism and her choice of Singapore as home are significant in the novel's challenge to the reader's horizon of expectation, it is Suyin who embodies the novel's vision of a new future. Symbolically conceived in racial chaos, Suyin is a hybrid of Asia and America living in a modern Asian city that is similarly a hybrid of Asian and Western cultures. Moreover, Suyin, by the novel's conclusion, is given two fathers, one Asian and the other American. Henry comes into her life at the death of Suyin's grandmother, as Henry becomes the executor of her will. Through their interaction over legal matters and Grandmother Yeh's funeral, Henry comes to finally accept Suyin as his daughter now that he is remarried and has a child of his own: "Suyin was a backward family bond; but Henry, being now a good Chinese father, would not refuse that bond" (Lim 2001: 303). At the same time, Chester travels from America to seek his daughter. Li An allows Chester to take Suyin out while he is in Singapore and eventually Suyin grasps that Chester is her father. Chester's invitation for Suyin to come to America for a visit seems to stand as an open invitation for Suyin to move to America when and if she chooses to do so.

Suyin, by the end of the novel, does not simply have an Asian mother, but she has an Asian father and an American father. Ellen, Li An's good friend who acts as Suyin's second parent, criticizes Li An for allowing the two men into Suyin's life:

> You have her all confused. One father in Kuala Lumpur, one father in New York. It was better when she did not know about either of them. (2001: 304)

But Li An comes to the conclusion that it is better for Suyin to have choices. In the end, the choice is Suyin's. She is, at novel's end, an eleven-year-old hybrid girl with a transnational identity.

Joss & Gold's diasporic and transnational vision valorizes choice and mobility. The happy note on which the novel ends is that Suyin, unlike her mother who never belonged in the country of her birth, belongs to *both* Asia *and* America. With the help, moreover, of her mother's financial success and the inheritance she will receive from her grandmother's will, Suyin has the freedom and the ability to move between Asia and America, her two symbolic fathers. America remains a possible choice for Suyin, not an identity — and the text in no way marks America as the obvious or even the best choice.

Read as an Asian-American diasporic text, *Joss & Gold* interrogates US identity in at least several significant ways. First, the United States is displaced as an object of immigrant desire. The US remains a possible choice for several characters in the novel, but it is not the "Gold Mountain" of Asian aspirations. *Joss & Gold*'s substitution of an Asian city-state for the United States as the preferred site of migration questions "orientalist geography" by refusing the East/West binary (Li 1998: 196). The novel's redefinition of America as one of several possible choices rather than the unavoidable solution challenges the claiming America thesis with its assumptions of a shared national destiny and identity (Li 1998: 196). Second, the United States has not cornered the market on human rights, and specifically on female rights. The Asian female is independent and strong without the legitimization of US democracy and US feminism. If anything, the novel suggests that certain brands of US feminism may be inferior to certain brands of Asian feminism. As discussed above, Meryl's US feminism, in contrast to Li An's, is restrictive, self-indulgent, anti-community, and anti-family. Third, United States nationalism need not be the locus of identity for an Asian-American text, even if we continue to call it an Asian-American text. My claim is that *Joss & Gold* performs a critique of American nationalism and of ethnic nationalist rhetoric within Asian-American literary studies when it is read not simply as a diasporic, cosmopolitan, or global text, but as an Asian-American diasporic text. *Joss & Gold*'s transnational structure and challenge to the claiming America thesis (however we might judge the effectiveness or validity of that challenge) can be fruitfully read within Asian-American literature's turn to diaspora. The questions raised about its categorization are precisely the kinds of questions a non-nationalist diasporic text is meant to raise.

9

Writing the Chinese and Southeast Asian Diasporas in Russell Leong's *Phoenix Eyes*

Walter S. H. Lim

The age of globalization, that familiar if not somewhat overdetermined appellative used to describe the conditions of late twentieth and early twenty-first century (post)modernity, appears to have caused a degree of anxiety for some writers and critics involved in the ideological production of Asian American literature. This anxiety is registered in the critical debates on the nature of the relationship between the so-called "claiming America" and "claiming diaspora" projects. There is, at least on one level, the sense that the increasing push to adopt a diasporic perspective may generate a denationalizing impulse that is in fact inimical to the political gains made thus far in energizing and defining Asian American studies itself.[1] It has been cautioned that one must not lose sight of the significance of the "local" or "national" in the face of the palpable pressures exerted by the presence of the "global" and "transnational."[2] Globalization, which by definition entails reducing the vastness of the world into a compact space of unhindered interactions facilitated by IT and the Net as well as by the creation of free trade blocs, is not embraced unambivalently by all. Globalization, as Saskia Sassen puts it, has "its discontents," which in popular parlance translates to mean the reality of a widening gap between society's haves and its have-nots.[3] With all its valorized rhetoric concerning the improvement of the lives of people today, globalization has been viewed by some in terms of the economic hegemony of powerful industrialized and developed nations of the world over less privileged ones.

The age of globalization etches its presence in Asian American literature in the writing of a new mobility, where America no longer signifies as the concluding point of a teleological narrative predicated upon the idea of the migrant quest. In the discourse of this new mobility, national and cultural identity is no longer always defined by a controlling historiography that charts and engages the early coming of an immigrant group to the New World. Instead of Asia functioning as the launch pad for the search of a better life, America now begins to constitute the starting point for accessing different geopolitical and economic spaces making up the globalized community of nations. Taking off from America to plug into opportunities offered by the tiger economies of the Asia Pacific, for example, rewrites the narrative of America as land of promise guaranteeing socioeconomic equality. Positing the implied premise of a more level playing field that is the result of the emergence of various robust Asian economies then entails unavoidable compromising of the glamour defining America's mythic plenitude.

One of the things achieved by transnational mobility is an increase in the power of subjects to contest the hegemonic hold exerted over individual lives by the nation-state. In an era marked by infinitely quicker and strikingly denser transactions energizing the operations of the world economy, international travel and movement seriously interrogate the authority of the nation-state as exclusive locus of political organization and action. What it also does is give to the subject a certain freedom in fashioning his or her own identity that is not fully anchored in the cultural logic of the nation-state, a freedom intertwined with release into the spaces of diaspora.[4] Robin Cohen (1997: 135) identifies a distinctive feature of diaspora in the age of globalization: "Forms of international migration [now] emphasise contractual relationships, intermittent postings abroad, and sojourning, as opposed to permanent settlement and the exclusive adoption of the citizenship of a destination country." Postcolonial discourse itself posits the existence of a type that is a close relative to Cohen's diasporic subject, the exilic self usually associated with the errant intellectual seeking to position himself or herself in what Ihab Hassan (1995: 250) has referred to as "an interactive earth; a patchwork of values; a hash of habits, traditions, histories; a mess of interests." If the rootlessness of being in the condition of mobility can be anxiety-stricken, it also embeds the experience of exhilaration.

In the context of Asian American literature in the age of globalization, which is the focus of my consideration in this chapter, Russell Leong is one writer who has registered deep interest in the themes of exile and diaspora. In his collection of short stories, *"Phoenix Eyes" and Other Stories* (2000), Leong expands the identification of the Old World with China to encompass migrants from Hong Kong and Vietnam as well as jet setters and political exiles who flit from country to country in Southeast Asia. Leong's expansion of focus constitutes an important readjustment of the narrative of migration found in such canonical texts as *The Woman Warrior*, *China Men*, and *The Joy Luck Club*, which locate China as the point of origin of the Chinese migration experience in the United States, and where the motif of travail on the part of the first-generation migrant informs the literary meditations on individual, cultural, and social identity. In Leong's fiction, the struggles of the first-generation (im)migrant do not appear to be of primary concern. He also does not make it a point of engaging the entire issue of negotiating the cultural differences between generations, between those who made their way to the United States from across the ocean and those who are born American.

In general, Leong's (im)migrant brings with him or her a different history from the ones brought, for example, by Brave Orchid and the aunts of *The Joy Luck Club*. First of all, Leong is interested in a history linked not only to China but the countries in Southeast Asia. The experience of the history of the Southeast Asian diaspora is a much more recent one when compared to the coming of the Chinese to America in the nineteenth century, a history that gets associated at a popular level with America's disastrous involvement in the Vietnam War. Belonging to the generation involved in that war, Leong invokes the Vietnamese presence in his writings to highlight that contemporary American interactions with the Southeast Asian immigrant continue to be colored by myths, expectations, and other cultural baggage that have developed around the Vietnam War as controlling historical referent. With the implied social and political backdrop of the many Vietnamese refugees and immigrants presently living in the United States evoked as informing context, Leong engages the contemporary Vietnamese presence on relationships other than the historical reference point of war. In "Geography One," one of the short stories in *Phoenix Eyes*, we encounter the interactions of two male lovers, one Chinese American and the other Vietnamese, in his consideration of the possibilities of relationships between an American and the Vietnamese, worked out on the bases of shared histories and love. Leong suggests that while migration and movement may provide a way of looking at social and individual transformations, transnationals code cultural experiences that are not limited to and by the migration experience. Significantly, the transnational experience is also colored by individual histories, generational difference, family dynamics, and sexual orientation.

In *Phoenix Eyes*, all of these motifs are harnessed to give nuance to the experience of subjects negotiating their relationships to nation-states within the context of the transnational experience and of globalization. If the age of globalization confers an important capacity for mobility, facilitating the attainment of a freedom (within limits) that stands in contrast to the motifs of imprisonment found in a poem like "Fire" in Leong's *The Country of Dreams and Dust* (1993), it does so through the (re)claiming of the sexual body. Where, in *The Country of Dreams and Dust*, sex appears inextricable from the experience of historical victimization and cultural violation, in *Phoenix Eyes* one gets the much stronger sense that it is not so much determined by circumstantial exigencies as expressive of the very important freedom to choose. The choice of deciding one's sexual preference is directly tied to the enlargement of social space(s) facilitated by the capacity for transnational movement. It is possible to have lovers, and multiple ones at that, anywhere in the world.

In *Phoenix Eyes*, the production of pleasure, which is tied directly to the celebration of freedom predicated upon transnational mobility, is most definitely affirmative at one level. In Leong's writings in general, gay sexuality constitutes, at least on one level, an important symbolic locus for the celebration and affirmation of individuality, selfhood, and identity. It appears that self and identity become most powerfully assertive at those moments when the body experiences the greatest sensations of pleasure, as when the narrator of the short story "Camouflage" masturbates himself on the dancing floor that is the public/private space of a male strip-joint and spa. Choice marks the experience of Terence, the male narrator in the short story "Phoenix Eyes," who chooses his own path in life and ends up in Taipei because he had fallen in love with an airline steward based in that city. Terence's decision to live in Taipei with his male lover is a direct response to the demands of desire and one's particular sexual predilections.

But if "Phoenix Eyes" is about the affirmations of subjectivity underwritten by the autonomous subscription to libidinal desire, it is also, importantly, about the marginalization of perceived aberrant sexuality in the conventional Chinese family. In this story, Terence figures his (aberrant) sexuality with reference to the specific delineations of his eyes:

> I myself was called *feng yen* or "phoenix eyes" because of the way the outer folds of my eyes appeared to curve upward like the tail of the proverbial phoenix. Such eyes were considered seductive in a woman, but a deviation in a man. (Leong 2000: 135)

One finds implied in this association of seductive eyes in a man with deviancy the reason for the narrator's familial marginalization. When Terence flew in to Seattle to celebrate his father's seventieth birthday, he recognized that he had not been seen at a family banquet for some twenty-odd years. And then rather self-consciously, he begins imagining the questions that must be going through the minds of the party guests: "Where are his wife and children? Why isn't he married yet? Does he make money? What exactly does he do for a living?" (2000: 142). In contradistinction to this normative space associated with the valorization of conventional familial expectations and a clearly defined value system is the space of freedom associated with the so-called *hung kung hsien*, "the international call line" (2000: 132) of high-priced prostitutes servicing well-heeled clients throughout the major cities of Southeast Asia.

The banquet referred to here in this episode signifies the cultural logic of the Confucian family, locus of order and controlling center of kinship ties. Celebratory though it may be, the joyous banquet also provides an occasion for scrutiny and stocktaking, not exactly pleasant for Terence who finds himself the primary object of a familial and social gaze. Part of the issue here has to do with the impossibility of familial accommodation of particular kinds of lifestyle, which leads to forms of ostracism. More importantly, however, it has to do with the reality that lies beneath the surface of the idea of the stable family, a reality directly tied to the experiences of a character like Terence who inhabits a space that can best be termed the "underworld." This "underworld" is that cultural and experiential space viewed as taboo by the legislative spaces of official culture, embodied in the Chinese family. Characters who are gay inhabit this "underworld" together with prostitutes.

In "Daughters," Leong depicts a family selling its daughter into prostitution. Financial need, identified as the obligation to pay off an outstanding debt, is the ostensible reason given to explain the family's compulsion to do this. The barter of the daughter's body signifies a familial patriarchalism that clearly privileges the welfare of sons over daughters. "Daughters" can be read as a compressed and dark version of the *bildungsroman*, in which a young woman undertakes a journey of self-discovery within the dark spaces of the soul-numbing brothel. The narrative of victimization that grounds Haishan's experience as a prostitute is significantly complemented by the (limited) affirmations of a subjectivity tied to the ability for articulation, registered in the forceful assertion of her rights to the woman who controls the destiny of the prostitutes under her charge. If a central aspect of the sexual experience in Leong's representations of the subject has to do with forms of violation as figured through harrowing images of imprisonment, it also narrativizes the struggles entered into by victims to wrest some degree of control over their lives. When Haishan finally finds herself in Los Angeles, she becomes part of a small community of women, also prostitutes, enjoying a degree of much-needed support and the sense of solidarity not readily afforded her in the real world.

Despite the obvious narrative differences separating "Daughters" from "Phoenix Eyes," the two stories share one common thematic linkage — the relationship of the family to the "underworld" entered into by daughters and sons because of their perceived sexual deviations. It is interesting to note that both Haishan and Terence, who are defined by the sordidness and pains of this "underworld," contribute to the sustenance of the immediate family. They both transmit money to their respective families, fulfilling the demands of filial obligations even though their families have not accorded them due recognition. In both "Daughters" and "Phoenix Eyes," the space of the "underworld" exists in complicity with the normative articulations of official culture, facilitating in effect its very existence. And it also functions as a critique of the myth of the family as the bedrock that grounds the "Asian" side of the Chinese American's hyphenated identity.

In the stories of *Phoenix Eyes*, the concept of the viable and stable Confucian family is interrogated by the difficulties of grappling with the defining parameters of what constitutes maleness and masculinity. Leong registers a powerful impulse to want to revise conventional notions of masculinity and fatherhood. In "Hemispheres," Bryan, despite being gay, receives offers from three lesbian friends to father their children. The freedom to apply one's body to the demands of the procreative mandate or simply the pull of sexual desire is, however, not a straightforward one. Sometimes sexual freedom, the complete liberation from prescribed social codes governing acceptable sexual behavior, makes it difficult to find meaning in the body. As Bryan comments: "it disturbed me that bodies and beauty were so provisional — women reached a time in which they had to make a choice about birthing, just as men reached a time in which they had to commit to something other than themselves" (Leong 2000: 85). Sexual freedom can never, in the final analysis, be completely free from the legislative spaces of official culture with which it is in constant negotiation. Bryan finds out emphatically that he is prevented from pursuing a relationship with Vinny and raising their child because he is bisexual.

Sexual choices, whether freely undertaken or forced into by circumstance, may entail consequences, like dying of AIDS. In the space that I've referred to as the "underworld," distanced from the gaze of official culture, people and friends die of the disease. The story "Camouflage" deals with how a male dancer and stripper, whose identity is shaped by sexual abuse, ecstasy, and Valium, finally engages in unprotected sex with an HIV-positive man in a moment of uncontrollable desire — a powerful example of the tragic that shades quite a number of Leong's stories. As highlighted in "Phoenix Eyes" and in "Aloes," Asian families relegate those close to them who are dying of AIDS to oblivion, conveniently forgotten and simply not talked about. There is a systematic cultural excision of AIDS sufferers from familial recognition and, after their passing, from familial memory.

Part of Leong's ideological project in *Phoenix Eyes* then involves the reinsertion and recuperation of (deviant) sexual identities via the conferral of normative valences. Sexual(ized) identities, and for that matter appreciation of beauty, are relative, not absolute:

> It didn't matter. We were beads on a string. A rosary of flesh. We gave up our youth to those who desired youth. There was some room for variation, for beauty was in the eye of the beholder. (2000: 135)

This resonant line also captures succinctly the important and characteristic weaving of sexuality and religion that defines much of the cultural and diasporic thematics of Leong's short stories. Specifically, the sexuality that is generally defined by the interplay of violence and pleasure, entrapment and freedom, intersects the Buddhist concept of *samsara* that informs much of the religious underpinnings of these stories.

Samsara refers to the cycle of death and rebirth from which the self seeks liberation. The ultimate goal in this philosophical understanding is the total cessation of desire and the elimination of attachment to and belief in the existence of the illusory self. Successfully eliminating such attachment means that the effects of karma, the system of cause and effect in which all actions have consequences, will have nothing to attach themselves to, thus enabling the attainment of nirvana.

While Leong's invocation of Buddhist references and allusions may be meant to offer a critique at some level of the norms and forms of Western philosophical thought, specifically the cultural imperialism associated with the Judeo-Christian tradition, it finally finds its place in a literary production predicated upon a series of paradoxes: concealment and revelation, appearances and essences, enslavement and liberation. If at one level, sexuality and spirituality (the two are deeply enmeshed) constitute forms of imprisonment, at another they can prove to be liberative. Like sexuality, the experience of religion entails the convergence of contradictory drives, producing situations in which the subject experiences a kind of pleasure in religious discipline. Violence and pleasure, entrapment and freedom — such contradictions find themselves engaged in complex dialectical interactions in Leong's writing.

As a philosophical system, Buddhism offers a way out of the suffering in which being is locked, a belief inscribed in the controlling imagery and metaphor of the world as red dust and as the dream (*meng chen*) of illusory existence from which the self seeks complete extrication. The question remains, however, as to whether this system is indeed capable of doing so. The connoted idea is that the entire world we call reality is actually just one vast and spacious but essentially empty illusion made up of dust, related to the Buddhist concept of nothingness. Given this nothingness, in which everything is dust — and this includes all tangible material possessions and our very own corporeal bodies as well — transcendence becomes necessary.

In *The Country of Dreams and Dust,* Leong's 1993 collection of lyric utterances united by the controlling narrative of the historical and imagined journey, America, the land of dreams because of its promise of greater economic and social opportunity, is also the land of dust where dreams and expectations disintegrate. If in Buddhism there is the dust of empty illusions, in the experience of migrancy there is also the dust of shattered dreams. The social, cultural, and political experience of diaspora, entailing the leaving of an ancestral homeland and being propelled into the space of international dispersal, finds its spiritual homology in the condition of being flung out from a center of being into the world of dust. Spiritual decentering, tied to the desire (ironic in a Buddhist context) to invest existence with meaning, entails a kind of floating, wavering between heaven and hell, or earth. For Leong, the concept of diaspora is not to be limited to cultural and political modes of understanding. It must be viewed from within a spiritual perspective as well.

If, typically speaking, spiritual experience is that which is sought after for its ability to afford transcendence, its invocation in *Phoenix Eyes* only serves to reinforce the reality of being locked in time and space, defined by the corporeality of the body as imaged through the immersion in sensuous details that come thick and fast in the pages of various texts. In Leong's writings, the body is always fully aware of itself as body, an awareness concretized by the experiences of sexual pleasure as well as violation. This body also defines itself by resisting the pull of the demands of the nation-state by literally and metaphorically throwing itself into the conditions of transnational mobility. We notice that the figure of Leong's immigrant is always on the go, always on the move, constantly crossing (inter)national boundaries. This figure represents a striking departure from the familiar Asian American discourse that deals with the experience of migration to the United States, or another that imagines conciliatory possibilities in the bridging of cultures. Distanced from the direct effects of the defining parameters of the cultural logic of the nation-state, the identity of Leong's Asian American is established with reference to the process of globalization, which facilitates the maintenance of open diasporic links. The multiple affiliations and associations facilitated by globalization produce indefinite and unstable identities that are, at the same time, paradoxically affirmative.

The dismantling of borders is consistent with the general impulse in

Leong's writings to deconstruct generic delineations and demarcations. Discrete gender, ethnic, and national boundaries break down to make way for fluid interminglings and hybrid interactions. Interactions between peoples in the Far East and Southeast Asia as well as in the United States itself are at best complex social and cultural processes and transactions — different nationalities come into close and often intimate contact; characters are of mixed racial origin; even sexual habits are defined by their general resistance to the straightforwardness of the heterosexual paradigm. Leong implicitly accepts then Homi Bhabha's theoretical premise that an inherent instability governs all interactions transpiring between two terms of a binary opposition owing to unavoidable spillages and reabsorptions. This instability, in Bhabha's (1995) formulation, generates an indeterminate third force of hybridity between the polarities it attempts to keep in being. Bhabha's "hybridity" complicates and gives nuance to the concept of "Orientalism" and its reverse face, "Occidentalism," when postulating that the dominant culture that defines its own identity by setting itself off against an Other always has the Other already implicated in and contaminating its exclusivist definition.

Belonging categorically within the canon of Asian American literature, the stories in *Phoenix Eyes* engage in some detail the implications of living in diasporic spaces and under the conditions of globalization. Meditating on diasporic realities, Leong imagines the pulls and tensions defining the site at which the impulses of transnationalism intersect the defining power that continues to be exerted, albeit with destabilizations, by the nation-state. Clearly, an important impulse in Leong's writings is to recuperate for the individual subject a degree of freedom, manifested in the disengaging of direct familial ties and in the alacrity with which national boundaries get crossed. And he does this through the informing paradigms of postcolonial thinking, postmodernist poetics, and gay theory.[5] Exile is, at one level, a liberating condition predicated upon the premise of a decentered and multiple subjectivity. The most distinctive form of this subjectivity is the hybrid, which Leong figures in the familiar terms of gender poetics and gay politics. Most importantly, freedom in *Phoenix Eyes* is coded in the control one possesses over one's sexuality.

While Leong's foregrounding of the sexual(ized) self in the representation of diasporic subjectivity participates in the deconstruction of binary oppositions in a series of narrative contexts that inscribe the dissolution of generic and gender boundaries, it leaves unresolved the ubiquitous problematic of the figuration of Asia's cultural identity. If the age of globalization and (inter)national connectedness has yielded "new" types of the Asian — the "astronaut husband," "parachute kids," the affluent businessman and woman — these types only manage to make the significance of their presence felt in Leong's writings in a marginal manner, being generally overshadowed by the deep(er) interest in sexual(ized) subjectivities. In Leong the figuration of Asia in sexual terms generates the effect of replacing the colonial paradigm of the feminine East with a radically hybrid one. On one level, invoking the sexual body to enforce an ideological statement has an important place — it demands that attention be paid to its presence and the particular forms of its legitimacy. On another level, however, such figuration continues to ensure Asia never gets itself extricated from an imagistic and symbolic matrix that is sexual in origin and definition, producing inadvertent *Orientalist* resonances. If part of Leong's ideological impulse in *Phoenix Eyes* is to disrupt the idea of America as *raison d'être* of the migration quest and to open up Asia as a contemporary space of infinite possibilities, it cannot finally transcend the *Orientalist* inflection of the East as an inchoate cultural space that supports thriving deviant sexualities.

As a work that belongs to the canon of Asian American literature, *Phoenix Eyes* finally takes on board some of the implications of the pressures exerted by the contemporary conditions of transnationalism and globalization, readjusting the centrality formerly accorded the historical narrative of the coming of Chinamen to seek their fortune in Gold Mountain, a narrative typically viewed as formative in constituting the beginnings of Asian America. It rightly complexifies the character of the Asian in America, with his or her own distinctive point of national and ethnic origin, with his or her own individual reason for migration. It does not offer a naive and idealistic reading of America as *telos* of the migration quest; neither does it sugarcoat the experiences and character of the Asian migrant. Leong's project of highlighting the complexities involved in any effort to define cultural identity is salutary, functioning as a literary example that inscribes important diasporic and transnational interests. Its ideological premises can be built upon to greater substantive effect in the production of a literature that brings into conjunction Asian American politics and the realities of a globalized world, where perhaps the thing to do is not only to further tease out and fine-tune different theoretical matrices and their ideological implications, but also to represent the effects of the emergence of an Asian Pacific cultural and economic viability upon meditations and representations of (Asian) American cultural identity.

10

Diasporic Communities and Identity Politics: Containing the Political

Ryan Bishop and John Phillips

The "deportees" in the "camps" of our urban wastelands are . . . merely indicating the irresistible emergence of a previously almost unknown level of deprivation and human misery. They are waste-products of a military-industrial, scientific civilization which has applied itself for almost two centuries to depriving individuals of the knowledge and skill accumulated over generations and millennia, before a post-industrial upsurge occurred which now seeks to reject them on the ground of definitive uselessness. (Paul Virilio, *Strategy of Deception*)

What marks the diasporic experience as *diasporic*? What shapes diasporic communities in ways unique to them? Perhaps the answer can be found in the violence of community formation, the traumas that led to migration and the terrors of carving out a space in a new country and culture, the inevitable rending wrought by forced evacuations from and insertions into the complex webbing of geopolitical sites, the tearing of roots from the earth's surface coupled with the tenuous act of transplanting. The patterns evoked here contain synchronic similarities worth noting, but the diachronic differences — i.e., the specificities of events — are the stuff of collective memory essential to diasporic experience.

The violence inscribed on Asian diasporic communities reads, appropriately enough, like a list of trials and punishments in the Torah. Floods, droughts, civil war, and rebellions in mid-nineteenth century China poured forth massive numbers of émigrés to a range of locations. Some of these ended up on the west coast of the US, and anti-Chinese violence perpetrated by white workers in the 1870s helped transform Chinatown in San Francisco from an inchoate clustering of shops and residences into a segregated ethnic enclave that provided protection from a hostile social environment. This violence, too, spurred Chinese migration in the US toward the east coast, eventually making New York's Chinatown the largest such community in the world. The end of the nineteenth century saw the US military brutally and bloodily taking hold of the Philippines from first the Spanish and then Filipino nationalists, causing flight from the archipelago that was to be sustained for almost a hundred years. Japan's self-imposed isolation ended, of course, at the hands of Perry's gunboat policies, starting a period of interaction with the external globe that exacerbated political crises within the country. Meiji modernization policies created agricultural pressures and landlessness among farmers, leading to nefarious dealings in conscripted labor to work in Hawaii, Guam, and California, where laborers were treated brutally by bosses and coworkers alike. Korea suffered invasions from without as well as religious rebellions from within, especially in the late nineteenth century, not to mention the Sino-Japanese war which was fought on their soil in the first decade of the twentieth. Again, the export of laborers played a pivotal role in the formation of Korean diasporic communities during these periods, and again, violence surrounds the experience of life in the new sites. When the Cold War became a hot war for the first time, in the Korean peninsula, new diasporic groups came from there as well. A second major hot war of the Cold War was also fought on Asian soil, leading to massive diasporic movements from Laos, Cambodia, and Vietnam — once more, with violence being the bookends of the diasporic experience. This is but a brief, grossly truncated list of atrocities that led to the formation of Asian diasporic communities and that marked their reception.

We would draw attention in this list to the complex interaction of economic, technological, state, and martial forces at play in the constitution of all of these Asian diasporic communities. This is what we will call *the insignia of the military,* which inscribes diasporas past and present. The term "insignia" probably comes from two Latin roots: *signum*, which is "a distinguishing mark" and *sec-*, "cut." The distinguishing mark, then, is a cut, forming an integral connection to the severing operative in diasporic experience. The "military" involved in our analysis is both the military-as-entity, and the military-as-techne (or organizing, operating, and executing principle). Regardless of whether we are discussing actual military operations or events that have militaristic logic, violence is the tool of implementation, and a severing of sorts results. Thus, even when diasporic communities result from civic conflict, e.g., religious or ethnic violence resultant from political decisions, such as the partition that created Pakistan, we would argue the insignia of the military marked the event of diasporic sufferings. The "spontaneous" outbreak of violence and the dislocation of millions of people during the 1947 event had both militaristic origins and implementations. And the distinguishing marks of this event that severed peoples from lands long held as familial property were sustained physical and symbolic violence.

The marks inscribed as insignia of the military cannot always be easily distinguished from those of civil or ecclesiastical insignia — either as manifestations or as significations (senses that anyway overlap and recall each other). While the dominant insignia — the uniforms, arms, units, divisions, armies — help to play this distinguishing role by marking out an armed and mobile force in the service of some sovereign state, the insignia of the military in fact disperse in fragments into all aspects of experience, emerging for instance both in the form of monuments (memorial structures, museums, coats of arms, titles, tombs, and public marches) and in the form of ruins and remains (bunkers, rubble, cripples, killing fields, and dispersion). The overlaps between monument and ruin, one standing for the other falling, help to mark out the sense of *abbreviation* that the insignia of the military imposes, cutting short or cutting out. In some very important ways, the power of the state is borne by and through the abbreviation of the insignia of the military. The abbreviation reveals the state's sovereignty to cut out, to mark citizens, territory, and language; i.e., to cut short lives, borders, and words.

Diasporic communities result from the power of sovereignty to expunge those who oppose it, and are, indeed, the manifestation of this power. Because the military provides the most crucial and visible means of implementing state sovereignty, the very existence of diasporas reveals the insignia of the military through the state sovereignty manifest in and apparent through its creation of wandering peoples. The insignia of the military, then, is part of the invisible trace diasporic communities bear *in* and *for* their "home" sites, as well as in the sites of exile. In this fashion, Ambrose Bierce's definition of an exile as "one who serves his country by residing abroad, yet is not an ambassador" is as accurate as it is satiric.

The singular unit of the military, the *miles* (or soldier) must be employed to bear arms potentially against other soldiers, but not necessarily. Thus it is that civilians also can bear the marks of the military. Everyone is potentially a soldier, especially with the advent of "total war." From this fact derives the *power of sovereignty*, which thus shapes political communities according to the relative capabilities that individuals can acquire, a point that manifests itself in a range of institutions. It is no accident that the word *discipline* (from *disciplina* — instruction or teaching) finds its most appropriate usage today with reference to the modern military whose armies command great skill and great force and so must be managed through the exercise of great discipline. In this way the insignia of the military inscribes itself on the academic disciplines too, and it is this aspect that tends to get lost in the identity politics of contemporary intellectuals. In the university qua institution, a cool debate about who and what we are serves the military function of drill, and a delimited debate about "the political" effectively serves as an abbreviation of *thinking* about "the political."

The insignia of the military in diasporic community formation operates in a continuum of ways, from the visible to the invisible, from the explicit to the implicit. Direct military conflict — such as the Taiping Rebellion, or Perry's arrival in Japan, or China and Japan at war on Korean soil, or the Vietnam War — is only the most blatant means through which the insignia of the military results in diasporic movements. But when the insignia of the military manifests itself in other systemic forms, for example, technology, economics, political apparatuses, or global linkages, then the full complexity of the phenomenon and its capacity to shape human organization can be glimpsed. The recent bombing of Kosovo, for example, by an international force deploying the most advanced high-tech weaponry resulted in large-scale movements of people who were not welcome within any nation's borders, except in the most minimal numbers. This war that was not a war resulted, therefore, in refugees who were not refugees. That is, other, systemic dimensions of the insignia of the military prevented the conflict from being defined as a war and its wandering victims as refugees worthy of designation as diaspora. Alternatively, the transfer of Hong Kong to China led to thousands of wealthy Hong Kong Chinese fleeing to North America and Australia. In this case, the peaceful transfer of power meant to facilitate both state sovereignty and market access resulted in a new diasporic community significantly different from most Chinese immigrants past and from those huddling along Macedonia's borders: that is, it is well-heeled and therefore capable of attaining (or purchasing) diasporic status.

Another densely complex example of how the insignia of the military creates diasporic communities can be found in the 1997 Southeast Asian economic crash. The globalization thrust that allows for "real time" military surveillance of the earth necessary for waging the Cold War also provides the means for uniting the earth in interrelated markets. Technologies designed to take snap-second decisions out of human hands in military situations function in a similar fashion for currency exchange markets and other global investment mechanisms. Maximum control of these technologies led to maximum economic meltdown in 1997, resulting in capital taking the mantle of the diaspora. Capital fled the region and, as it always can and does, found harbor elsewhere. Human others who suffered the adverse effects of this flight did not always have the advantage of flight themselves — capital having the inherent attribute of mobility that people do not, unless it is forced upon them. The insignia of the military, then, provides a means for reading a myriad of diasporic phenomena in subtly but profoundly interconnected ways, thus keeping a range of causes and effects, forces and resistances, and modes of violence simultaneously under consideration. In other words, the insignia of the military does not isolate the political solely within the domain of the individual; rather, it reveals how the political cannot be so easily contained in that specific site while examining a multitude of systems that shape the individual as individual (including those discursive and ideological ones that foreground the individual).

The traumas that birthed Asian diasporic communities play an integral role in identity formation for these communities. They are firmly woven into the warp and woof of the communities' understandings of themselves in relation to the past and the present, the global and the local. These violent acts provide an essential context for reading diasporic texts. Yet, much current research into diasporic writing and diasporas almost completely elides this violence, or relegates it to "backdrop" rather than context or text. Following a general trend in recent humanities and social sciences research, diasporic inquiry has privileged the concepts of the individual and identity formation (at the individual level) over and above the military, economic, technological, and ideological apparatuses (i.e., the insignia of the military) in the shaping of diasporic experience. What operates as the domain of the political in much contemporary humanities and social sciences research is, in fact, a containment of the political subject in the image of the individual and individual identity.

Again, diasporic studies is by no means unique in this delimiting of the political, but it seems a particularly odd, unnecessary, and even dangerous narrowing of the objects of inquiry — an abbreviation of inquiry itself — when one is concerned with diasporas (as our all-too-brief list above reveals). If diasporic writing contests the optimistic assumptions of cosmopolitanism *exclusively* under the rubric of individual identity politics, then it displaces the larger forces found in the insignia of the military that actually shape political identity, and abandons these for an inquiry into subjectivity. We argue, therefore, that if diasporic writing is to have the kind of political purchase that is often claimed for it, scholarship will have to recognize the wider horizons on which diasporic experience is played out.

Diaspora? This would always have been a curse. In its current sense, originating in *Deuteronomy*, diaspora itself (from the Greek translation of *za'avah* in the Hebrew scroll) is one among the catalog of curses that would befall the chosen people if they did not submit to the commandments: "thou shalt be a diaspora (or dispersion) in all kingdoms of the earth" (Deut. 28: 25). And in a rare moment of humor in John, when Jesus proposes to disappear to join "the Father who sent me," the response of the Jews to is to assume that he intends to go "into the diaspora among the gentiles" (John 7: 35). The humor can help lessen the sense of what is at stake here. One purpose of the testament of John is to demonstrate how Jesus fulfils the conditions set out in *Deuteronomy*: to show that this man was not a false prophet but the real thing. The pertinent sign must strictly be neither a sign nor a wonder, but it must make itself apparent in the absolute disappearance of Jesus from the temporal sphere. The relative disappearance of the diaspora would be the sign only of a curse. This is what resolves the difference between Old and New Testament. Jesus' disappearance must be absolute both apparently (as a sign of absence in the absence of a sign) and conspicuously (as a wonder). In this way the dichotomies of *Deuteronomy* between the law and its disobedience are resolved only in their repetition — the absolute alterity of the atemporal divine in dichotomy with the mortal dislocations of law, sovereignty, and identity in time.

It is probably no accident that this pattern, inscribed in the deep historicity of the Judaic and Christian traditions, seems to be replicated in the patterns of diaspora that we are calling Asian. The curses described in *Deuteronomy*, recognizable in contemporary contexts as the direct consequences of disasters like war (poverty, famine, displacement, separation, criminality, death, dispersion, and a host of other consequences), are formulated as a kind of deterrence. The curses will not only have been a verbal deterrence against erring from the commandments but they also would be, in their actuality, the promise of their fulfillment in advance — they would make examples of their victims: "they shall be upon thee for a sign and for a wonder [*mopheth*, i.e., something conspicuous], and upon thy seed for ever" (Deut. 28: 46).

So the law that outlines this horrific catalog of consequences for disobeying it is always and everywhere made evident by a sleight of hand that identifies existing woes as evidence for the power of the Father to visit them upon disobedient victims. Thus the curses of war, plague, famine, and drought become the signs for the powerful wrath of an almighty authority. In the phrase coined by Franco Moretti, these signs and wonders might just as well be the "signs *taken* for wonders" that ground the mystical foundations of authority that Moretti examines in his book of that title. Alluding to Moretti, Homi Bhabha addresses the issue of the ambivalence of authority in his "Signs Taken for Wonders" (Bhabha 1994), in which he analyzes three moments when texts of the civilizing mission meet with their own dislocation: the printed Bible distributed and dispersed among the colonized people of Delhi in 1817, Joseph Conrad's Marlowe coming across Towson's *Inquiry into Some Points of Seamanship*, and V. S. Naipaul's discovery of the same text in "Conrad's Darkness":

> Written as they are in the name of the father and the author, these texts of the civilizing mission immediately suggest the triumph of the colonialist movement in early English Evangelism and modern English literature.

> The discovery of the book installs the sign of appropriate representation:
> the word of God, truth, art creates conditions for a beginning, a practice
> of history and narrative. But the institution of the Word in the wilds is also
> an *Entstellung*, a process of displacement, distortion, dislocation, repetition
> — the dazzling light of literature sheds only areas of darkness. (1994:
> 105)

One interesting aspect for us in Bhabha's analysis is the way he shows
how the authorized colonial text — the word of the law itself — becomes
subject to its own curse in diaspora. In this case the distortions,
displacements, and dislocations are revealed to be functions of the law
itself — its repeatability and the inevitable difference in each repetition
as it disperses into the future of its legislations. *Deuteronomy* is already
the embodiment of its own curse in this sense, as the literal meaning of
"Deuteronomy" is "second law," but is based on a misinterpretation at a
crucial stage of the translation process. The *Devarim* (or Words) identify
themselves as a repetition by Moses of his original law. The possibility
of repetition can be seen, then, as both blessing and curse because it
gives the law its legislative possibility while simultaneously exposing it
to dislocations as it disperses into the wild.

The pattern of Bhabha's analysis turns up again in a later essay,
"Dissemination," this time locating the force of *dis*location no longer in
the structural repeatability of the law but now — much more
problematically — in the figures of the various diasporic peoples of the
contemporary world:

> At this point I must give way to the *vox populi*: to a relatively unspoken
> tradition of the people of the pagus — colonials, postcolonials, migrants,
> minorities — wandering peoples who will not be contained within the
> *Heim* of the national culture and its unisonant discourse, but are
> themselves marks of a shifting boundary that alienates the frontiers of the
> modern nation. (Bhabha 1994: 164)

And here we raise a flag of caution. This attempt to shift from a structural
phenomenon to a subjectivity resultant from it — which throughout
Bhabha's work runs alongside his more meticulous analyses of the
paradoxes of law under colonialism — works like a kind of hallucination
of alterity in the figure of the diasporic wanderer. Just as the Jews thought
that Jesus was going to disappear into the diaspora, Bhabha locates the

law's own ambivalent alterity in the figure of diasporic people. But diasporic peoples are hardly ever marks of a shifting boundary. Diaspora more often marks the steadfastness of modern national boundaries as well as the fecund reproducibility of boundaries as these boundaries re-emerge like high fences around refugee camps. We draw attention to this only to show that the valorization of alterity in contemporary work on hybridity, multiculturalism, diaspora, and so on, runs the risk of attempting in all the traditional ways to separate the blessing from the curse.

Returning briefly to the curse, what we find in *Deuteronomy* is an account of alienation:

> The stranger within thee shall get up above thee very high; and thou shalt come down very low [*ger qereb àlah maàl maàl yarad mattah mattah*]. He shall lend to thee, and thou shalt not lend to him: he shall be the head, and thou shalt be the tail. (Deut. 28: 43–4)

What this passage makes clear (despite some peculiar but interesting translation decisions among the recent Anglo-American texts) is that the question of identity can be grasped as a struggle of sovereignty, in which the force of a relative alterity plays against the force of a relative identity. The very high (*maàl maàl*) and the very low (*mattah mattah*) constitute a topology, which corresponds to an economic system (lending and borrowing) and a dynamic (heads and tails). What is at stake is the relation between sovereign and subject, which can thrive when the stranger within (*ger qereb*) is subordinate (as the borrower and the tail). The curse manifests in the stranger becoming the lender. The ascendance of the stranger within — this relative alterity — would be the curse of those dispossessed of their sovereignty — the wandering peoples identified in the citation from Bhabha — forever in debt to their own foreignness. The thing to underscore here would be that the stranger cannot be separated from its opposite — *our identity*. The blessings and curses are so constructed to reveal these alternatives as belonging to each other. For each blessing there corresponds a curse, and each correspondence follows the form of an inversion. Diaspora would thus have always been the inversion of sovereignty. And in the dialectic of the inverted world the inversion is revealed as a repetition of the same from a different viewpoint.

The *hallucination* of alterity in the figure of the diasporic wanderer, therefore, finds analogous form in the *image* of the individual that passes for the political subject in much recent research. That is, the diasporic sign of relative alterity is taken for the wonder of radical, absolute alterity and, thus, mirrors the containment of the political in individual identity politics, as if alterity could be made conspicuous in the sign of hybrid identity. Diasporic communities do not necessarily and inherently challenge the insignia of the military or the sovereignty of the nation; in fact, they do just the opposite. *They are the necessary result of state sovereignty and prove its power through their existence.* They are the cursed that prove the blessings of the state's sovereignty, and, just as important, they are the potential existential condition of the blessed. How their lives and horizons have been abbreviated — cut out and cut short — serves as warning to those still in the sovereign's good graces. Bhabha's valorization of diasporic individuals as in and of themselves challenging the "unisonant discourse" of the nation valorizes the effects of structural and systemic forces that reveal state sovereignty. The valorization of the effects diverts attention from the structural and systemic forces — the insignia of the military — and, therefore, contains and abbreviates the political subject within the domain of the individual. Such a theoretical move is itself a sign taken for a wonder because it reads the relative alterity of diaspora as a blessing rather than a curse. The state's sovereignty is not undermined by such an interpretation, only repeated — as the repetition of the law already enacted in the translation of *Devarim* as "Deuteronomy" suggests. Such readings, however, risk converting diasporic research into thaumatology, the study of wonders.

The sheer conspicuousness of diaspora leads writers like Bhabha to what seems to us to be a hasty valorization of the symptom as an alternative to, rather than as a consequence of, structural and historical conditions that also account for the generalizable global phenomena of sovereign states at war with each other. Global war is conducted in many ways (and at a range of temperatures between cold and hot) that include those conditions that we sometimes call "peace." For this reason it would be a mistake to neglect Bhabha's motivation — which in line with a number of political theorists today provokes his attempt to rethink political philosophy and political community beyond the historical precedence of sovereignty, identity (of whatever kind), and state.

Political frontiers expose communities to their others — undoubtedly — but the radical structural condition of the *frontier* itself is rarely considered to take precedence over the communities bounded by it, despite the fact that sovereignty is dependent upon the defining, policing and defense of frontiers. Communities who are dispossessed of their sovereignty of the frontier might well be taken as signs for the inadequacy of current thinking and current international practice (as in Bhabha's argument), but they probably should not be mistaken as the marks of the frontier itself. What is so enigmatic and powerful about political frontiers is that they resist such identifications. So long as there is a frontier, there is an "other" — whether any particular other shows itself or not, whence the perpetual "othering" of neighbors. But the alterity of the frontier is not itself the identity of others on the other side. Here we have an a priori condition, an irreducible structural condition that, without being identifiable as such, gives us identities in contrast with others. The relative alterity of being in-contrast-with — simultaneously a relative difference and a relative identity — simply serves the thought of the sovereign over and above the stranger inside you: the subaltern in the service of the sovereign.

The extent of the problem can be indicated if we look at a short "Postscript" to an essay, "Against the Lures of Diaspora," by Rey Chow (Chow 1993). Chow's work is relevant here because it represents a sustained attempt to address the problems of cultural displacement on a globe marked by the multiple legacies of imperialism. Chow's work often draws attention to the continued and often paradoxical imbalances produced in interactions between the West and the East: the role of Western critical discourses and the way that role changes with the subject of enunciation; the role of Western technologies in enabling non-Western cultural development; the postmodernist replication of orientalism, and so on. She too argues against the valorization of minority positions, especially those of intellectuals in diaspora, because as she sees it the valorization masks a number of hegemonic relations. Chow articulates, in conclusion, a statement that at first sight would be entirely in support of our own critical position. She writes that:

> Any attempt to deal with "women" or the "oppressed classes" in the "third world" that does not at the same time come to terms with the historical conditions of its own articulation is bound to repeat the

> exploitativeness that used to and still characterizes most "exchanges"
> between "West" and "East." (1993: 119)

The marked terms here indicate the way the mask works: women, oppressed classes, Third World, exchanges, East and West. In their valorization, these terms operate as "intangible goods," values that intellectuals trade in, a form of exchange and hegemonic oppression that simply repeats those of imperial and colonial power. And she accurately identifies how these diasporic signs can be taken for wonders:

> Like "the people," "real people," "the populace," "the peasant," "the poor,"
> "the homeless," and all such names, these signifiers *work* insofar as they
> gesture towards another place (the lack in discourse-construction) that is
> "authentic" but that cannot be admitted into the circuit of exchange.
> (1993: 118)

In Chow's account, then, these *relative* alterities give rise to the hallucination of an *absolute* alterity. But, like the alterity of the political frontier, this "other place" outside the circuit of exchange is just *not there*.

So how does Chow reconcile this admirable critical vigilance against what she calls "the lures of diaspora" with her position as a Chinese diasporic intellectual? She would seem to be taking almost exactly the contrary position to Bhabha. Bhabha's critique of the law and its dislocation in repetition certainly corresponds with Chow's critique of the hegemonic repetition of imperial force in the figure of the diasporic intellectual. But where Bhabha locates an irreducible dissonance in the figure of the homeless wanderer, in the irreducible hybridity of hybrid identity, in what he calls the "third space," Chow comes down on the side of political identity. Her counter to charges of essentialist identity politics is to affirm and avow a political identity grounded in historical materialism. It is not by chance that she can ground her position with an appeal to Hegel's dialectic:

> If we describe the postcolonial space in Hegelian terms, we can say that
> it is a space in which the object (women, minorities, other peoples)
> encounters its Notion [i.e., Concept] (criterion for testing object), or in
> which the "being-in-itself" encounters the "being-for-an-other." (Chow
> 1993: 115)

In Hegel's dialectic of experience, consciousness eventually must come to terms with itself. For Chow, Third World intellectuals in diaspora must achieve the status of conscious subjects of knowledge at the cost of the discovery of their long-term historical object-hood: "Third world intellectuals acquire and affirm their own 'consciousness' only to find, continually, that it is a 'consciousness' laden with the history of their objecthood" (1993: 115).

When they also have to come to terms with the fact that, in the "First World," they continue to be "beheld as other," the lure of diaspora no longer beckons:

> For "third world" intellectuals especially, this means that recourse to alterity
> — the other culture, nation, sex, or body in another historical time and
> geographical space — no longer suffices as a means of intervention simply
> because alterity as such is still the old pure "object" (the being-in-itself)
> that has not been dialectically grasped. Such recourse to alterity is
> repeatedly trapped within the lures of a "self"-image — a nativism — that
> is, precisely, imperialism's other. (Chow 1993: 116)

This is an ingenious explanation, the old object now valorized as interventionist diasporic subject (and thus objectified all over again).

But Chow now takes it one step further. The diasporic intellectual, lured by her own objectivity, now reproduces the hegemonic relation between orientalist discourses and the East by disguising the oppression that continues unabated in the so-called "native" lands; that is, by supporting the myth of the Chinese *zuguo*, the glorious native homeland. In other words, as we have been arguing, the hallucination of alterity in diaspora has many ways of masking wideranging political conditions. For this reason Chow recommends an unmasking policy:

> We need to unmask ourselves through a scrupulous declaration of self-
> interest. Such declaration does not clean our hands, but it prevents the
> continuance of a tendency, rather strong among "third world" intellectuals
> in diaspora as well as researchers of non-western cultures in "first world"
> nations, to sentimentalize precisely those day-to-day realities from which
> they are distanced. (1993: 117)

Here, however, it is difficult to see how Chow has escaped her own charge of essentialist identity politics. Beneath the mask (hybrid identity contributing to the sentimental image of the minority Third World subject) lies a more authentic version of Chinese diasporic identity: the one she is arguing for. (Chow's habit of putting words like "authentic" in demystifying quotation marks lends its own force to the sense of truth beneath the mask). Unmasking and demystification are both essential components of a critical vigilance against the lures of diaspora, but what now is the ground of the unmasking identity? This revelatory unmasking remains the action of the identifiable agent of identity politics. Critical and ingenious as the circuit might be, it remains circular, beginning with valorized diasporic Asian identity, passing through the revelation of unmasking, before returning that agency back to its original identity (diasporic Asian). For it would seem that no other has access to this critique. Similarly, Chow's move to separate herself from the essentialized otherness she delineates as institutional practice ironically reveals the sovereignty of the university to incorporate and domesticate dissent, in much the same way that the state displays its sovereignty through the existence of diasporas. There would seem to be no end to the power of the law to repeat itself through its dichotomies and no end to the number of shapes taken by the oscillation between sovereignty and diaspora. The canonical New Testament attempt to separate out an absolute atemporal alterity from the relative forces of the contingent temporal world emerges in a number of ways in contemporary discourses. Bhabha's hallucination of alterity in the wandering peoples of the earth and Chow's attempt to unmask the diasporic intellectual are but two such ways. Chow takes the side of contingent forces, which at least has the advantage of rendering the insignia of the military conspicuous, but which leads her to a strategy of unmasking that simply recreates the objectivity found in the Cartesian subject. And Bhabha takes the side of irreducible alterity, which has the advantage of locating the irreducible condition of the law in repetition, but which moves the focus of analysis from the structural, historical, and systemic forces that shape subjectivity to their effects.

In each case, an identity politics threatens to draw attention away from the powerful processes played out between the state and the war machine that are materialized in the insignia of the military, processes that will turn out to have little to do with individual identities but that nonetheless ground the politics of national as well as transnational identity in simultaneously diachronic and synchronic ways — in the diachrony of diasporic histories and the synchrony of globally overdetermined social relations. We are not arguing the irrelevance of individual identity in diasporic research, but rather pointing toward what is elided by an overemphasis on it and what is risked in the process of unduly and unnecessarily delimiting the diasporic research enterprise. Diasporic communities require a widened reading of their experience if the utopian discourse of cosmopolitanism operative within globalization is to be substantively challenged. If diasporic research is not so widened, and if the political remains contained in the image of the individual, diasporic communities will not only remain, as they always have, the tragic and cursed results of violence that proves the power of sovereignty; they will suffer a similar fate at the hands of our own academic research community that examines so narrowly, that so abbreviates, their situation. All that has political potential in this research will have been, therefore, successfully contained.

Notes

CHAPTER **1**

1. "The two principal factions contesting for national political power in the
   wake of British colonial administration in Singapore – a Communist faction,
   later grouped as the Barisan Socialist Party, and the social democrats
   organized as the People's Action Party, or PAP ... – both harnessed feminist
   issues to their national platforms. The first created a Singapore Women's
   federation as a front organization for revolutionary activity, and the second
   sponsored a women's league and women's subcommittees in 1956 under
   the direction of central PAP party leadership" (Heng 1997: 34–35).

CHAPTER **2**

1. Thus Menkhoff and Gerke (2002: 3–4) show that myths of the overseas
   Chinese as being all "successful economic actors" and "excellently
   networked" conceal the reality of significant disparities between different
   overseas Chinese communities and of real failures in Chinese businesses,
   and raise fears of absolute tribal loyalties among the diasporic Chinese.
2. As Saggar (1992: 120) observes, one plank of Margaret Thatcher's Tory
   regime was the presentation of a "more hospitable image towards potential
   supporters among the ethnic minorities," who became partners in the
   entrepreneurial project of the nation. Power (2001: 30) notes that *Britain's
   Richest Asians 2000*, published by Eastern Eye, is striking proof of the
   integration of at least the top echelons of Asian businessmen into the
   financial life of the nation.

3. There are numerous examples of these, representative of which are "Chinatown Video" (http://www.chinatownvideo.com.au), whose homepage features the rear view of a topless Asian woman dressed in leathers and an ammunition bandolier and carrying a gun; and "Chinatown Dreams" (http://www.asianbeauties.nu/porn/Chinatowndreams/index-adultsights.html), a bondage pornography site explicitly featuring Asian women.

4. This parallel is neither a thing of the past (of the 1960s Chinese migrant scene in Britain that is Mo's setting), nor a fictional stretch, but continues to characterize the image of the Triad today. A recent editorial in Hong Kong's *South China Morning Post*, responding to the recruitment of children by gangs lately, explains this with the fact that gangs "become a perverted substitute for family," especially if the biological family is characterized by the "poverty," "limited potential," and "broken home" that is often the case among both the poor in Hong Kong and working-class Chinese migrants overseas (reprinted in *Today*, 3 September 2001: 11).

5. There are biographical parallels: Mo's own father (as a Cantonese man who married an English woman, and moved the family to England when Mo was ten years old) similarly bears the burden of that family's cultural-geographical attenuations, and within the novel's symbolic logic would be yet another risk-bearing candidate for ritualistic violence and sacrifice.

CHAPTER 3

1. The popular conception of immigration, outlined by Robbie Goh in his introduction to this volume, as "influx of lowly qualified members of a workforce who ... will take on low-paying jobs, live in abject conditions, and contribute to urban problems," constitutes the other dimension to the particular form of economic migration that I discuss here.

2. Integration, however, remains a problematic and highly contentious issue because of vested interests inherent in multiculturalism that apparently conflict with expectations of migrants to "integrate" or "assimilate." For a discussion of the tensions arising from this conflictual desire to see migrants integrate and yet remain separate, see Hage (2000).

3 The type of nationalist rhetoric to which I am referring is explained by Ernest Gellner: "nationalism is a theory of political legitimacy," based on the principle "that the political and the national unit should be congruent" (1983: 1).

4. Gellner identifies, as "some traditions of social thought," "anarchism, Marxism — which hold that even, or especially, in an industrial order the state is dispensable" (1983: 5). Globalization, as advanced, sophisticated

industrialization, epitomizes those processes contributing to the demise and (eventual) dispensability of the state.

5. Many critics have pointed to the "subversive" and empowering effect that the concept of ambivalence introduces into grand narratives and totalizing discourses. The "openness" inherent to such a concept has been criticized for feting apolitical versions of diversity, rendering the subject the subject a free-floating signifier who stands for all and nothing at once.

6. Ambivalence here becomes twofold: that which governs the nation's drive to exclude its perceived Others, compounded by the ambivalent supplementarity of the diasporic community's status.

7. For a detailed discussion of the uses (and abuses) of positivistic images in and of grand narratives, see Zizek (1989). The hostland's positivity lies in the myth that it constructs for the imagination of a homogeneous self untainted by foreign elements. While social reality attests to a plurality of Other voices and cultures, the national imaginary locates its existence within an idealized spatiality and temporality, the boundaries of which it tries to "fix" (by nationalist rhetoric and narratives). The nation therefore idealizes and mythologizes itself, in and as an act of positive affirmation for its members, people deemed appropriate and desirable for a particular constitution that it wants inscribed onto its (imaginary) national space. The imaginary may not materialize, because its function is purely mythical; to exist as the "homeland" for which its diaspora may retain positive images, while also acting as a propagandist vehicle for (re)validating the nation as an ideal space, in which its people are encouraged to remain. By constantly projecting positive images of itself, the nation (as homeland) is able to generate a sense of empowerment for both its local and diasporic communities. The homeland thus provides an image-based ("imaginary") identification for the diaspora, while mnemonic devices (memory, distortion, and idealization) and past events work to enhance that image-based identification of the homeland, thereby imbuing the image with symbolic significance/signification. I would argue that this is where imaginary and symbolic identification can be said to have collapsed into each other, because where there once was a physical image, retrospection has led to an accumulation of other images, or a distortion of that image, so that it now takes on mythical qualities, and past events take on a "supernatural reality" (Brennan 1990: 45).

8. Diasporic relocation is not always a consequence of economic factors, as highlighted by recent political upheavals. Under these conditions, the extent to which the diaspora idealizes its homeland will be considerably attenuated. Even so, relocation to a new country can still generate feelings of resentment by those "left behind."

9. Amy Tan's *The Hundred Secret Senses* (1996) expresses the opinion that "it's hip to be ethnic," and which has been literalized in North America, where "Hapa," or mixed-race Asians, are fast gaining street credibility and are becoming a prominent feature of the demographic landscape. Inundated with images of Hapa youth in fashion magazines and on billboards, a Vancouver daily has hailed the Hapa face as the ultimate fashion accessory one can acquire (*Vancouver Sun* 26 May 2001: E11). Yet, we have to note that the cultural capital derived from being ethnic is available to only those familiar with and able to access popular culture (and its language), i.e., a specific demographic. This sort of cultural capital does not accrue, however, to other sectors of the diaspora, such as older-generation migrants.

10. In the Hapa instance, the minority literally becomes an "absolute entity" whose image is a commercially viable and exploitable resource.

11. On the "fakeness" of experience, see Brah (1996), who argues that "experience does not reflect a pre-given 'reality' but is the discursive effect of processes that construct what we call reality" (Brah 1996: 11). However, the question then follows, "how do we think about the materiality of that which we call real?"

12. See Chow (1993), Chapter 2. "Where Have All the Natives Gone?"

13. This is also the same charge leveled against Charles Taylor's advocating of "equal recognition" in "The Politics of Recognition" (1994).

14. This observation is true to some extent because many novels written and published by the old diaspora were concerned with recovering their histories, a recuperative project aimed at (re)telling the tales of the first-comers to the new land (although written/narrated by the later generations).

15. Several recent films have highlighted the politics and problematics of diasporic cross-cultural experience, most significantly of Indians in Britain (I am referring to the films *East is East* [1999] and *Bend It Like Beckham* [2002]). Diasporic Asians in North America have had aspects of their lives portrayed in films such as *The Wedding Banquet* (1993), *Double Happiness* (1994), and in Australia, *Floating Life* (1995) and William Yang's autobiographical photo-documentary *Sadness* (1996).

16. In *White Nation*, Hage shows how the lack of a mainstream political language has led to the experience of white multiculturalism as loss. Coupled with "the discourse of Anglo-decline" (Hage 2000: 20), the political language that emerges is one of "a home-grown Australian neo-fascism."

17. In Australia, Prime Minister John Howard's tough stand against asylum seekers has ensured election victory (in the November 2001 elections), while others, especially those in the business sector, have suffered economically for taking a sympathetic stance on the refugee issue (as highlighted at a

public forum, "Let's Talk About Race — Culture, Privilege and Prejudice," held in Perth, Western Australia, 12 September 2002).

18. Most notably in *The Joy Luck Club* by Amy Tan, which contextualizes and juxtaposes historical border crossings with present-day events. Other Chinese-North American works include Wayson Choy's *The Jade Peony*, Denise Chong's *The Concubine's Children*, and to a certain extent, Sky Lee's *Disappearing Moon Cafe*.

19. This concept of a future tense is derived from, and also supplements, Paul Gilroy's discussion of diaspora in his "It Ain't Where You're From, It's Where You're At … : The Dialectics of Diasporic Identification" (1991).

20. Echoing Radhakrishnan's point "[all] hybridities are not equal" (1996: 159).

CHAPTER **4**

1. The Immigration Restriction Act, also known as the White Australia policy, was the first act passed by the newly federated Australian Parliament in 1901. It was gradually eased after World War II, but it was not until the early 1970s that the Whitlam government removed all reference to ethnic origin from its immigration policy.

2. I am referring specifically to the *Tampa* incident of August-September 2001, when the Norwegian ship *Tampa* rescued almost 500 asylum seekers, mostly from Afghanistan, bound for Australia on a nonseaworthy Indonesian vessel. The *Tampa* was refused entry to an Australian port, and the asylum seekers were eventually taken to the tiny island of Nauru for Australian authorities to process their applications. In order to ban their entry, the government had to rush through Parliament legislation similar to that of Premier Henry Parkes in his effort to ban entry to the Chinese would-be immigrants of 1888. In the subsequent weeks, several groups of boat people were intercepted by the Australian navy and turned away from Australia. The matter became a major issue in the run-up to the Australian election of 10 November 2001. Most commentators agree that the election victory of Prime Minister John Howard can in large part be attributed to his uncompromising stand on the question of asylum seekers (for a detailed analysis of the *Tampa* affair, see Marr and Wilkinson 2003).

3. The "banana," whether evoked in scorn, jest, or pride, is the East Asian version of the "coconut" of the black diaspora: an image for someone who is "yellow" (i.e., racially marked) on the outside, but white on the inside, that is, culturally assimilated to a Western way of life and Western standards of thinking.

4. I am once again referring to the *Tampa* affair and subsequent debates in the Australian media.

5. It is common for British and American migrants to wait for decades before seeking citizenship, whereas immigrants from, for example, the People's Republic of China generally take out Australian citizenship as soon as they become eligible.

6. For a detailed discussion of the Giese and Sang Ye compilations, see Ommundsen 2002.

7. I would like at this point to acknowledge the contribution of Dr Ouyang Yu. Without his linguistic and cultural competence, and his extensive research skills, this project would not have been possible.

8. A large number of PRC migrants initially came to Australia in the late 1980s and early 1990s on temporary visas to attend short-term English courses. After the events of Tiananmen Square in June 1989, their visas were extended and many (some 40,000 to 50,000) have since obtained permanent residence or citizenship.

CHAPTER 5

1. For the involvement of intellectuals in peasant rebellions see Spivak (1985) and Devi (1995). For a history of the Naxalites see Banerjee (1984), Franda (1971), and Sen et al. (1978).

2. A comparison between Mukherjee's novel and Mahasweta Devi's short story "Draupadi" (1995) reveals an alternate treatment of the topic of subaltern agency and female participation in the Naxal movement. In Devi's story, Dopdi, a female revolutionary, is raped by several members of the police force and in her defiance, Dopdi refuses to clothe herself in front of the Senanayak or the police chief, thus challenging the masculinity of her rapists.

3. Thomas Macaulay's 1835 "Minute" proposed to form "a class of interpreters between us and the millions whom we govern – a class of persons Indian in blood and colour, but English in tastes, in opinions, in morals and in intellect" (cited in Bhabha 1994: 87).

4. In her interview with Michael Connell, Mukherjee says: "There is no reason why we should have to appropriate – wholesale and intact – the white, upper-middle-class women's tools and rhetoric" (Connell et al. 1990: 22). She later adds: "But I do disapprove of the imperialism of the feminists, American, and perhaps European feminists, but especially the American feminists of the mid-70s who felt that they could go to Iran and tell the Iranian women what to do" (1990: 23). But as I have shown, Mukherjee does appropriate the tools and rhetoric that she so disdains in her interview.

5. Such notions about Third World literature are not uncommon among cultural critics themselves. See Saba Mahmood's refutation of Stuart Hall's

comments in "Cultural Studies and Ethnic Absolutism: Comments on Stuart Hall's 'Culture, Community, Nation'" (Mahmood 1996). Mahmood criticizes Hall for possessing "the suspicion and dismissal with which most intellectuals of widely divergent political persuasions treat contemporary social movements" (1996: 2).

6. A cover blurb quoted from a review in the Baltimore *Sun* describes *Jasmine* as: "Poignant ... Heartrending ... The story of the transformation of an Indian village girl whose grandmother wants to marry her off at 11, into an American woman who finally thinks for herself." Ideals of south Asian women are marketed not only as an exploited and oppressed group but also as a foil for the free and independent "American woman."

CHAPTER 7

1. In the Ahmad text, Homi Bhabha is cited from *The Location of Culture* (1994: 187).
2. In particular the chapter "Post-Colonial DestiNations," 160–89.
3. Here reference is made to the late eighteenth-century Farsi novel *Nashtar*, literally "the surgeon's knife," that is the tragic separation of a pair of lovers, whose plight is reminiscent of Romeo and Juliet, insofar as their forbidden love comes to an end because of mischance and misunderstanding.

CHAPTER 8

1. As in the Chinese Exclusion Act of 1882, the ban on Japanese and Korean immigration in Teddy Roosevelt's "Gentleman's Agreement" of 1907, the "Asiatic Barred Zone Act" of 1917, the National Origins Act of 1924, the Tydings-McDuffie Act of 1934 that recategorized Filipinos as aliens.
2. As in the Cooper's Act of 1902 prohibiting Filipinos from owning property, voting, operating businesses, etc.; and the internment of American citizens of Japanese ancestry under Executive Order 9066.
3. For a discussion of related issues, see David Leiwei Li's analysis of Asian-American citizenship in the introduction to his book *Imagining the Nation: Asian American Literature and Cultural Consent* (1998).
4. Li An's confrontation with English language and literature parallels Shirley Lim's own experience as a student in Malaysia, one of many such autobiographical crossovers in the novel. In the preface to her book *Writing South/East Asia in English*, Lim makes reference to her "conversion" experience at the University of Malaya in 1966: "This undergraduate conversion, the belief in the necessity for a literature of one's own, has remained my unshakable creed, even as the identity of 'one' — under the

multiple deconstructive interrogations of psychology, anthropology, sociology, global economics, politics, linguistics, revisionist history — has grown progressively more shaky" (1994: xi). Lim's autobiography, *Among the White Moon Faces*, reveals more nonfictional crossovers with the fictional world of the novel.

5. The teasing Suyin endures works within *Joss & Gold* to highlight the existence of racism within Asia, and to therefore mark Singapore *as relatively tolerant* in comparison to the Malaysia and United States constructed by the novel. Intolerance in the US toward immigrants is suggested by several conversations in the New York segment of the novel, for instance when Dan argues that it is dangerous to let Indian immigrants work on US defense systems, whereas European immigrants are acceptable because they are "from our part of the world" (Lim 2001: 125). Even so, I find it difficult to reconcile the novel's portrayal of intolerance with personal and anecdotal evidence I have gathered on the acceptance of Eurasian children in Singapore schools. Students in my Transnational Literature module at the National University of Singapore expressed surprise at Suyin's mistreatment; they concurred with one another that Eurasian children were not teased, but were actually privileged in their schools by teachers and peers alike.

CHAPTER **9**

1. A consideration of the potential problems for the politics of Asian American studies as generated by a move toward favoring diasporic perspectives is offered in Wong (1995).
2. Dirlik (1999) registers this point; for further discussion of transnational and national paradigms in Asian American literary studies, see Lee (1999).
3. For an important meditation on the complex relationship of gender, migration, and information technology to the phenomenon of the global city, see Sassen (1998).
4. According to Ong (1999: 6), "'Flexible citizenship' refers to the cultural logics of capitalist accumulation, travel, and displacement that induce subjects to respond fluidly and opportunistically to changing political-economic conditions."
5. For an important work analyzing the intersection of feminist theory with modernist, postmodernist, and postcolonialist discourses, see Grewal and Kaplan (1994). A fine collection of critical essays dealing with the relationship between gay literature and the thematics of AIDS is offered in Murphy and Poirier (1993). For a contribution to the building of an artistic and critical tradition predicated upon the gay experience, see Bergman (1991).

References

INTRODUCTION

Alexander, C. (2000) "(Dis)Entangling the 'Asian Gang': Ethnicity, Identity, Masculinity." In *Un/settled Multiculturalisms: Diasporas, Entanglements, Transruptions*. Ed. B. Hesse. London: Zed Books, 123–47.

Bakhtin, M. M. (1981) *The Dialogic Imagination*. Ed. M. Holquist. Trans. C. Emerson and M. Holquist. Austin: University of Texas Press.

Bhabha, H. (1994) *The Location of Culture*. London: Routledge.

Chua, B. H. (1998) "Culture, Multiracialism, and National Identity in Singapore." In *Trajectories: Inter-Asia Cultural Studies*. Ed. K.-H. Chen. New York: Routledge, 186–205.

Chuh, K. and K. Shimakawa. (2001) "Introduction: Mapping Studies in the Asian Diaspora." In *Orientations: Mapping Studies in the Asian Diaspora*. Ed. K. Chuh and K. Shimakawa. Durham, N.C.: Duke University Press, 1–21.

Croucher, S. L. (1997) *Imagining Miami: Ethnic Politics in a Postmodern World*. Charlottesville: University Press of Virginia.

Economist, The (2002) "Who Gains From Immigration?" *The Economist* 29 June–5 July, 55–6.

Goldsmith, W. W. (2000) "From the Metropolis to Globalization: The Dialectics of Race and Urban Form." In *Globalizing Cities: A New Spatial Order?* Ed. P. Marcuse and R. Van Kempen. Oxford: Blackwell, 37–55.

Holston, J. and A. Appadurai (1999) "Cities and Citizenship." In *Cities and Citizenship*. Ed. J. Holston. Durham, N.C.: Duke University Press, 1–18.

Kain, G. (ed.) (1997) *Ideas of Home: Literature of Asian Migration*. East Lansing: Michigan State University Press.

King, A. D. (1976) *Colonial Urban Development: Culture, Social Power and Environment*. London: Routledge and Kegan Paul.

Li, D. L. (1998) *Imagining the Nation: Asian American Literature and Cultural Consent*. Stanford, Calif.: Stanford University Press.

Ling, J. (1998) *Narrating Nationalisms: Ideology and Form in Asian American Literature*. New York: Oxford University Press.

Lyotard, J.-F. (1992) "Answering the Question: What is Postmodernism?" In *Modernism/Postmodernism*. Ed. P. Brooker. London: Longman, 139–50.

Ong, A. (1999) *Flexible Citizenship: The Cultural Logics of Transnationality*. Durham, N.C.: Duke University Press.

Parker, D. (2000) "The Chinese Takeaway and the Diasporic Habitus: Space, Time and Power Geometries." In *Un/settled Multiculturalisms: Diasporas, Entanglements, Transruptions*. Ed. B. Hesse. London: Zed Books, 73–95.

Perry, M., L. Kong, and B. Yeoh. (1997) *Singapore: A Developmental City State*. New York: Wiley.

Pinderhughes, D. M. (1997) "Race and Ethnicity in the City." In *Handbook of Research on Urban Politics and Policy in the United States*. Ed. R. K. Vogel. Westport, Conn.: Greenwood Press, 75–108.

Ratcliffe, P. (1997) "'Race, Housing and the City." In *Transforming Cities: Contested Governance and New Spatial Divisions*. Ed. N. Jewson and S. MacGregor. London: Routledge, 87–99.

Sassen, S. (1999) "Whose City Is It? Globalization and the Formation of New Claims." In *The Urban Moment: Cosmopolitan Essays on the Late-Twentieth-Century City*. Ed. R. A. Beauregard and S. Body-Gendrot. Thousand Oaks, CA: Sage Publications, 99–118.

Sung, G. (2001) "Immigrants Take the Rap for Europe's Ills." *Straits Times* 2 October, 11.

Van Hear, N. (1998) *New Diasporas: The Mass Exodus, Dispersal and Regrouping of Migrant Communities*. London: UCL Press.

Virilio, P. (1998) *The Virilio Reader*. Ed. J. Der Derian. Malden, Mass.: Blackwell.

Yeoh, B. S. A. and S. Huang (1998) "Negotiating Public Space: Strategies and Styles of Migrant Female Domestic Workers in Singapore." *Urban Studies* 35: 3, 583–602.

CHAPTER 1

Ang, I. (1992) "On not Speaking Chinese: Diasporic Identification and Postmodern Ethnicity." Paper resented at the conference "Trajectories: Towards an International Cultural Studies," Taipei, Taiwan, 5–19 July.

————. (1993) "The Differential Politics of Chineseness." *Communal/Plural* 3. 1: 17–26.

————. (1996) "The Curse of the Smile: Ambivalence and the 'Asian' Woman in Australian Multiculturalism." *Feminist Review* 52 (Spring): 36–49.

Ang, I. and J. Stratton (1995) "Straddling East and West: Singapore's Paradoxical Search for a National Identity." In *Asia and Pacific Inscriptions*. Ed. S. Perera. Melbourne: Meridian Books.

Ang-Lygate, M. (1997) "Charting the Spaces of (Un)location: On Theorizing Diaspora." In *Black British Feminisms: A Reader*. Ed. H. S. Mizra. London: Routledge.

Ashcroft, B. (ed.) (1995) *The Post-Colonial Studies Reader*. New York: Routledge.

Ashcroft, B., G. Griffiths, and H. Tiffin (1989) *The Empire Writes Back: Theory and Practice in Post-colonial Literatures*. London: Routledge.

Bhabha, H. (1994) *The Location of Culture*. New York/London: Routledge.

Brooks, A. (2003) "Intersecting Tensions of Gender, Race, Ethnicity and Class in Southeast Asia." *Asian Journal of Social Sciences* 31: 86–106.

————. (1997) *Postfeminisms: Feminism, Cultural Theory and Cultural Forms*. London: Routledge.

Derrida, J. (1978) *Writing and Difference*. London: Routledge and Kegan Paul.

Dirlik, A. (1997) "The Postcolonial Aura: Third World Criticism in the Age of Global Capitalism." In *Dangerous Liaisons: Gender, Nation and Postcolonial Perspectives*. Ed. A. McClintock, A. Mufti, and E. Shohat. Minneapolis: University of Minnesota Press.

Goh, C. T. (1993) "Guarding the Sacred Institutions of Marriage and the Family." In *Speeches: A Bi-Monthly Selection of Ministerial Speeches*, May-June: 28–33.

Hall, S. (1996) "When Was the "Post-colonial"? Thinking at the Limit." In *The Post-Colonial Question*. Ed. I. Chambers and L. Curti. New York: Routledge.

Heng, G. (1997) "'A Great Way to Fly': Nationalism, the State, and Varieties of Third World Feminism." In *Feminist Genealogies, Colonial Legacies, Democratic Futures*. Ed. M. J. Alexander and C. T. Mohanty. London: Routledge.

Heng, G. and J. Devan (1995) "State Fatherhood: The Politics of Nationalism, Sexuality and Race in Singapore." In *Bewitching Women and Pious Men: Gender and Body Politics in Southeast Asia*. Ed. A. Ong and M. G. Peletz. Berkeley: University of California Press.

Lyons, L. (2000) "Disrupting the Centre: Interrogating an 'Asianist Feminist Identity.'" *Communal/Plural* 8. 1: 65–79.

Morris-Suzuki, T. (1998) "Invisible Countries: Japan and the Asian Dream." *Asian Studies Review* 22. 1 (March): 5–22.

Ong, A. (1999) *Flexible Citizenship: The Cultural Logics of Transnationality*. Durham, N.C.: Duke University Press.

Purushotam, N. (1998) "Between Compliance and Resistance: Women and the

Middle Class Way of Life in Singapore." In *Gender and Power in Affluent Asia*. Ed. K. Sen and M. Stivens. London: Routledge.

Said, E. (1978) *Orientalism*. Harmondsworth: Penguin.

――――. (1993) *Culture and Imperialism*. London: Vintage.

Spoonley, P. (1995) "The Challenges of Post-Colonialism." *Sites: A Journal of South Pacific Cultural Studies* 30 (Autumn): 44–68.

Stivens, M. (1998) "Theorising Gender, Power and Modernity in Affluent Asia." In *Gender and Power in Affluent Asia*. Ed. K. Sen and M. Stivens. London: Routledge.

――――. (2000) "Reinventing the 'Asian Family': 'Asian Values,' Globalisation and Cultural Contest in Southeast Asia." Paper given at the conference on "Families in the Global Age," Singapore, 4–6 October.

Stratton, J. and I. Ang (1994) "Multicultural Imagined Communities: Cultural Diversity and National Identity in Australia and the U.S.A." *Continuum* 9. 2: 124–58.

Suleri, S. (1995) "From 'Women Skin Deep: Feminism and the Postcolonial Condition.'" In *The Post-Colonial Studies Reader*. Ed. B. Ashcroft, G. Griffiths, and H. Tiffin. New York: Routledge.

Teo, H.-M. (2000) *Love and Vertigo*. St. Leonards, N.S.W.: Allen and Unwin.

Trinh T. M. (1991) *When the Moon Waxes Red: Representation, Gender and Cultural Politics*. London: Routledge.

CHAPTER 2

Alexander, C. (2000) "(Dis)Entangling the 'Asian Gang': Ethnicity, Identity, Masculinity." In *Un/settled Multiculturalisms: Diasporas, Entanglements, Transruptions*. Ed. B. Hesse. London: Zed Books, 123–7.

Chaliand, G. and J.-P. Rageau (1995) *The Penguin Atlas of the Diasporas*. Trans. A. M. Berrett. New York: Viking.

Cunningham, S. and J. Sinclair (ed.) (2001) *Floating Lives: The Media and Asian Diasporas*. Lanham, Md.: Rowman and Littlefield.

Deleuze, G. and F. Guattari (1984) *Anti-Oedipus: Capitalism and Schizophrenia*. Trans. R. Hurley, M. Seem, and H. R. Lane. London: Athlone Press.

FindFamilyFun (Online) "Ethnic Adventures — Chinatown — Vancouver." Http://www.findfamilyfun.com/chinatown.htm [date accessed: 1 September 2001].

Foong, W. W. (2001) "Jet's Set to Soar." *The Straits Times*, 16 July: L4.

Goldsmith, W. M. (2000) "From the Metropolis to Globalization: The Dialectics of Race and Urban Form." In *Globalizing Cities: A New Spatial Order?* Ed. P. Marcuse and R. Van Kempen. Oxford: Blackwell, 37–55.

Hall, S. (2000) "Conclusion: The Multi-Cultural Question." In *Un/settled*

Multiculturalisms: Diasporas, Entanglements, Transruptions. Ed. Barnor Hesse. London: Zed Books, 209–41.

Hartmann, P. and C. Husband (1974) *Racism and the Mass Media*. London: David-Poynter.

Ho-Down Chinatown (Online) "The Ultimate Monkey Style Kung-Fu School." Http://www.utero.se/kungfu/index.html [date accessed: 1 September 2001].

Holston, J. and A. Appadurai (1999) "Cities and Citizenship." In *Cities and Citizenship*. Ed. J. Holston. Durham, N.C.: Duke University Press, 1–20.

Kingston, M. H. (1990) *Tripmaster Monkey: His Fake Book*. New York: Vintage International.

Kotkin, J. (1993) *Tribes: How Race, Religion, and Identity Determine Success in the New Global Economy*. New York: Random House.

Lee, A. (2001a) "Asians in British Town Riot after Cabby is Beaten." *Straits Times*, 26 June: 9.

————. (2001b) "Glasgow Youths Kill Turkish Asylum Seeker." *Straits Times*, 8 August: 15.

Lester, M. L. (dir.) (1991) *Showdown in Little Tokyo*.

Lever-Tracy, C., D. Ip, and N. Tracy (1996) *The Chinese Diaspora and Mainland China: An Emerging Economic Synergy*. Houndmills: Macmillan.

Menkhoff, T. and S. Gerke (2002) "Introduction: Asia's Transformation and the Role of the Ethnic Chinese." In *Chinese Entrepreneurship and Asian Business Networks*. Ed. T. Menkhoff and S. Gerke. London: RoutledgeCurzon, 3–20.

Mo, T. (1982) *Sour Sweet*. London: Sphere Books.

Parker, D. (2000) "The Chinese Takeaway and the Diasporic Habitus: Space, Time and Power Geometries." In *Un/settled Multiculturalisms: Diasporas, Entanglements, Transruptions*. Ed. Barnor Hesse. London: Zed Books, 73–95.

Partridge, J. (1999) "The Changing Horizon of Literary Chinatown: Reception and the Ethnic-Author Function." Unpublished Ph.D. thesis, National University of Singapore.

Power, C. (2001) "The House Divided." *Newsweek*, 13 August: 30–1.

Saggar, S. (1992) *Race and Politics in Britain*. New York: Harvester Wheatsheaf.

Sassen, S. (1996) "Analytic Borderlands: Race, Gender and Representation in the New City." In *Re-Presenting the City: Ethnicity, Capital and Culture in the Twenty-First Century Metropolis*. Ed. A. D. King. Houndmills: Macmillan, 183–202.

————. (1999) "Whose City Is It? Globalization and the Formation of New Claims." In *The Urban Moment: Cosmopolitan Essays on the Late-Twentieth-Century City*. Ed. R. A. Beauregard and S. Body-Gendrot. Thousand Oaks: Sage Publications, 99–118.

Solomos, J. (1989) *Race and Racism in Britain*. Houndmills: Macmillan.

Straits Times, The (2001) "Gang Rapists to Face Harsher Penalties in Aussie State." *Straits Times,* 27 August: 11.

Wilson, C. C. and F. Gutierrez (1995) *Race, Multiculturalism, and the Media: From Mass to Class Communication.* Thousand Oaks, CA: Sage Publications.

Wilson, S. (Online) "Crime-Z-Landmap" (An Art Installation). Http://userwww.sfsu.edu/~netart/crimezy/crimemap2.html [date accessed: 1 September 2001].

CHAPTER 3

Ang, I. (1992) "Migrations of Chineseness." *SPAN* 34 and 35 (October/May): 3–15.

————. (2001) *On Not Speaking Chinese: Living Between Asia and the West.* London: Routledge.

Appadurai, A. (ed.) (1986) *The Social Life of Things: Commodities in Cultural Perspective.* Cambridge: Cambridge University Press.

Bhabha, H. (ed.) (1990) *Nation and Narration.* London: Routledge.

————. (1994) *The Location of Culture.* London: Routledge.

Brah, A. (1996) *Cartographies of Diaspora: Contesting Identities.* London: Routledge.

Brennan, G. (1993) "The Baby Trade: The Political Economy of Inter-Country Adoption." In *Multicultural Citizens: The Philosophy and Politics of Identity.* Ed. C. Kukathas. St. Leondard's, N.S.W.: Multicultural Research Program, Centre for Independent Studies, 159–73.

Brennan, T. (1990) "The National Longing for Form." In *Nation and Narration.* Ed. H. Bhabha. London: Routledge, 44–70.

Chicago Cultural Studies Group (1992) "Critical Multiculturalism." *Critical Inquiry* 18. 3: 530–55.

Chong, D. (1995) *The Concubine's Children.* Toronto: Penguin.

Chow, R. (1991) *Woman and Chinese Modernity: The Politics of Reading Between West and East.* Minneapolis: University of Minnesota Press.

————. (1993) *Writing Diaspora: Tactics of Intervention in Contemporary Cultural Studies.* Bloomington: Indiana University Press.

Choy, W. (1995) *The Jade Peony.* New York: Picador.

Derrida, J. (1992) *Acts of Literature.* Ed. D. Attridge. New York: Routledge.

Fanon, F. (1970) *Black Skin, White Masks.* London: Paladin.

Fish, S. (1997) "Boutique Multiculturalism, or Why Liberals Are Incapable of Thinking About Hate Speech." *Critical Inquiry* 23. 2: 378–95.

Gellner, E. (1983) *Nations and Nationalism.* Oxford: Blackwell.

Gilroy, P. (1991) "It Ain't Where You're From, It's Where You're At …: The Dialectics of Diasporic Identification." *Third Text: Third World Perspectives on Contemporary Art and Culture* 13 (Winter): 3–16.

————. (1993) *The Black Atlantic: Modernity and Double Consciousness.* Cambridge, Mass.: Harvard University Press.

Gordon, A. and C. Newfield (ed.) (1996) *Mapping Multiculturalism.* Minneapolis: University of Minnesota Press.

Gunew, S. (1993) "Against Multiculturalism: Rhetorical Images." In *Multiculturalism, Difference and Postmodernism.* Ed. G. L. Clark, D. Forbes, and R. Francis. Melbourne: Longman, 38–53.

Hall, S. (1990) "Cultural Identity and Diaspora." In *Identity: Community, Culture, Difference.* Ed. J. Rutherford. London: Lawrence and Wishart, 222–37.

Hage, G. (1994) "Locating Multiculturalism's Other: A Critique of Practical Tolerance." *New Formations* 24 (Winter): 19–34.

————. (2000) *White Nation: Fantasies of White Supremacy in a Multicultural Society.* Sydney: Routledge.

Huyssen, A. (2000) "Present Pasts: Media, Politics, Amnesia." *Public Culture* 12. 1: 21–38.

Lee, S. (1991) *Disappearing Moon Cafe.* Seattle: Seal Press.

Radhakrishnan, R. (1996) *Diasporic Mediations: Between Home and Location.* Minneapolis: University of Minnesota Press.

Renan, E., (1990) "What is a nation?" *In Nation and Narration.* Ed. H. Bhabha. London: Routledge, 8–22.

Spivak, G. C. (1993) *Outside in the Teaching Machine.* New York: Routledge.

Tan, A. (1989) *The Joy Luck Club.* New York: Ballantine Books.

————. (1996) *The Hundred Secret Senses.* London: HarperCollins.

Taylor, C. (1994) "The Politics of Recognition." In *Multiculturalism: Examining The Politics of Recognition.* Ed. A. Guttman. Princeton, N.J.: Princeton University Press, 25–73.

Trinh, M.-H. (1989) *Woman, Native, Other: Writing Postcoloniality and Feminism.* Bloomington: Indiana University Press.

Vancouver Sun, The (2001) "Eurasian Persuasion: A Worldwide Trend." *Vancouver Sun,* 26 May: E11.

Zizek, S. (1989) *The Sublime Object of Ideology.* London: Verso.

CHAPTER **4**

Ang, I. (2001) *On Not Speaking Chinese: Living Between Asia and the West.* London: Routledge.

Balibar, E. (1991) "Is There a 'Neo-Racism'?" In *Race, Nation, Class: Ambiguous Identities.* Ed. E. Balibar and I. Wallerstein. London: Verso.

Broinowski, A. (2001) "Chinese Remonstrances." In *Bastard Moons: Essays on Chinese-Australian Writing.* Ed. W. Ommundsen. Melbourne: Otherland Publications, 7–22.

Castro, B. (1983) *Birds of Passage*. Sydney: Allen & Unwin.

Cunningham, S. and J. Sinclair (ed.) (2000) *Floating Lives: The Media and Asian Diasporas*. St. Lucia: University of Queensland Press.

Delanty, G. (2000) *Citizenship in a Global Age: Society, Culture, Politics*. Buckingham: Open University Press.

Docker, J. and G. Fischer (ed.) (2000) *Race, Colour and Identity in Australia and New Zealand*. Sydney: University of New South Wales Press.

Donald, J. (1996) "The Citizen and the Man About Town." In *Questions of Cultural Identity*. Ed. S. Hall and P. du Gay. London: Sage, 170–90.

Giese, D. (1997) *Astronauts, Lost Souls and Dragons*. St. Lucia: University of Queensland Press.

Hage, G. (1998) *White Nation: Fantasies of White Supremacy in a Multicultural Society*. Sydney: Pluto Press.

Ip, D. et al. (1994) *Images of Asians in Multicultural Australia*. Sydney: Multicultural Centre, University of Sydney.

Khoo, T. (2001) "Re-siting Australian Identity: Configuring the Chinese Citizen in Diana Giese's *Astronauts, Lost Souls and Dragons* and William Yang's *Sadness*." In *Bastard Moons: Essays on Chinese-Australian Writing*. Ed. W. Ommundsen. Melbourne: Otherland Publications, 95–109.

Li, D. L. (2001) "On Ascriptive and Acquisitive Americanness: *The Accidental Asian* and the Illogic of Assimilation." Paper presented to the conference "Asian Diasporas and Cultures: Globalization, Hybridity, Intertextuality." National University of Singapore, 5–7 September.

Ling, C. (2001) *Plantings in a New Land: Stories of Survival, Endurance and Emancipation*. Brisbane: Society of Chinese Australian Academics of Queensland.

Marr, D. and M. Wilkinson (2003) *Dark Victory*. Sydney: Allen and Unwin.

Morley, D. (1996) "EurAm, Modernity, Reason and Alterity." In *Stuart Hall: Critical Dialogues in Cultural Studies*. Ed. D. Morley and K.-H. Chen. London: Routledge, 326–60.

Ommundsen, W. (ed.) (2001) *Bastard Moons: Essays on Chinese-Australian Writing*. Melbourne: Otherland Publications.

————. (2002) "Of Dragons and Devils: Chinese-Australian Life Stories." *JASAL* 1. 1: 67–80.

Pakulski, J. (1997) "Cultural Citizenship." *Citizenship Studies* 1. 1: 73–86.

Parker, D. (2003) "Dissidence and the Danger of Cosmopolitanism." *Asian Studies Review*. 27.2: 153–79.

Rolls, E. (1992) *Sojourners*. St. Lucia: University of Queensland Press.

————. (1996) *Citizens*. St. Lucia: University of Queensland Press.

Rose, N. (1996) "Identity, Genealogy, History." In *Questions of Cultural Identity*. Ed. S. Hall and P. du Gay. London: Sage, 128–50.

Sang, Y. (1996) *The Year the Dragon Came*. St. Lucia: University of Queensland Press.

Sheehan, P. (1998) *Among the Barbarians: The Dividing of Australia*. Sydney: Random House.

Shen, Y. (2001) *Dragon Seed in the Antipodes: Chinese-Australian Autobiographies*. Melbourne: Melbourne University Press.

Stevenson, N. (1997) "Globalization, National Cultures and Cultural Citizenship." *The Sociological Quarterly* 38. 1: 41–66.

————. (2001) "Culture and Citizenship: An Introduction." In *Culture and Citizenship*. Ed. N. Stevenson. London: Sage, 1–10.

Stratton, J. (1998) *Race Daze: Australia in Identity Crisis*. Sydney: Pluto Press.

Turner, B. S. (2001) "Outline of a General Theory of Cultural Citizenship." In *Culture and Citizenship*. Ed. N. Stevenson. London: Sage, 11–32.

CHAPTER 5

Ahmad, A. (1992) *In Theory: Classes, Nations, Literatures*. New York: Verso.

Ashcroft, B., G. Griffiths, and H. Tiffin (1989) *The Empire Writes Back: Theory and Practice in Post-Colonial Literatures*. London: Routledge.

Banerjee, Sumanta. (1984) *India's Simmering Revolution: The Naxalite Uprising*. London: Zed.

Bhabha, H. K. (ed.) (1990) *Nation and Narration*. London: Routledge.

————. (1994) *The Location of Culture*. New York: Routledge.

Bhatnagar, R., L. Chatterjee, and R. S. Rajan (1990) "Interview with Gayatri Spivak." In *The Post-Colonial Critic: Interviews, Strategies, Dialogues*. Ed. S. Harasym. New York: Routledge, 67–74.

Brennan, T. (1989) "Cosmopolitans and Celebrities." *Race and Class* 31. 1: 1–19.

Connell, M., J. Grearson, and T. Grimes (1990) "An Interview with Bharati Mukherjee." *Iowa Review* 20. 3: 7–32.

Devi, M. (1995) "Draupadi." In *Imaginary Maps: Three Stories*. Trans. G. C. Spivak. New York: Routledge.

Fanon, F. (1990) *The Wretched of the Earth*. Trans. C. Farrington. Harmondsworth: Penguin.

Franda, Marcus F. (1971) *Radical Politics in West Bengal*. Cambridge: MIT.

Grewal, I. (1995) "The Postcolonial, Ethnic Studies, and the Diaspora: The Contexts of Ethnic Immigrant/Migrant Cultural Studies in the US." *Socialist Review* 4. 4: 45–75.

Guha, R. (1982) *Subaltern Studies* 1: *Writings on South Asian History and Society*. Delhi: Oxford University Press.

Gunew, S. (1990) "Questions of Multi-Culturalism: Interview with Gayatri Spivak." In *The Post-Colonial Critic: Interviews, Strategies, Dialogues*. Ed. S. Harasym. New York: Routledge, 59–66.

Jameson, F. (1986) "Third World Literature in the Era of Multinational Capitalism." *Social Texts* 15. 3: 65–88.

Mahmood, S. (1996) "Cultural Studies and Ethnic Absolutism: Comments on Stuart Hall's `Culture, Community, Nation.'" *Cultural Studies* 10. 1: 1–11.

Mani, L. (1987) "Contentious Traditions: The Debate on *Sati* in Colonial India." *Cultural Critique* 7: 119–75.

Mohanty, C. T. (1991) "Under Western Eyes: Feminist Scholarship and Colonial Discourses." In *Third World Women and the Politics of Feminism*. Ed. C. T. Mohanty, A. Russo, and L. Torres. Bloomington: Indiana University Press.

Mukherjee, B. (1972) *The Tiger's Daughter*. Boston, Mass.: Houghton Mifflin.

———. (1988) "Immigrant Writing: Give Us Your Maximalist!" *New York Times Book Review*, 28 August: 28–9.

———. (1992) *Darkness*. New York: Fawcett Crest.

———. (1997) "Beyond Multiculturalism: Surviving the Nineties." *Journal of Modern Literature* 2. 1: 16–18.

Radhakrishnan, R. (1992) "Ethnicity in an Age of Diaspora." *Transition* 54: 104–15.

Sen, Samar, et al., eds. (1978) *Naxalbari and After: A Frontier Anthology*. Vol. 5. Calcutta.

Spivak, G. C. (1985) "Subaltern Studies: Deconstructing Historiography." *Subaltern Studies* 4. Delhi: Oxford University Press.

Trinh, T. M. (1989) *Woman, Native, Other: Writing Postcoloniality and Feminism*. Bloomington: Indiana University Press.

Viswanathan, G. (1989) *Masks of Conquest: Literary Studies and British Rule in India*. London: Faber and Faber.

CHAPTER **6**

Bhabha, H. K. (1994) *The Location of Culture*. London: Routledge.

Chambers, I. (1990) *Border Dialogues: Journeys in Postmodernity*. New York: Routledge.

Childs, P. and R. J. P. Williams (1997) *An Introduction to Post-Colonial Theory*. Hertfordshire: Prentice Hall/Harvester Wheatsheaf.

Egan, S. (1997) *Mirror Talk: Genres of Crisis in Contemporary Autobiography*. Chapel Hill: University of North Carolina Press.

Gilmore, L. (1994) "The Mark of Autobiography: Postmodernism, Autobiography, and Genre." In *Autobiography and Postmodernism*. Ed. K. Ashley, L. Gilmore, and G. Peters. Amherst: University of Massachusetts Press, 1–18.

Giltrow, J. and D. Stouck (1992) "'Mute Dialogues': Michael Ondaatje's *Running in the Family* and the Language of Postmodern Pastoral." In *Postmodern Fiction in Canada.* Ed. T. D'haen and H. Bertens. Amsterdam: Rodopi-Antwerpen, 161–79.

Hall, S. (1993) "Cultural Identity and Diaspora." In *Colonial Discourse and Post-Colonial Theory: A Reader.* Ed. P. Williams and L. Chrisman. London: Harvester Wheatsheaf, 392–403.

Hutcheon, L. (1985) "*Running in the Family*: The Postmodernist Challenge." In *Spider Blues: Essays on Michael Ondaatje.* Ed. S. Solecki. Montreal: Véhicule Press, 301–19.

———. (1988) *The Canadian Postmodern: A Study of Contemporary English-Canadian Fiction.* Toronto: Oxford University Press.

Jewinski, E. (1994) *Michael Ondaatje: Express Yourself Beautifully.* Toronto: ECW Press.

Kamboureli, S. (1988) "The Alphabet of the Self: Generic and Other Slippages in Michael Ondaatje's *Running in the Family.*" In *Reflections: Autobiography and Canadian Literature.* Ed. K. P. Stich. Canada: University of Ottawa Press, 79–92.

Mishra, V. (1995) "New Lamps for Old: Diaspora's Migrancy Borders." *Studies in Humanities and Social Sciences* 2. 1: 147–64.

———. (1999) "Mourning Becomes Diaspora." In *Impossible Selves: Cultural Readings of Identity.* Ed. J. Lo et al. Melbourne: Australian Scholarly Publishing, 46–71.

Mukherjee, B. (1982) "Ondaatje's Sri Lanka is Prospero's Isle." *Quill and Quire* 48: 30–8.

Ondaatje, M. (1980) *Rat Jelly and Other Poems 1963–78.* London: Marion Boyars.

———. (1984) *Secular Love.* Toronto: The Coach House Press.

———. (1993) *Running in the Family.* New York: Vintage.

Pesch, J. (1997) "Mediation, Memory and a Search for the Father: Michael Ondaatje's *Running in the Family.*" *Quarterly of Language, Literature and Culture* 45. 1: 56–71.

Snelling, S. (1997) "'A Human Pyramid': An (Un)Balancing Act of Ancestry and History in Joy Kogawa's *Obasan* and Michael Ondaatje's *Running in the Family.*" *Journal of Commonwealth Literature* 32. 1: 21–33.

Virilio, P. (1998) *The Virilio Reader.* Ed. J. Der Derian. Malden, Mass.: Blackwell.

CHAPTER 7

Ahmad, A. (1997) "The Politics of Literary Postcoloniality." In *Contemporary Postcolonial Theory.* Ed. P. Mongia. Delhi: Oxford University Press, 276–93.

———. (1999) *In Theory.* Delhi: Oxford University Press.

Dayal, S. (1998) "The Emergence of the Fragile Subject: Amitav Gosh's *In an Antique Land.*" In *Hybridity and Postcolonialism: Twentieth-Century Indian Literature*. Ed. M. Fludernik. Tübingen: Stauffenburg Verlag, 103–33.

Fludernik, M. (1998) "The Constitution of Hybridity." In *Hybridity and Postcolonialism: Twentieth-Century Indian Literature*. Ed. M. Fludernik. Tübingen: Stauffenburg Verlag, 19–53.

Göbel, W. (1998) "Beyond Hybridity? Chance as a Literary Stereotype in Novels of India, and Chaos on the Rebound." In *Hybridity and Postcolonialism: Twentieth-Century Indian Literature*. Ed. M. Fludernik. Tübingen: Stauffenburg Verlag, 55–77.

Hall, S. (1997) "Cultural Identity and Diaspora." In *Contemporary Postcolonial Theory*. Ed. P. Mongia. Delhi: Oxford University Press, 110–21.

Mukherjee, B. (1990) *Darkness*. New Delhi: Penguin India.

Morey, P. (2000) *Fictions of India: Narrative and Power*. Edinburgh: Edinburgh University Press.

Moore-Gilbert, B. (1997) *Postcolonial Theory*. London: Verso.

Mistry, R. (1996) *A Fine Balance*. London: Faber and Faber.

Stilz, G. (1998) "'Truth? Hell, You Will Get Contrast, and No Mistake!' Sanitarizing the Intercultural Polylemma in G. V. Desani's *All About H. Hatterr* (1948/ 72)." In *Hybridity and Postcolonialism: Twentieth-Century Indian Literature*. Ed. M. Fludernik. Tübingen: Stauffenburg Verlag, 79–101.

CHAPTER **8**

Bakhtin, M. M. (1987) *The Dialogic Imagination*. Ed. M. Holquist. Trans. C. Emerson and M. Holquist. Austin: University of Texas Press.

Cheung, K.-K. (ed.) (1997) *An Interethnic Companion to Asian American Literature*. Cambridge: Cambridge University Press.

Gadamer, H.-G. (1989) *Truth and Method*. 2nd rev. ed. Trans. J. Weinsheimer and D. G. Marshall. London: Sheed & Ward.

Kingston, Maxine Hong (1976) *The Woman Warrior: Memoirs of a Girlhood Among Ghosts*. New York: Knopf.

———. (1977) *China Men*. New York: Vintage.

Li, D. L. (1998) *Imagining the Nation: Asian American Literature and Cultural Consent*. Stanford, Calif.: Stanford University Press.

Lim, S. G. (1994) *Writing South East/Asia in English: Against the Grain*. London: Skoob.

———. (1997) "Immigration and Diaspora." In *An Interethnic Companion to Asian American Literature*. Ed. K.-K. Cheung. Cambridge: Cambridge University Press, 289–311.

———. (1999) "Writing out of Turn." *Profession 1999* (PMLA): 214–24.

———. (2001) *Joss & Gold*. Singapore: Times Books International.

Lowe, L. (1991) "Heterogeneity, Hybridity, Multiplicity: Marking Asian American Differences." *Diaspora* 1. 1: 24–44.

Ong, A. (1999) *Flexible Citizenship: The Cultural Logics of Transnationality.* Durham, N.C.: Duke University Press.

Skenazy, P. and T. Martin (ed.) (1998) *Conversations with Maxine Hong Kingston.* Jackson: University Press of Mississippi.

Wilson, R. (1996) "*Goodbye Paradise*: Global/Localism in the American Pacific." In *Global/Local: Cultural Production and the Transnational Imaginary.* Ed. R. Wilson and W. Dissanayake. Durham, N.C.: Duke University Press, 312–36.

Wilson, R. and W. Dissanayake (1996) "Introduction: Tracking the Global/Local." In *Global/Local: Cultural Production and the Transnational Imaginary.* Ed. R. Wilson and W. Dissanayake. Durham, N.C.: Duke University Press, 1–20.

Wong, S. C. (1995) "Denationalization Reconsidered: Asian American Cultural Criticism at a Theoretical Crossroads." *Amerasia Journal* 21. 1 & 2: 1–27.

CHAPTER **9**

Bergman, D. (1991) *Gaiety Transfigured: Gay Self-Representation in American Literature.* Madison: University of Wisconsin Press.

Bhabha, H. (1995) *The Location of Culture.* London: Routledge.

Campomanes, O. V. (1992) "Filipinos in the United States and Their Literature of Exile." In *Reading the Literatures of Asian America.* Ed. S. G. Lim and A. Ling. Philadelphia, Pa.: Temple University Press.

Cohen, R. (1997) "Diasporas, the Nation-State, and Globalization." In *Global History and Migrations.* Ed. G. Wang. Boulder, Colo.: Westview Press.

Dirlik, A. (1999) "Asians on the Rim: Transnational Capital and Local Community in the Making of Contemporary Asian America." In *Across the Pacific: Asian Americans and Globalization.* Ed. E. Hu-DeHart. Philadelphia, Pa.: Temple University Press.

Grewal, I. and C. Kaplan (ed.) (1994) *Scattered Hegemonies: Postmodernity and Transnational Feminist Practices.* Minneapolis: University of Minnesota Press.

Hassan, I. (1995) *Rumors of Change: Essays of Five Decades.* Tuscaloosa: University of Alabama Press.

Lee, R. C. (1999) *The Americas of Asian American Literature: Gendered Fictions of Nation and Transnation.* Princeton, N.J.: Princeton University Press.

Leong, R. (1993) *The Country of Dreams and Dust.* Albuquerque, N. Mex.: West End Press.

————. (2000) *"Phoenix Eyes" and Other Stories.* Seattle: University of Washington Press.

Murphy, T. F. and S. Poirier (ed.) (1993) *Writing AIDS: Gay Literature, Language, and Analysis.* New York: Columbia University Press.

Ong, A. (1999) *Flexible Citizenship: The Cultural Logics of Transnationality*. Durham, N.C.: Duke University Press.

Sassen, S. (1998) *Globalization and Its Discontents: Essays on the New Mobility of People and Money*. New York: The New Press.

Wong, C. S. (1995) "Denationalization Reconsidered: Asian American Cultural Criticism at a Theoretical Crossroads." *Amerasia Journal* 21: 1–27.

CHAPTER **10**

Bhabha, H. (1994) *The Location of Culture*. London: Routledge.

Bierce, A. (1958, 1881) *The Devil's Dicctionary*. New York: Dover.

Chow, R. (1993) *Writing Diaspora: Tactics of Intervention in Contemporary Cultural Studies*. Bloomington: Indiana University Press.

Moretti, F. (1983) *Signs Taken For Wonders: Essays in the Sociology of Literacy Forms*. Trans. S. Fischer, D. Forgacs, and D. Miller. London: Verso.

Virilio, P. (2000) *Strategy of Deception*. Trans. Chris Turner. London: Verso.

Contributors

Ryan Bishop is an Associate Professor of English and American studies at the National University of Singapore. Among his publications are works on international sex tourism in Thailand, critical theory, rhetoric, urbanism, visual culture, and the history of technology in relation to the university, the military, and aesthetics.

Ann Brooks has published extensively in the area of globalization, gender and organizational change, citizenship and social justice, academic women and equity, contemporary feminisms, cultural theory and politics, and postcolonialism and feminism. Dr Brooks is the author of *Academic Women*; *Postfeminisms: Feminism, Cultural Theory and Cultural Forms*; and with Alison Mackinnon, *Gender and the Restructured University: Changing Management and Culture in Higher Education*.

Robbie B. H. Goh (Ellgohbh@nus.edu.sg) teaches at the National University of Singapore. His recent publications include *Sparks of Grace: The Story of Methodism in Asia*; *Singapore Space and the Dialogics of Culture* (forthcoming); and various articles on Asian studies, gothic literature, and popular culture.

Regina Lee is currently in the process of completing her PhD in English and comparative literature at Murdoch University, where she has also taught in the School of Arts and School of Media, Communication and Culture. Her research and teaching interests include the Chinese diaspora, film and literary narratives, multicultural/race and representational issues.

Carol E. Leon is a lecturer, and currently head, of the English Department at the University of Malaya. She teaches postcolonial literature and theory as well as travel writings and eighteenth-century literature. Among her more recent publications are "Travel Writing and the Humanities" in *Ideya* (2002) and "Textual Travel: Creating the Homespace and the Search for Belonging in Michael Ondaatje's *Running in the Family*," in *Asian Journal of Social Science* (2003).

Walter S. H. Lim is an Associate Professor of English literature at the National University of Singapore. He teaches English Renaissance literature and Asian-American literature, and is the author of *The Arts of Empire: The Poetics of Colonialism from Ralegh to Milton* (1998).

Rajeshwar Mittapalli teaches English in Kakatiya University, Warangal, India. He has authored *The Novels of Wole Soyinka* and *Indian Women Novelists and Psychoanalysis* and edited more than 20 anthologies of essays on a wide range of literary topics. He is currently the editor of the well-known literary journal *Atlantic Literary Review*.

Alessandro Monti teaches Shakespearean drama in the Department of Oriental Studies at the University of Turin. He is the Italian translator of Raja Rao and collaborates with Indian publishers and academic institutions. His books include *Durga Marga* and *The Time after Cowdust*. He has also edited two collections of essays: *Hindu Masculinities across the Ages* (2002) and *Migrating the Text: Hybridity as a Postcolonial Literary Construct* (2003).

Wenche Ommundsen teaches literary and cultural studies at Deakin University, Australia. She is the author of *Metafictions: Reflexivity in Contemporary Texts* (1993) and the editor (or co-editor) of *Refractions: Asian/ Australian Writing* (1995), *From a Distance: Australian Writers and Cultural*

Displacement (1996), *Appreciating Difference: Writing Postcolonial Literary History* (1998), and *Bastard Moon: Essays on Chinese-Australian Writing* (2001). She is currently completing a book on cultural citizenship in diasporic populations.

Jeffrey F. L. Partridge is an Assistant Professor of English at Central Connecticut State University. He teaches American literature and specializes in Asian-American literature. He lived and taught in Singapore from 1992 to 2002.

John Phillips teaches at the National University of Singapore. He has published books and articles on philosophy and literature, postmodernism, postcolonialism, critical theory, urbanism, aesthetics, and military technology, and has recently edited, with Ryan Bishop and Wei-Wei Yeo, two books on urbanism in Southeast Asia.

Rebecca Sultana received her PhD in postcolonial theory and literature from Texas Christian University and is now a Professor of English at East West University in Dhaka, Bangladesh. Her interests include south Asian English literature, diaspora literature, and immigration and gender issues. She also teaches contemporary American and British literature.

Shawn Wong is the author of two novels, *Homebase* and *American Knees*. *Homebase* won both the Pacific Northwest Booksellers Award and the Governor's Writers Day Award. He is also the editor or co-editor of six anthologies of literature, including the landmark book *Aiiieeeee! An Anthology of Asian American Writers*. Wong is currently working on a third novel and finishing a feature-length screenplay of *American Knees*. He is a Professor in the Department of English and Director of the University Honors Program at the University of Washington.

Index